EQUIPPED FOR BATTLE

from
Generation to Generation

A Military Devotional

By Lamar Creel and Ray Hanselman

the Peppertree Press
Sarasota, Florida

All scripture references are from The Holy Bible;
KJV (King James Version) and
ESV (English Standard Version)

DEDICATION

To our son and grandson
Zachary Joseph Hanselman, USMC

ACKNOWLEDGMENT

This type of undertaking does not occur without the help of many people along the way. We would first like to thank our wives, Jana and Catty, and our families who have endured the hardships of men who have given their lives to serving others. Their commitment and love is appreciated at all times. Ray would also like to thank inspiring teachers such as: Dr. B.R. Minton, Dr. Fred Hadley, Pastor Chuck Smith, Pastor Kent Nottingham and others who taught him the importance of knowing and following the Scriptures. Ray would also like to thank his father-in-law, Lamar Creel, for his tireless effort and noteworthy example of what it is to live the Christian life. It has been Ray's pleasure to cooperate in such an undertaking as this devotional book.

Lamar Creel added: I am indebted to the congregations of three churches (El Bethel, Gastonia First Assembly and Oak City), who gave me the opportunity to serve and grow in the Lord with them. They allowed me to grow in the calling and gifts God placed in my life. The list of individuals who have contributed to my spiritual journey would be extensive. I thank my son-in-law, Ray Hanselman, whose idea gave birth to this endeavor, and for inviting me to share in this project.

The actual writing has been done while serving the awesome congregation of Oak City in Tallahassee, Florida and Pastor Matt Campbell. Pastors Fred Hadley and Clayton Wilkinson were instrumental in mentoring my formative years in the ministry. Personal friends, Otis Mott and David Stewart, spoke God's Word to me by their example and friendship. The person who, apart from the Lord Jesus Christ, has contributed the most and over the longest period of time is my wife, Catty Creel. Without her unconditional love and faithful support, I would have crashed and burned years ago.

I thank God for a wonderful family—being a parent and a grandparent is awesome. A special thanks to Zachary Hanselman, whose dream to be a Marine provided the inspiration for this devotional. I pray that you'll find encouragement and maybe, a word or two of wisdom from someone who has made lots of mistakes.

Finally, we would like to thank our Savior and Lord Jesus Christ for life and His salvation plan. Without the inspiration and breath that comes from Him, there would be no book to write, and it is for His pleasure that each word has been written.

TABLE OF CONTENTS

Military Devotional
FOREWORD

The journey of this book began as I thought about my son entering the military. I wondered, "If I were to be with my son every day he is in the military, what would I say? Would I give him advice on living? Would there be days of reflection, inspiration, exhortation, or encouragement? Would there be days where longevity and endurance were the themes? How about integrity and making good choices?"

I'm sure that after thinking about it for a while, one might think of many other directives. However, mostly each one would be served with a love that a father has for his son and, therefore, this venture must begin.

After the writing began, I thought of how interesting it would be to include a military son's grandfather in this offering. It was then that Lamar Creel was offered the opportunity to share thoughts from his heart that would inspire his grandson while he was in the military.

The following is a compilation of very short devotionals that are meant to be read within a minute every day. Each devotional includes a Bible verse, a thought about that verse, and a prayer. Understanding the time constraints that military personnel incur, this well-thought-out undertaking will quickly inspire a thought that can be meditated upon during the day. Those who take advantage of this book will be inspired, challenged, motivated and directed in the principles given throughout the Bible. Having this devotional as part of one's life will keep an individual on the path of eternal life that pleases God Almighty, who is the Supreme Authority.

May the readers be blessed as they read and ponder the writings of this book.

PRIORITY

*Seek ye first the kingdom of God and His righteousness,
and all these things shall be added unto you.*

Matthew 6:33

Command is supreme and supreme command is priority. The higher the rank, the higher the respect must be. Whoever rejects the command of the higher ranking officer will pay the penalty, and the outcome will not be enjoyable.

Our Heavenly Father is the highest in command. His directives never succumb to another for He is the Supreme authority. When He speaks, His commands are because He has greater knowledge, greater insight, and even better, greater understanding of the future. His motivation is love for His subjects of whom we are, and His intent is the best path for any to live.

When we understand the Heavenly Father's rank and the benefits to following His orders, we have aligned ourselves with the Author and Finisher of life itself. Without Him, none would exist to seek His kingdom or His righteousness, which are priority commands for those who will follow Him.

PRAYER

Dear Heavenly Father, teach me today to understand Your supreme position and help me to follow Your directives. In Jesus' name I pray. Amen.

_____

_____

_____

_____

GRANDSON

And he said to them, 'Take care, and be on your guard against all covetousness, for one's life does not consist in the abundance of his possessions.

Luke 12:15

One danger of being young is to overlook the wisdom and rich experience of family and friends available to a person. A folly of old age is to feel entitled to give advice, whether it's asked for or not. Most parents desire to leave an inheritance to their children. The question that dominates my thoughts is, "What can I pass on that will have lasting value?"

Money? It can be both a blessing and a curse. Property? My house may not fit your lifestyle, and it too is a short-term commodity. When I look at the people who have made a lasting impact on my life, their contributions haven't been material, neither did they offer unsolicited advice, but each one spoke volumes by the way they lived. An old preacher once said, "Some things are better caught than taught!"

My most valuable lesson has been that I am a sinner and I need a Savior. You'll find that your grandfather has failed to live what he has preached in many ways, but know also that he has received the super-abounding grace of God's forgiveness. Because He has forgiven me, I know that no matter what or how you fail, His grace will be sufficient for you.

The Bible says that children are a reward to their parents and grandparents. I consider that to be true in my life. The greatest gift I could give you is to point you to the Lord Jesus Christ! Everything else will pass away, but His word will last forever.

PRAYER

Dear Heavenly Father, I am thankful for the wonderful gift of family, especially my grandchildren. I pray that each one will know and obey Your word. In Jesus' name I pray. Amen.

January 3

NEW YEAR

Therefore, if anyone is in Christ, he is a new creation. The old has passed away; behold, the new has come.

2 Corinthians 5:17

The start of New Year's Day, at midnight, is heralded by fireworks, parties and special events which are often televised. A few dedicated people have to work on the day itself. For many it is a day of recovery from the New Year's Eve celebrations from the previous night. In some towns and cities, parades are held and special football games are played. The birth of the first baby in the New Year is often celebrated with gifts to the child's parents and accompanied with appearances in local newspapers and on local news shows. Many people make New Year's resolutions. These are usually promises to themselves that they will improve something in their own lives. Common New Year's resolutions are to stop smoking or drinking alcohol, to lose weight, exercise more or to live a healthier lifestyle.

New Year's resolutions last about as long as the celebrations. Usually they are made with sincere intentions to make them a part of the lifestyle. However, old patterns and habits aren't easily broken. The rigorous training of bootcamp is designed to make permanent new habits of discipline. Soldiers have their new habits reinforced by accountability to a commanding officer.

How well we do in making our New Year's resolutions a new lifestyle is seen when there's nobody checking up on us. A new way of thinking and living ensures that our resolution has a beneficial result. The Scriptures give us a key to permanent and positive change. Through receiving a new nature by faith in Christ, the old nature passes away, and the new is come.

PRAYER

Dear Heavenly Father, I have made many resolutions to do better, and each time I fail. You promise that I can become a new person and that's what I need. In Jesus' name I pray. Amen.

SACRIFICE

I appeal to you therefore, brothers, by the mercies of God, to present your bodies as a living sacrifice, holy and acceptable to God, which is your spiritual worship.

Romans 12:1

What was appealing as we considered joining the military? Career opportunity? Education? Travel? Adventure? Maybe the recruiter convinced us that midnight hikes, grueling exercise and eight-month oversea deployments would be exciting and fun. How influential was the idea of sacrifice and self-denial in our decision?

In sports there's a cliché that says, "There's no 'I' in team." Building a team requires sacrifice for the welfare of the unit. Individual goals must be incorporated into the objectives of the team. The concept that a team can accomplish more that any one individual must prevail over the ambitions of each individual.

My contribution to the success of the team will require personal sacrifice. If I reject the notion of sacrifice and self-denial as a value, then I will not contribute to the success of the team. The Apostle Paul urges teamwork as he calls us "brothers" and appeals to us to become a *living sacrifice, holy and acceptable to God.*

PRAYER

Dear Heavenly Father, I don't always want to sacrifice my desires. Truthfully, I struggle with the idea that You ask me to deny myself and follow You, but I know You have my interest in mind. Help me to present my body as a living sacrifice. In Jesus' name I pray. Amen.

NEW

Therefore, if anyone is in Christ, he is a new creation, old things have passed away; behold, all things have become new.

2 Corinthians 5:17

This is what we need to recapture: confidence in what God has done, is doing, and will complete! Paul, the apostle, and author of this Scripture, declares this world as we know it had "had it" and that the new order that would last forever had already begun.

He was not talking about a newness that was merely cosmetic, like a new hairdo or new clothes—rather he was talking about an inner change that only God could make. It is newness that ties together our past, our present and our future.

In verses 18 and 20 of chapter five, we find our assignment, *He gave us a ministry of reconciliation* and *we are ambassadors.* Paul is telling us; if we see people—even Christians who disappoint us—they may be inconsistent and even unfaithful to their profession of faith. Don't give up on them! Don't lose confidence in mankind.

We must renew our hope in God's redemption plan! The old is passing away, and the new is coming!

PRAYER

Dear Heavenly Father, I have looked at the old long enough! Make me new and help me to bring the good news of reconciliation to the people in my world. In Jesus' name I pray. Amen.

_____

_____

_____

_____

_____

January 6

OATH

*…but it is because the Lord loves you and is keeping the oath that
he swore to your fathers …*

Deuteronomy 7:8a

When you entered the military, you were asked to take the oath
of enlistment, which was something like the following: "I, (*name*),
do solemnly swear (*or affirm*) that I will support and defend the
Constitution of the United States against all enemies, foreign and
domestic; that I will bear true faith and allegiance to the same; and
that I will obey the orders of the president of the United States and
the orders of the officers appointed over me, according to regulations
and the Uniform Code of Military Justice. So help me God."

There was a time in our history when we were more united and
secure in this country. Very few homes had security systems, cars
could be left unlocked and a person could walk down the streets of
our cities safely. The public school system was a safe environment
where students could learn and pursue their educational dreams.
This period wasn't without its problems, admittedly—discrimina-
tion squashed the dreams of many of our minorities.

We have gained much in the rich diversity of our multinational
immigrants and our nation is better as a result. However, we have
experienced some alarming losses in unity, morality, discipline and
integrity. Respect for authority is at an all-time low. Violent crime
continues to plague our cities and disrupt our educational institu-
tions. Our oath to support and defend our nation against all enemies
requires our unselfish dedication.

The people of the United States of America owe a huge debt to the
diligence of the men and women who serve in the military, both past
and present, who have honorably protected this nation. We must never forget that our safety is also the concern of Almighty God. He has
declared his love in an oath for all people of every tribe and tongue.
His kingdom is big enough to include all races and all nations.

PRAYER

*Dear Heavenly Father, we gratefully acknowledge the
dedicated men and women who defend our nation. Thank
You for loving the world and sending Jesus to save us. In
Jesus' name I pray. Amen.*

PUNCTUALITY

Preach the word; be instant in season, out of season; reprove, rebuke, exhort with all longsuffering and doctrine.

2 Timothy 4:2

From the first sound of reveille in the early morning, a military person learns the value of punctuality. Without a prompt and quick response, there will be a heavy price to pay. Being on time is essential and is regarded as highly important when it comes to fulfilling even the slightest of missions. And so it is with the Christian every day.

Christians must live their lives in such a manner that their light is ready to respond any time there is a call for it. A time to witness may come in the spur of a moment, and the opportunity to lead someone to a relationship with Jesus Christ may occur at any time.

If one is in a ready response position and lives a life that is a reflection of Jesus Christ, punctuality will be no problem at all. But, if there is a nonchalant attitude and being on time doesn't matter, the times that come out of nowhere will pass by, and there will be no one to share in that moment.

PRAYER

Dear Heavenly Father, help me today to understand the importance of being punctual. In Jesus' name I pray. Amen.

QUESTION

Search me, O God, and know my heart!
Try me and know my thoughts!

Psalm 139:23

Remember the feeling of anxiety when the teacher would say, "Clean off your desk and take out a sheet of paper and a pencil. We're having a pop quiz!" No matter how prepared we were, those words always brought a degree of uncertainty, a little bit of doubt. Self-examination can motivate better preparation and lead to greater success, both in the classroom and in life.

What are the questions that interest us? Great breakthroughs in science, industry and education are possible when someone asks the right question. The great inventions that resulted in the Industrial Revolution came as result of inquisitive minds seeking to expand their knowledge. A sincere questioner will be good learner.

The Scriptures offer us some helpful advice in the psalm that says, *Search me ... try me ... know my heart and know my thoughts.* If facing the exam in a classroom setting can be intimidating, what about asking a Holy God to check us out? Our questions here are, by nature of our finite existence, limited and narrow. God is not limited by things that are, He will make all things new!

PRAYER

Dear Heavenly Father, I am ashamed that my thoughts are so filled with limitations and doubt. When I consider Your greatness, I can only say, Have Mercy on me a sinner! In Jesus' name I pray. Amen.

EXCEL

So he listened to them in this matter, and tested them for ten days. At the end of ten days it was seen that they were better in appearance and fatter in flesh than all the youths who ate the king's food. Because an excellent spirit, knowledge, and understanding and wisdom like the wisdom of the gods were found in him, ...

Daniel 1:14-15; 5:12a

The Reader's Digest has a section in each publication for humor. My favorite tells of a teenager who has just been given his first car. On his first solo drive, he puts the petal to the metal and is pulled over by a state trooper. The trooper walks up to the young driver and says, "I've been waiting for you!" To which the fast thinking teenager replied, "I got here as fast as I could." The officer couldn't suppress his laughter and announced to his offender, "For that answer, I'm not giving you a ticket—just slow down."

A spirit of excellence begins early in life with small chores, but it pays dividends throughout our entire life. Some people are satisfied to run with the pack, fit in with the crowd, but never excel at anything. These individuals are always looking for the easy way out. They only work when someone is watching and are the first to slack off when unsupervised.

The Bible tells about Daniel and his three friends who desired to eat a simpler, but healthier diet. Although their choice wasn't on the king's menu, they were permitted to follow their own preference, provided they compared favorably with the other servants. The results vindicated their choice, as they proved to be superior in spirit, knowledge and understanding.

The king assigned them greater responsibility and they performed with greater skill. Some have an attitude that says, "I'll excel when I get the promotion or the big job," but if we don't do the small things with excellence, we may never get the big job.

PRAYER

Dear Heavenly Father, I want to be the best I can at every task I'm assigned. I want to have the spirit of excellence. In Jesus' name I pray. Amen.

HELMET

*But since we belong to the day, let us be sober, having put
on the breastplate of faith and love, and for a helmet the hope
of salvation.*

1 Thessalonians 5:8

How should we live? This question requires another important consideration: How will we die? Visit any cemetery, where three bits of information are on every grave marker: name, date of birth and date of death.

How we live can be described in two ways: living in the light or living in darkness. Those living in the light are like people living with electricity. (All the appliances are functioning, we can see, the television works, computer connects to the internet and we can take a hot bath.) Those living in darkness can be pictured as sleeping and being drunk. When we sleep, we are pretty much out of touch with the world, except through our dreams. The drunk has lost control of the ability to make wise decisions and to make appropriate responses.

In warfare, a wise soldier utilizes all available equipment to protect self and comrades. When a soldier goes into battle unprepared or ill-equipped, it endangers the individual soldier and the platoon. Our equipment for living in the day is the breastplate of faith and love, and for a helmet, we have the hope of salvation.

PRAYER

Dear Heavenly Father, I would be a fool to expose myself to the enemy without all available protection. I'm asking for the protection that You provide for my body and soul. In Jesus' name I pray. Amen.

_____

_____

_____

PAST

Brethren, I count not myself to have apprehended: but [this] one thing [I do], forgetting those things which are behind, and reaching forth unto those things which are before,

Philippians 3:13

There is a tendency within man to look to the past. This happened or that occurred. Warriors and sports personalities are some of the best at sharing old stories. The past is a reminder of events that a person or people have been involved. However, Paul the Apostle has a different approach to the past.

Paul says, *I count not myself to have apprehended* and *forgetting those things which are behind.* The difference between Paul and most human thinking is that he does not rest upon his past failures or his accolades. The bent of most people is to talk about how good this was or how bad that was, and in doing so, they lose sight of what is being accomplished now. In other words, resting upon the past, whether there are successes or losses, only robs a person of what may be executed today.

The wise individual allows the past to be motivation in today's activities, and reaching forward unto those things which are before becomes the marching mantra of those making stories today that will be fuel for the future.

PRAYER

Dear Heavenly Father, help me to forget those things that are behind and apprehend that which You have in mind for me today. In Jesus' name I pray. Amen.

January 12
FAMOUS

And the fame of him went out into every place of the country round about.

Luke 4:37

Fame and fortune are pursued by people every day. He knows her and they know him. He has this and she has that are common conversations and make for interesting fodder for television talk shows. However, there is a fame for which anyone who is wise will aspire—the fame that is known by the Heavenly Father.

Jesus grew in reputation on the earth, and his fame "went out into every place of the country" as more people heard about him. Those who do heroics like Jesus are usually held high on a pedestal. The interesting thing about Jesus' fame is that it did not last in a favorable way. Even those who heralded Him at the triumphal entry, less than a week later were shouting out, "Crucify Him!"

Fame is a fleeting quality, and those who aspire to it find themselves only famous for a short while. Those who realize how temporary fame is would be much better served by concentrating on being famous before the Lord Jesus who has eternal destiny in mind for those who are known by Him.

PRAYER

Dear Heavenly Father, please help me today to continue to focus on that which is eternal rather than the temporary benefit that being famous extends. In Jesus' name I pray. Amen.

_____

_____

_____

_____

_____

APPROACH

Do not boast about tomorrow, for you do not know what a day may bring.

Proverbs 27:1

I was piloting a boat out of the Gulf of Mexico into a fresh water harbor. Buoys marked the channel into the dock. Navigating safely requires lining up two buoys at a time. It was tempting to look too far ahead. If I did, very quickly the boat was in shallow water and in danger of hitting a sandbar.

The greatest example of living is found in the life of Jesus. He said, *do not be anxious about tomorrow, for tomorrow will be anxious for itself. Sufficient for the day is its own trouble.* (Matthew 6:34) In other words, don't borrow trouble from the future.

Keeping our focus on the task at hand will keep us in the channel. Tomorrow we'll see more clearly the directions for that day.

PRAYER

Father, I don't need to know the future. Increase my faith to obey what I know to do. In Jesus' name I pray. Amen.

January 14
PLAN

*For I know the thoughts that I think toward you, saith the
LORD, thoughts of peace, and not of evil,
to give you an expected end.*

Jeremiah 29:11

An old country preacher used to say, "God's got a plan, and he's gonna work it out." Whether a person thinks about it or not, everyone has a life plan. Because of certain circumstances, many people believe that their lives are random, without meaning and purposeless. This is not so.

As with any military operation, there is a certain amount of planning, design and strategy. One who operates without any training, instruction or preparation is doomed to fail. A key component to victory is in the planning stages and not all the components to the plan are revealed at one time. In other words, mission will follow mission until the objective is met.

The Heavenly Father above knows and gives the direction for a person's life. If anyone turns to Him to seek out the plan, He will reveal it in the quantity He knows to be best. Trust is involved, and though one does not know the full details, the Heavenly Father is completing His mission. Wise soldiers will trust their superiors and fulfill the directives given for today.

PRAYER

Dear Heavenly Father, I know You have a plan for my life. Help me today to fulfill Your purposes according to Your will. In Jesus' name I pray. Amen.

FICKLE

A double-minded man [is] unstable in all his ways.

James 1:8

Should I choose this? Should I choose that? Which way should I go? Which way should I turn? If I go this way, this will happen. If I goes that way, that will happen. Has the reader ever been in these situations? Being fickle is as unstable as water in an earthquake. Those who cannot make up their minds generally go out of their minds trying to decide which way to go.

Sometimes decisions must be made. Although there are alternatives with each choice, the one alternative must be to choose one of the alternatives. There will be costs associated with decisions no matter which way one chooses. Every "yes" to one side is a "no" to the other. The careful person will be wise enough to evaluate in advance those advantageous and disadvantageous parts before making a decision.

When a difficult decision must be made, go to the prayer closet and bring the decision before the Lord above. Then choose one way or the other. By bringing the concern before the Almighty, the results will be in His hands. Even if the choice is not the best one, He knows how to turn the worst of decisions into ones that are good.

PRAYER

Dear Heavenly Father, I bring all my decisions before You. Help me to choose according to Your will, and should I not, help even those choices to work out for good. In Jesus' name I pray. Amen.

PRIVATE

But thou, when thou prayest, enter into thy closet, and when thou hast shut thy door, pray to thy Father which is in secret; and thy Father which seeth in secret shall reward thee openly.

Matthew 6:6

There is something wonderful about quiet time alone with God, when no one else is around, and nothing is disturbing. When nothing else is competing for one's time, and there are no obligations to fulfill, there, in the private time, God speaks. God shares and communion is enjoyed between man and his Maker like at no other time.

Being private and alone with God is a key component to finding the will of God. Jesus Himself went off alone to be with the Heavenly Father before making many huge decisions such as just before He chose His disciples and before that fateful time on the cross in Gethsemane. Jesus knew the benefits of praying "in thy closet."

There will be times when a person feels alone. Those who are wise will note that this quiet time, this alone time, this private time may be the most beneficial moments ever spent on this earth. Those who realize this benefit early in life will be at their best in this world.

PRAYER

Dear Heavenly Father, help me to recognize the benefits of being alone in my closet with You. I desire to seek Your face in the private times. In Jesus' name I pray. Amen.

_____

_____

_____

_____

_____

ATTENTION

Listen to advice and accept instruction, that you may gain wisdom in the future.

Proverbs 19:20

How many of us have ever experienced a rumble strip? A rumble strip is a continuous strip of shallow grooves along each side of the roadway. If our vehicle starts to leave the highway, the grooves generate a loud roar and severe vibration throughout the vehicle, which alerts the driver to impending peril. Some people humorously call this driving by Braille.

Life can be compared to a highway and God's will is the safe zone. There are times we momentarily are distracted or become sleepy and drift away from God's chosen path. For our safety, God installs rumble strips along our highway. Notice these aren't retaining walls to hold us on course—we still must choose to obey. However, the Holy Spirit has many ways of alerting us and calling us to attention. It may be a friend, commanding officer, or a minister who serves as a rumble strip.

PRAYER

Dear Heavenly Father, thank You for the warning! I was drifting and headed for disaster. In Jesus' name I pray. Amen.

_____

_____

_____

_____

_____

_____

_____

January 18

COMMANDER

And the child grew and became strong, filled with wisdom. And the favor of God was upon him.

Luke 2:40

The most basic lesson that every soldier must master is to "follow orders!" From the moment we step onto the bus at our induction until we're discharged, someone is giving orders. It is natural to aspire to be the one who gives the orders. That day will not come unless we learn quickly to obey our commanders.

The childhood of Jesus provides a valuable lesson in obeying those in charge. In the Jewish tradition, every boy at the age of twelve underwent a rite of passage called, "bar mitzvah." Upon completion of this instruction, he would be accepted into the religious community. At the age of twelve, Jesus is found in the temple discussing the Scriptures with the synagogue leaders. His parents assumed that he was accompanying them as they traveled home.

A basic principle of Christianity is that Jesus was both man and God. He was born as a babe, but He existed eternally with God. Mary was his birth mother, but He is God. His mother was upset that Jesus wasn't with the family, and she rebuked Jesus and ordered him to return home with the family. Luke records this in chapter 2:41-51. Jesus recognizes that He has a mission from His heavenly Father, but He is submissive to Mary and Joseph. He who would one day say, "All authority in heaven and earth is given unto me," learns obedience at the hands of a mother.

The observation of those who were eyewitness to the life of Jesus tell us that he *grew and became strong, filled with wisdom. And the favor of God was upon him.* (Luke 2:40) The connection between his submission to authority and becoming strong and filled with wisdom is not a coincidence.

PRAYER

Dear Heavenly Father, if Jesus, who came to earth as a man, could place himself under the human authority of Mary and Joseph, then I can obey my commander. Teach me the lesson of submission to authority. In Jesus' name I pray. Amen.

CHALLENGE

I appeal to you therefore, brothers, by the mercies of God, to present your bodies as a living sacrifice, holy and acceptable to God, which is your spiritual worship.

Romans 12:1

Every four years, teams from the nations of the world are assembled to compete in the Olympics. These games bring together the best competitors, and each athlete dreams of bringing home the gold metal. What qualities separate the medal winners from the rest of the athletes?

These athletes are a part of their country's team—maybe the best of their country, but most will never be in the running for a medal. There are 10 or 11 countries that win 10 to 60 medals each (teams include the U.S., China, Australia, France, Russia, Germany, and Great Britain). Another ten nations win 5-10 medals; and then about 30 nations are awarded 1 or 2 medals. What keeps them coming back to the Olympics?

What does it mean to be an Olympian? Olympians dedicate themselves to one thing. Someone who determines to be the best they can be in their chosen competition. This requires years of dedication and work with no days off. They know that in the end, there will be only three medalists, of which just one is a gold medal winner.

They do all that for a perishable prize. Paul calls us to a similar dedication, but for a superior goal. Our goal is not for a medal but for a life acceptable to God.

PRAYER

Dear Heavenly Father, I present my body in worship to You. Those who train for athletic competition sacrifice to excel. I want to do no less for You. In Jesus' name I pray. Amen.

_____

_____

FROWARD

*With the pure thou wilt shew thyself pure; and with the
froward thou wilt shew thyself froward.*

Psalm 18:26

One misunderstood principle within the ability to engage in battle is the need for purity, and yet with some clarification, that need will be realized. For example, what if the gun barrel is not straight or the compass is off just one degree in a battleship? What if the tolerances for error on a scope are misaligned, causing the target to be missed by several yards? What if the intelligence is off by just a sentence or two? The idea of purity and singleness, perfect in accuracy, is essential to winning the battles and those who deal with such tolerances know the importance of purity.

So it is with the Christian's life. When a Christian's life is off just a little, or misaligned just a tiny bit, the impurity affect upon others who watch this transformation is catastrophic. A froward or impure, misaligned, distorted, twisted witness is no witness at all and may be a deterrent to someone coming to Christ as their Savior.

In Christianity, not one is perfect, but nonetheless, let purity be the standard, and let all frowardness of heart disappear.

PRAYER

Dear Heavenly Father, I desire to put away all frowardness and to become pure before You. Help me to keep my mind upon things that are pure in Your eyes and to put aside all things that are froward. In Jesus' name I pray. Amen.

REFUGE

God is our refuge and strength, a very present help in trouble.

Psalm 46:1

The United States National Park Service provides a refuge for wild life. A visit to Yellowstone National Park offers visitors an up-close view of bear, buffalo and other wildlife native to that locale. The refuge provides protection and food for the animals and the park system allows visitors to see wildlife in their native habitat.

Whether we're privileged or poor, whether life is great or our world is falling apart, we need a place of safety, a quiet place. Increasingly, we live in toxic, hostile and dangerous environments. Work places, schools, airports and even our homes have become targets of violence. The war zone is not limited to military operations.

The Scriptures describe a provision God made for the descendants of Jacob. They were called cities of refuge. These certain cities were each designated as a safe zone, where a person could flee when in trouble. They would be assured of protection until their situation could be heard by an impartial judge. The Bible tells us that is what God offers us! He is our city of refuge, who promises that we will be judged by our Advocate, Jesus Christ!

PRAYER

Dear Heavenly Father, thank You for providing a safe place for me. You have provided for my sins to be forgiven through my faith in Jesus Christ. In Jesus' name I pray. Amen.

_____

_____

_____

_____

_____

_____

POTENTIAL

Beloved, now are we the sons of God, and it doth not yet appear what we shall be: but we know that, when he shall appear, we shall be like him; for we shall see him as he is.

1 John 3:2

What a person *is* does not always determine what that individual shall *become*. As a baby, no one except God really knows a child's destiny. Though there may be early indications in one direction or another, there is no absolute determination. There is potential, however, not always definite knowledge.

The Lord knows the potential of every person, and that potential is directly related to an individual relationship with the Heavenly Father. It is the "sons of God" who are in great favor. Those who know the premier importance of being related to God are those who will reach a potential that is far beyond both man and personal expectations. In other words, those who have the Heavenly Father within them are the ones who will live beyond mediocrity.

No one knows the advancement that God has in mind. Examples such as the shepherd boy, David, who would be king, the Moabite servant, Ruth, who would be David's great-grandmother, or Jesus, who was a simple carpenter's son, serve as the precipice of potential when the Heavenly Father is involved.

PRAYER

Dear Heavenly Father, please help me to understand that my potential is directly related to my relationship with You. Help me to be all that I can be. In Jesus' name I pray. Amen.

_____

_____

_____

_____

THINKING

Thou wilt keep [him] in perfect peace, [whose] mind [is] stayed [on thee]: because he trusteth in thee.

Isaiah 26:3

What is it that most people think about? When they ponder, what has the attention of their minds? What is on the forefront of the frontal lobes? Whatever it is, does it bring peace or anxiety? The results are defining, so those who are prudent will examine the effect of their thoughts on a daily basis.

The Bible is clear about the state of peace. Oh, it never states that there will always be peaceful situations and circumstances. However, there is a place where we can put thoughts that will lead us to rest, no matter what is going on in the surrounding world.

The key is to have our minds "stayed" upon the Lord. There should be no drifting, no wavering, and no doubting. The moment anxieties are allowed, peace will flee and rest will escape, because our capacity to handle issues has been pushed out of the mind.

PRAYER

Dear Heavenly Father, I place all my situations and circumstances before You. Please help me to keep You in my thoughts as I meet every challenge that life serves my way. In Jesus' name I pray. Amen.

_____

_____

_____

_____

_____

_____

_____

_____

SURVIVAL

I lay down and slept; I woke again, for the Lord sustained me.

Psalm 3:5

Lieutenant Douglas "Pete" Peterson, U.S. Air Force, an F-14 pilot during the Vietnam conflict, was shot down over Hanoi. He spent 7½ years as a POW in the infamous Hanoi Hilton. Pete, as he is known to his family, spent the first 4 to 5 years without his family knowing whether he was alive or dead. He had a son born while he was a prisoner and he didn't see him until his son was 7 years old. Upon his release, due mainly to the efforts of Ross Perot, he was asked, "How did you survive the torture, loneliness, and the dysentery?"

Pete's reply was: "Faith in God, prayer and knowing my family was waiting for me." We may never experience torture or prison, but it's very likely that we will face loneliness. What sustains us when life throws us a curve? To whom do we turn for comfort when we are lonely?

The writer of Psalms was sustained by the reality of his faith in God. In those times when we're alone and in those times when we face overwhelming trouble, our strength will come from within. Though our families cannot always talk to us and our comrades won't always be able to protect us, God will never leave us nor forsake us.

PRAYER

Dear Heavenly Father, I will never be in a situation where I'm isolated from Your presence. Whatever I face, whether it's good or bad, my faith in You will sustain me. In Jesus' name I pray. Amen.

_____

_____

_____

January 25
MISSION

Open your mouth for the mute, for the rights of all who are destitute. Open your mouth, judge righteously, defend the rights of the poor and needy.

Proverbs 31:8-9

Our military's mission is to fight and win our Nation's wars by providing prompt, sustained land dominance across the full range of military operations and spectrum of conflict in support of combatant commanders. The reasons for fighting a war are varied and often complex, but underlying the willingness to serve, send and support our military is the idea expressed in our Declaration of Independence: "… secure life, liberty and the pursuit of happiness."

These truths have their origin in the Scriptures. Solomon, king of Israel, known for his wealth and wisdom passed along something he learned from his mother. She taught him that leaders have a responsibility to speak on behalf of the poor and defend those who aren't able to protect themselves. A nation that enjoys prosperity is responsible to share with those in poverty.

Some sincere objections are raised to the violence of war, but we cannot escape the charge given by God to defend the rights of the poor and needy. This command doesn't give permission for the slaughter of everyone who disagrees with our point of view, but it does mandate that the recipients of great blessings are to share those blessings. The only lasting peace for the world is that offered by the one known as the Prince of Peace. *Peace I leave with you; my peace I give to you. Not as the world gives do I give to you* … (John 14:27)

PRAYER

Dear Heavenly Father, I haven't thought of my military service as being a mission for You. I want to be Your partner, defending the rights of those who are unable to defend themselves. In Jesus' name I pray. Amen.

LISTEN

Listen to advice and accept instruction, that you may gain wisdom in the future.

Proverbs 19:20

The human brain has a mechanism called Reticular Activating System (RAS). Simply put, it is the automatic mechanism inside our brain that brings relevant information to our attention. It also facilitates our ability to tune out unimportant noise. For example, if an individual is in a busy airport with many people talking, loud announcements, and luggage carriers making lots of noise, how much of this noise is noticed? Not much. But when a new announcement comes over the public address system broadcasting our name or flight number, our attention is suddenly full on. The RAS alerts the body to relevant information.

Several types of information are so important that they automatically pass through this built-in filter. They are things that are unique, things we value, and things that we find threatening. In Luke 16, Jesus tells the story of a rich man and a poor man. The rich man had every thing in life he needed. The poor man had nothing and is left to beg for the crumbs from the rich man's table. Both the rich man and the poor man died. The rich man's focus was on himself and his riches. He neglected to attend to his soul. The beggar, although impoverished materially, discovered eternal riches.

The lessons Jesus taught us in this story are: 1) Love Sees - the rich man passed the beggar every day and never saw him until it was too late, 2) Love Acts - the rich man never acted on his need for God until it was too late, and 3) Love Heals - the rich man saw his family's need too late.

PRAYER

Dear Heavenly Father, give me ears that hear, eyes that see and hands that reach out to those in my world who need charity and, most importantly, hope. You are the way, the truth and the life. In Jesus' name I pray. Amen.

DIFFERENCE

And he said to him, 'Please, Lord, how can I save Israel?
Behold, my clan is the weakest in Manasseh, and I am the least
in my father's house.

Judges 6:15

During the Cold War era, the relations between the United States and the former Soviet Union were strained, to say the least. A central figure in the USSR was Nikita Khrushchev, the premier who followed Joseph Stalin as leader of the Communist world. History records the brutal suppression of any opposition during Stalin's rule. Khrushchev was one of his advisers and supported most of his policies.

I remember news reports of Khrushchev at the United Nations pounding the table with his shoe and shouting, "We will bury you!" It seemed that the USA and the USSR were on a collision course for another world war. A few years later, Khrushchev began to distance himself from the dark period of Stalin's rule. He publicly attacked his former comrade for his oppression. On one occasion where he denounced some of the former premier's actions, someone in the audience sent him a note. The note asked about his involvement and cooperation in those actions.

It was reported that Mr. Khrushchev demanded that whoever sent the note stand up. After several minutes of silence with no one moving, Khrushchev said to the audience and to the individual who sent the note, "I was doing what the writer of this note was doing, I did nothing because I was afraid to stand up."

Standing up for what is right is not easy, especially when the opposition is powerful and cruel. The Bible records the story of Gideon, who is asked to revolt against the oppression of the hordes from Midian. His personal resources were no match for the powerful invasion of these militant neighbors. Gideon is ill-equipped and outnumbered, but he is assured that God would be with him. His faith and obedience rallied the spirits of a demoralized people and resulted in the resounding defeat of Midian.

PRAYER

Dear Heavenly Father, one person can make a difference. You have promised to be with me and give me courage. Strengthen my faith and use me to stand for the right. In Jesus' name I pray. Amen.

CHAPTER

Whereas ye know not what [shall be] on the morrow. For what [is] your life? It is even a vapour, that appeareth for a little time, and then vanisheth away.

James 4:14

Training such as bootcamp; field training; and Special Ops School are all examples of chapters within a soldier's life. From one stage to the next, the soldier knows what it is like to move from one position to another one and then to another and another. The chapters written within a soldier's life can become the story of many soldiers, who give their lives for their country, thus serving many people whom they do not know. They are to be commended.

The Bible encourages people to focus on the purposes of the day in which they live. This day becomes a chapter for all who will serve the Living God. Tomorrow is uncertain, and whether a person makes it to the morrow is not really known in advance in most cases. The idea is to live within the chapter that is being written today. Many people squander today's activities by worrying about the things that might occur tomorrow.

Life is like a vapor—it vanishes quickly. Those who are wise will realize the benefit of living within the chapter that is being written in their lives right now.

PRAYER

Dear Heavenly Father, I desire to live within the chapter that You have written for me today. Help me to keep my focus in this day and not allow the concerns of tomorrow to ruin the chapter being written right now. In Jesus' name I pray. Amen.

_____

_____

January 29

BRAVE

Wait for the Lord; be strong, and let your heart take courage; wait for the Lord!

Psalm 27:14

A recent slogan popular on T-shirts and bumper stickers says, "No Fear." I remember being coached by my mother on the way to the dentist, "Now be brave. You're a big boy." The truth was I didn't like going to the dentist and I had some fear! Webster's definition of brave includes two words: "courage" and "endure." For me, the visit to the dentist required endurance, but it didn't mean, "No Fear."

Facing danger requires courage and endurance. Fear is not necessarily an undesirable quality, unless we are paralyzed by it. Being brave doesn't mean we have no fear, but it does mean that we aren't incapacitated in the face of a difficult assignment. Brave people have fear, but they respond with courage and endurance.

Many times, the Scriptures admonish us to be strong, take courage and endure. Accompanying this exhortation is another qualifying phrase, "wait for the Lord." Waiting on the Lord is not inactivity, but passionately seeking the wisdom of God's Word.

PRAYER

Dear Heavenly Father, when I am afraid, I will trust You. Help me to wait in Your presence and learn from Your Word. In Jesus' name I pray. Amen.

_____

_____

_____

_____

_____

_____

FATIGUE

When I am afraid, I put my trust in you. In God,
whose word I praise, in God I trust; I shall not be afraid.
What can flesh do to me?

Psalm 56: 3-4

Coach Vince Lombardi once said, "Fatigue makes cowards of us all." A word of military wisdom says: "Bravery is being the only one who knows you're afraid." (David Hackworth) Fear and fatigue are common enemies to the soldier and the athlete. The question is not, "Will you face fear and/or fatigue?" but "How will you deal with them?"

My high school basketball coach had a simple approach to fatigue. During conditioning drills, he would ask; "Are you tired?" If you answered, "No," he would reply, "You're loafing, give me twenty wind sprints." And if you answered, "Yes, I'm tired", he replied, "You're out of shape, give me twenty wind sprints." You were going to run twenty wind sprints (the length of the court) regardless of how you answered his question.

The lesson was that superior conditioning results in a better performance. We were less likely to experience fatigue and better prepared to overcome fear. Coach Bobby Bowden (FSU Hall of Fame former coach) said, "Don't depend on the un-dependables." All of us will experience fatigue, but we can prevent it from turning us into cowards. Condition! Train! Endure! Run some more!

PRAYER

Dear Heavenly Father, I will put my trust in You. You know when I am tired and afraid. Give me strength to endure. In Jesus' name I pray. Amen.

_____

_____

TOGETHER

Then we which are alive [and] remain shall be caught up together with them in the clouds, to meet the Lord in the air: and so shall we ever be with the Lord.

1 Thessalonians 4:17

Separation from loved ones can be one of the most difficult parts of life. Living without mother or father, wife or children, grandparents or friends can make a person feel alone, afraid, and very sad. Military people know this, and those who are away from their families for extended times have pains within that not many can describe.

There is a promise in the Bible for those who have been separated for some time, even if this separation is caused by death. The Christian shall "ever be with the Lord." The reunion of reunions is coming. All who know Jesus Christ will be there. Not one soul who has given their heart and life to Jesus will be separated, and there will never be a separation again.

Those who are wise know the importance of having their position with Jesus aligned now, for the key to being invited to the reunion is to have entry that is only given by accepting Jesus as our personal Savior. If we invite Him into our lives today, the reunion pass is ours.

PRAYER

Dear Heavenly Father, sometimes being separated from those I love is very difficult. I pray that my relationship with You will lead to a regathering of everyone whom I love and cherish. In Jesus' name I pray. Amen.

_____

_____

_____

_____

_____

FIRST

Seek ye first the kingdom of God, and His righteousness.
And all these things shall be added unto you.

Matthew 6:33

The key to being the best soldier that anyone will ever see or know is to be sure that the first things are first. Discipline, respect, honor, intestinal fortitude and integrity are a few of those characteristics to which all soldiers ascribe.

God Almighty understands the idea of first things being first, and Jesus Himself gave the words of greatest importance to all who will hear. There must be within those who will follow after Jesus a willingness to seek God's kingdom and His righteousness above all other pursuits. Most people receive the very things that Jesus promised would be provided. This happens when a person obeys the command to seek the kingdom of God and His righteousness before anything else.

"All these things" includes every necessary element to life. Such other trappings as food, clothing, shelter, and even relationships shall be provided when first things are first according to Jesus. The question becomes, "What is the master passion of our life, and does that master passion align with the one the Savior says will lead to every desire we may have?"

PRAYER

Dear Heavenly Father, I desire to seek Your kingdom and righteousness above all other desires within my life. Please help me to be conscious of this pursuit all throughout my days. In Jesus' name I pray. Amen.

_____

_____

_____

EYE

*The eye is the lamp of the body. So, if your eye is healthy, your
whole body will be full of light, but if your eye is bad, your whole
body will full of darkness. If then the light in you is darkness,
how great is the darkness!*

Matthew 6: 22-23

When anxious teenagers finally arrive at that "rite of passage into
adulthood called the driver's license," they are required to pass an
exam. This exam consists of three tests: written, driving and vision
(usually in that order). Does it seem odd that the eye exam is given
last? Does that mean that knowing the rules and operating a vehicle
are more important than being sure we can see where we're going?
Of course, that changes as we grow older. There comes a time when
experience and insight aren't enough—what's required is eyesight.

The eye is an amazing and important member of our body, but
the information behind the images the eye sees is processed by
our whole being. Every picture our eyes take is colored, focused
and framed by a lifetime of experiences and expectations. Just
ask any police officer trying to get eyewitness reports at the
scene of an accident. Vision can be very subjective. Ten witnesses
will give ten different versions of what they saw.

The eye can be diseased, thus requiring glasses or surgery. Like
the eye, our vision of life can be diseased, also. Jesus taught that
the spiritual health of the body depends upon our reception of
light. In Scriptures, light symbolizes truth, while darkness rep-
resents sin. *But if we walk in the light, as he is in the light, we have
fellowship with one another, and the blood of Jesus his Son cleanses
us from all sin.* 1 John 1:7

PRAYER

*Dear Heavenly Father, I once walked in darkness, not
knowing I was blind. Thank You for revealing the truth to
me and filling me with light. In Jesus' name I pray. Amen.*

February 3

SERVE

*For if you forgive others their trespasses, your Father will also
forgive you, but if you do not forgive others their trespasses,
neither will your Father forgive your trespasses.*

Matthew 6:14-15

Every day we're informed of earthquakes, tornadoes, floods and
other disaster around the world. The media flashes graphic images of suffering and death into our minds. How do we respond?
Are we one of those who ask, "What can we do?" We've been
taught to be responsible—so we may feel a personal responsibility to fix the problem.

A common reaction is to feel overwhelmed and powerless. Seeing
thousands of people suffering and dying may invoke a sense of hope-
lessness. For example, rebuilding Haiti after the recent earthquake
requires more resources than any single individual possesses. It requires equipment, food, money, manpower, and coordination.

Yet, in every disaster, there are some simple things that we can all
provide. People need love, acceptance and forgiveness. Jesus modeled these three things: Love—He loved people no one else would.
Acceptance—He never demanded people change before He loved
them. Forgiveness—He forgave those who rejected His teaching.
He also served those he loved, accepted, and forgave, symbolized by
washing the feet of His disciples. Jesus didn't come to be served as
the Commander in Chief, but to serve.

PRAYER

*Dear Heavenly Father, I can't do everything to heal the
suffering in our world, but I can do something. I can love
them. I can forgive them, and I can serve them. In Jesus'
name I pray. Amen.*

_____

_____

FRIEND

A man [that hath] friends must shew himself friendly: and there is a friend [that] sticketh closer than a brother.

Proverbs 18:24

Comradeship is one of the greatest benefits to being in the military. The relationships that are formed through boot camp, training and actual exercises rarely can be duplicated anywhere else in the world. Friendships are made for life, and the closeness that some soldiers feel toward others may be many times closer than brothers and sisters at home.

The Bible speaks of being a friend. Many people do not take advantage of the guidance found in Scriptures for friendships, They may spend their entire lives looking for just one or two people who will be friends with them. They employ techniques that are self-interested and not oriented towards others. In other words, to have friends, one must be friendly.

Jesus has shown Himself to be the friendliest person in history. "Greater love has no man than this that he lay down his life for his friends." Jesus laid down His life for everyone. This is the ultimate manner in reaching out to be friends with anyone and everyone.

PRAYER

Dear Heavenly Father, thank You for reaching out to me through Jesus Christ. I know that You consider all who call upon Your name as Your friends. I want to live my life as an attraction to You. In Jesus' name I pray. Amen.

_____

_____

_____

_____

_____

FORGIVE

But if ye forgive not men their trespasses, neither will your Father forgive your trespasses.

Matthew 6:15

Is there anyone who has done anything against another person? Is there anyone who has been wrongly treated, cheated or abused? Are there times when one person stands out above all the others and who excels all the rest in this area? Do angry thoughts come into one's mind when this person's name is said or that person is spoken about in any way? If so, there may be a cause for forgiveness.

When we have been wronged, one of the most difficult parts of living is to forgive. Many have stated, "I will never forgive ..." and they fill in the name. There is a great difficulty with this solid statement, and Jesus Himself spoke the words, *if ye forgive not men their trespasses, neither will your Father forgive your trespasses.* In other words, if we do not forgive, no matter how horrible the abuse was, we will not be forgiven by our Heavenly Father.

However, we have help with this difficult task. One, Jesus was the model: "Father, forgive them, for they know not what they do." Two, every sin that anyone committed Jesus paid for on the cross. Three, the Holy Spirit is there to remind all who will listen of everything that Jesus says. He will provide the power and strength to do what one cannot do alone. Finally, forgiveness takes the chains off the person who forgives. If we choose to remain in a state of unforgiveness those chains stay wrapped around us.

PRAYER

Dear Heavenly Father, help me to forgive others as You have forgiven me. May my life be a reflection of the grace that You have extended. In Jesus' name I pray. Amen.

February 6

FLIRT

And beheld among the simple ones, I discerned among the youths,
a young man void of understanding,

Proverbs 7:7

Testing the fate of a person's life is not only dangerous to ourselves, but also may be to others. Flirting with danger without proper regard is one of the reasons there is such firm discipline within the military ranks. All the yelling, screaming, studying, and following prescribed patterns of behavior are designed to teach soldiers to not flirt with objects, people and places that may get them or others around them killed.

The Bible speaks of people who flirt. Proverbs seven has an entire section devoted to the seduction of one who flirts. This action may seem so innocent at first, but it can turn quickly into deadly disaster or total devastation. Some flirting has a no-return policy attached. Once someone engages in this destructive behavior, there may never be a turning back again.

The key is not to be among the simple ones, but among the wise. The wise person plans in advance. They know the dangers of flirting are out there and plan, discipline, and study before the transaction or opportunity occurs. Those who flee such things will be safe, but those who engage in this type of activity will fall into a pit that has no bottom.

PRAYER

Dear Heavenly Father, please help me to guard my heart against flirting with dangerous people, places and things. I know there are traps set for me out there, and I want to always be trusting in and following You. In Jesus' name I pray. Amen.

February 7
FINE

I will make a man more precious than fine gold; even a man more than the golden wedge of Ophir.

Isaiah 13:12

Some equipment is more valuable than others. Who would dare compare the worth of an F-14 fighter plane to an old pot in the kitchen? Who would even start to compare the worth of a beat-up shovel to a nuclear missile? Each of these powerful weapons would greatly outshine the lowly pot or shovel, and the fine value of those more expensive items far exceeds the nominal worth of small things.

Precious. Valuable. Of worth. Expensive. Big-ticket. High-priced. Costly. All these words describe a person when measured by God's scales. Everyone is valuable to Him—all are worth saving, so everyone is placed within the "fine" category.

Everyone, however, is not as they should be, and that is where the master craftsman comes in. He promises to "make a man more precious than fine gold." This incurs a process that requires time. The fine work that He intends may not be seen for many weeks, months or years, but He is at work, on both the reader, and those the reader knows.

PRAYER

Dear Heavenly Father, I know that there is a process of refining that is going on in my life and others around me. Help me to see Your mighty hand at work at all times. In Jesus' name I pray. Amen.

_____

_____

_____

_____

_____

FEMALES

So God created man in his [own] image, in the image of God created he him; male and female created he them.

Genesis 1:27

When examining mankind, intelligence of great magnitude is not required to know that differences exist between men and women, boys and girls, and males and females. Each gender has its own special attributes and each, in general, becomes complimentary to the other. The Creator saw fit to design humans in this way. Those who recognize the benefits of these complimentary parts enjoy one another the most.

To be properly aligned with the Heavenly Father, we must employ a proper perspective when considering a relationship with someone of the opposite sex. Too often the opposite sex is taken for granted, abused, used or maligned, mainly for lack of understanding. Devaluing seems to be a mantra in this country as one gender tries to lower the worth of the other. Yet in God's economy, each is a tremendous treasure.

The image of the Heavenly Father is stamped upon male and female alike, and those who relish that image know the importance of giving honor to anyone upon whom the Lord has called His own.

PRAYER

Dear Heavenly Father, help me to give value to both males and females today, knowing that they are each of great importance to You. In Jesus' name I pray. Amen.

_____

_____

_____

_____

_____

FELLOWSHIP

And they continued stedfastly in the apostles' doctrine and fellowship, and in breaking of bread, and in prayers.

Acts 2:42

One of the greatest parts of human existence is the fellowship of friends. Comrades forged in the fellowship of the armed services last a lifetime. Those who have been in battle together have a bond like no other. A huge part of who we become is developed through the friendships we make. Those friends then become the people who will influence much of our lives.

Clothing, patches, shoes, activities, and other facets of daily living are usually similar among those who are in fellowship with one another. If the group likes the Pittsburgh Steelers, usually yellow and black is worn. If they like the Yankees, blue and white is worn. Those friends who like to play golf, soccer, football, baseball or other sports, usually play together. If it's movies they enjoy, whatever type of movie enjoyed best is what they see as a group. In other words, those in fellowship do things alike.

One of the key elements to the early church is that they had fellowship together. Those who are associated with members of one particular faith may be alike in other areas of life. The influences of the teaching of the Word of God are dominant in their lives. The key to fellowship is to note with whom one is in fellowship. Remember, those who hang around people of a certain ilk become like them, so the importance of selection is imperative from the beginning of any fellowship time.

PRAYER

Dear Heavenly Father, please help me to fellowship with those who will be like-minded with You. I ask You to remind me when my fellowship times are astray from Your Holy Word. In Jesus' name I pray. Amen.

PROMOTE

And the angel came in unto her, and said, Hail,
[thou that art] highly favoured, the Lord [is] with thee:
blessed [art] thou among women.

Luke 1:28

To enjoy the favor of someone, especially someone of great importance and means, can make the difference between advancement and decline, promotion and degradation. The soldier who knows the significance of being well-favored is wise and lives a life that will benefit from this knowledge.

Mary was highly favored by God Almighty. The Heavenly Father had a very extraordinary task for this very special lady to perform. Being mother to the Savior was one of the greatest honors ever bestowed to a woman and Mary was the recipient. God's favor shines on anyone who looks for His blessing. Special talents, gifts and abilities are awarded to people every day. The Heavenly Father is a master planner, and His ideas are superior to any leader or man. The conglomeration of different gifts and favors work out His purposes, which are eternal and not just for the mission on earth.

Seeking the favor of God is a proper mode. Each day should begin by asking the Lord for His favor. Life gels then. Life flourishes. Those who seek His favor will find a receptive and giving Father, Who loves to bless those who will just believe.

PRAYER

Dear Heavenly Father, I seek Your favor today and for all of my life. I know I cannot have a greater position than to be completely within Your favor. In Jesus' name I pray. Amen.

February 11
FAMILY

But as many as received him, to them gave he power to become the sons of God, [even] to them that believe on his name:

John 1:12

God wants a family—the idea of family was His originally. Those who are in the military know the meaning of an extended family, as cohorts in the military become like brothers and sisters united together. Within the ranks, there is comradeship and fellowship that rarely is realized in the civilian world.

So it is with the Heavenly Father. For those who receive Him, He gives the power to become the sons of God. There is an entrance into the family of God. Those who have been in the family for a while know the closeness that develops that may often exceed blood relations.

Unity and brotherhood are essential to functioning as a group. When one group member falls, another picks them up. Those who excel are applauded, When one is lost, the others search until they are found. God knows this, and He is constantly looking to add more to His family each and every day.

PRAYER

Dear Heavenly Father, thank You for allowing me into Your family. Help me to be the family member I should be with all my brothers and sisters. In Jesus' name I pray. Amen.

February 12

FAILURE

Against thee, thee only, have I sinned, and done [this] evil in thy sight: that thou mightest be justified when thou speakest, [and] be clear when thou judgest.

Psalm 51:4

People fail, so for anyone who attempts something of importance in life, there will be times of not succeeding. It's just the way it is. People make mistakes and accidents happen. The great question is, "What do we do in times of failure?"

Sometimes the battle was not executed correctly, so a re-planning session is necessary. When there is loss, a new game plan must be engaged. The key is to understand where one is in the present state. When David sinned against God in the ordeal with Bathsheba, he knew where the problem lay: "Against thee, thee only, have I sinned, and done this evil in thy sight." It took realizing where he was and to whom he had ultimately done this against to begin the recovery.

When failure comes, go to the Source of Life, the Heavenly Father. He already knows in advance of our failure. He knows in advance about that wrong move, and yet, He loves us in advance, during, and in the future, when other failures come into our lives.

PRAYER

Dear Heavenly Father, thank You for Your love for me even when I fail. I come to You humbly and with my whole heart to have You help me to be successful again. In Jesus' name I pray. Amen.

_____

_____

_____

_____

_____

BALCONY

Greater love has no one than this, that someone lay down his life for his friends.

John 15:13

A friend's value is most evident when we face adversity. Fair weather friends describe those acquaintances, who disappear when we suffer hardships or adversities. Success fosters the illusion that we have many friends. When fortune stops smiling and laughter turns into tears, we discover our true friends.

The proverbs of Solomon provide excellent insight for identifying the qualities of friends. *A friend loves at all times, and a brother is born for adversity.* (Proverbs 17:17) Solomon's experience teaches us that not everyone who surrounds us when we are successful, healthy and popular is our friend. A true friend remains loyal when we're a failure, sick and despised.

True friends not only stand beside us when others forsake us, but also inspire us to be "balcony" people. Some acquaintances live in the "basement." That is, they're always negative, everything is always bad, the world is awful. When we're around them, we're not inspired— we're depressed. Balcony people see the best in people. They live on the balcony and they encourage us to be a better person.

What kind of friend do we want? A basement friend or a balcony friend? What kind of friend are you?

PRAYER

Dear Heavenly Father, You have poured out Your love on us while we were enemies. You have made us Your friend by giving Your Son to die for our sins. Thank You! Now help me be a friend, a balcony friend. In Jesus' name I pray. Amen.

February 14
FLIGHT

Therefore, since we are surrounded by so great a cloud of witnesses, let us also lay aside every weight, and sin which clings so closely, and let us run with endurance the race that is set before us,

Hebrews 12:1

Insurance is supposed to protect us against loss. For example, we buy health insurance to protect us from the expense of hospital costs that often exceed our annual income. We endure the increasing cost of automobile insurance to protect us from the liability of personal and property damages. However, insurance cannot protect us from every loss or pain. (There's no earthy protection from the pain of losing a spouse, parent or child.)

Where do we find protection for our hope? Serving in the military requires exposure to danger. All the training and support of our unit cannot protect us from every risk or liability. How will we survive the inevitable losses in our life? Will we lose hope? Will it affect our courage?

Personally, I've found assurance in the Bible. First, when we know God's promises, we don't have to prove anything. Secondly, when we know God's faithfulness, we don't have to fear anything. Thirdly, when we know God's fellowship, we can handle anything, even losing a friend. Our courage and our hope are based in God, not in ourselves.

PRAYER

Dear Heavenly Father, thank You for the assurance that my security lies in trusting You. I cannot protect myself from every risk, but I can trust You in all situations. In Jesus' name I pray. Amen.

ACCEPTANCE

And the Spirit and the bride say, "Come." And let him that heareth say, "Come." And let him that is athirst come. And whosoever will, let him take the water of life freely.

Revelation 22:17

All people strive to be accepted in every walk of life. From the time of our birth until the day of our death, acceptance and love permeate our souls. Rejection by peers and castigation by others can make us sad, depressed and alienated. Basically, although we all may want to belong to a group, there are those who isolate themselves and thus become ostracized.

From the beginning to the end of the Bible, the redemption of man is the theme. In other words, Jesus wants everyone to know they are accepted by Him. Although many reject Jesus, His desire and passion is that all would come to Him, and His invitation is to *whosoever will*. Those who are wise know that not only are they personally invited, but also every soul with whom they come into contact is invited, too.

The beauty of Jesus is that people can receive acceptance from Him, if they will only come just as they are. When they do so, they find Him waiting with open arms to receive them.

PRAYER

Dear Heavenly Father, thank You for accepting and receiving me. Help me today to know that there are others with whom You want to share acceptance in this world. In Jesus' name I pray. Amen.

_____

_____

_____

_____

_____

February 16

ABSENT

We are confident, [I say], and willing rather to be absent from the body, and to be present with the Lord.

2 Corinthians 5:8

One of the most definite statistics in life is that ten out of ten people die. There is no escaping, and there is no alternative, other than rapture. But, what happens the moment we die? Do we go to heaven? Do we go to hell? Is there just non-existence, reincarnation, or some other unknown? The Bible is very clear when it discusses what happens with the Christian.

The Christian, the one who trusts in, relies upon, and clings to Jesus Christ goes immediately into the presence of the Lord the moment the last breath is taken. There is no purgatory, no penance, and no intermission. The follower of Christ when absent from the body will be present with the Lord.

The question is not whether we will die, but rather when. Those who have given their hearts to Jesus Christ shall have no worries. Those who have not shall have everything and more of which to be concerned.

PRAYER

Dear Heavenly Father, thank You for the provision that Jesus has given after my death. Please help me to live as though I shall see You face to face at any moment. In Jesus' name I pray. Amen.

ABLE

Now unto him that is able to keep you from falling, and to present [you] faultless before the presence of his glory with exceeding joy.

Jude 1:24

There are some tasks at which even the greatest of soldiers cannot do on their own. Although there are opportunities for soldiers to make a distinguished mark of excellence that may or may not be honored, some missions have been reserved for only one person to fulfill. That person is the Lord Jesus Christ, and He is able to do that which no other can do.

Try for a moment to never sin, never have a fault or never make a mistake—it's impossible. Those who pretend that they are perfect have failed in the attempt, because there is imperfection in the trying. Certain duties and responsibilities are reserved for God alone. The function of the obedient and wise is to realize and trust in the Almighty's ability—not their own.

God is able to deliver keep, and present His children in a manner that pleases His glory with exceeding joy.

PRAYER

Dear Heavenly Father, there are activities that I know are too great for me to do on my own. I trust in You, and You alone, to accomplish that which I cannot. In Jesus' name I pray. Amen.

_____

_____

_____

_____

_____

_____

PILGRIM

Set Your affection on things above, not on things on the earth.

Colossians 3:2

Some say, "He is so heavenly minded that he cannot be any earthly good," but rather it should be noted that most are "so earthly minded that they cannot be any heavenly good." Some people only live for this earth and never think about how things are going to be when they leave. The idea is similar to those who enter a battle, conquer their enemy, and then have no plan for what happens after they win. Thought must be given to what happens after the war *before* the victory is claimed.

Those who set their affections, their love, and their attention upon things that are above know that this world is not their home. They are simply passing through. Their love is directed to the aftermath, the swan song, the final curtain. No one knows when that time comes, but those who have heaven in mind keep their attentions upon the things of God and not on things of the earth.

Jesus knew that He was going to the Father and, thus, His purpose was to please the Father no matter what—*Thy will be done.* Those who are wise will follow His example all the way to the grave and beyond.

PRAYER

Dear Heavenly Father, help me to keep my focus and affections on things above and not be distracted by the things of this earth. In Jesus' name I pray. Amen.

_____

_____

_____

_____

February 19
ALIGNMENT

If you love me, keep my commandments.

John 14:15

A lot can be told about people who align themselves with those who have authority over them. One type of person murmurs and complains, while another type does the job without complaint. The difference is how they respond when commanded.

Jesus gives a charge and a challenge that is directly related to a love relationship. Love keeps commandments, while transversely, not keeping commandments implies lack of love. The implication is that not only keeping commands is important but also the way we align ourselves with keeping commands has a direct relationship to how we love.

Those who are wise understand who the Ultimate Authority is. By loving Him first, all other authorities are understood to be obeyed within a person's life. Though understanding may be absent, unless the authority goes directly against the Ultimate Authority, alignment is imperative or question arises as to one's love for the Supreme commandment giver.

PRAYER

Dear Heavenly Father, help me to understand that You are the Ultimate Authority, and may my love for You today align with those whom You have chosen to have in authority over me. In Jesus' name I pray. Amen.

_____

_____

_____

_____

_____

February 20

AGREEMENT

And Samuel said, Hath the LORD [as great] delight in burnt offerings and sacrifices, as in obeying the voice of the LORD? Behold, to obey [is] better than sacrifice, [and] to hearken than the fat of rams.

1 Samuel 15:22

When two or more individuals concur upon certain rules, regulations, patterns or ideas, they are said to be in agreement with one another. Contracts and treaties are filled with particulars that each party is supposed to sign and agree. The mutual consent of each side is imperative to the future relationship that is desired and expressed within that document.

When we obey the commands of God Almighty, in effect, we denote agreement with Him. There are rules and regulations given by God. When we know and obey them, we are agreeing that they are correct. To disobey God's contract or laws is to be in disagreement with Him, and those who do so are violators of the agreement.

Those who are wise know with whom to make an agreement, because violation and failure to perform are real possibilities when it comes to contracts and treaties. Lawsuits, divorces, and wars have been the result of non-compliance with previous agreements. Fortunately, God Almighty sent Jesus as one who was in full agreement with God and never failed to keep that agreement. It was Jesus who stood in everyone's place as One who completely fulfilled the law. It is to Jesus that all are in debt.

PRAYER

Dear Heavenly Father, Your law is right and good, and I want to be in agreement with You by obeying it. Help me today to be in agreement with You. In Jesus' name I pray. Amen.

CHAPERONE

Nevertheless I tell you the truth; It is expedient for you that I go away: for if I go not away, the Comforter will not come unto you; but if I depart, I will send him unto you.

John 16:7

Commanders and chiefs, sergeants and corporals, all have something in common. They serve as overseers or chaperones over a certain number of troops. Their responsibilities include leading and guiding people toward a specific mission or goal. They have the authority to make decisions that are supposed to be in the best interest of the people of whom they come alongside.

Jesus gave the disciples an authority that was to come alongside of them. He could no longer stay with them, because His fate upon the cross was imminent. That meant they might be alone to manage in this world without His guidance and leadership. Jesus expressed His concern for their inadequacies and gave the promise of the Comforter—the Holy Spirit. The Holy Spirit would now be their guide, their instructor, and their leader in authority. He would be their chaperone, and no one would ever lead in such a way as He.

The key for the disciples was to be wise enough to listen to the Holy Spirit's guiding, and then to obey whatever He spoke. The Holy Spirit is speaking today. Those who are wise disciples hear His voice and follow along, just as the disciples of long ago.

PRAYER

Dear Heavenly Father, help me to listen to Your Holy Spirit. I need a chaperone in my life, and I can receive none better that the Holy One You have provided. In Jesus' name I pray. Amen.

CHARITABLE

Every man according as he purposeth in his heart,
[so let him give]; not grudgingly, or of necessity:
for God loveth a cheerful giver.

2 Corinthians 9:7

Soldiers who travel overseas for military operations are often seen playing with children in the streets of foreign countries. Although they are dressed in full uniform and are very careful about their missions, these soldiers demonstrate the reason for securing nations and providing protection for the innocent. Their charitable times are some of the most precious recorded for others to see.

God loves those who are charitable, especially when it comes to giving. The Bible speaks specifically about the benefits to giving whether it be money, time or energy, and the key to giving is the attitude in which one gives. There should be no begrudging, no pressure or intimidation. The cheerful giver is the one whom God loves.

Some do not give at all, yet they want everything to come their way with no outlet to others. People like this bring upon themselves a forfeiture of one of the greatest blessings of all: the charitable nature of the Heavenly Father toward those who give.

PRAYER

Dear Heavenly Father, I give all my life to You cheerfully. You have provided life and all I have. Please help me to always be a cheerful giver no matter where I go in this world. In Jesus' name I pray. Amen.

February 23
CELEBRATION

And he saith unto me, "Write, 'Blessed [are] they which are called unto the marriage supper of the Lamb.'" And he saith unto me, "These are the true sayings of God."

Revelation 19:9

A military wedding has pomp and circumstance like no other. With swords drawn, dress uniforms pressed, and grandeur of décor like no other, soldiers bring a sense of charm, stature, and honor to such a momentous occasion. The celebration rivals every other event known to man.

There is a marriage spoken of in the Bible that will exceed all the marriages upon the earth. Those who know Jesus Christ as their personal savior shall be in attendance. The Bridegroom shall arrive, and the glorious union of Christ and His church will be complete. There will be a marriage supper there, and Jesus Christ shall serve everyone in the company. What a glorious day, and what a glorious event, and what a glorious invitation has been extended to all who will receive it.

The invitation to the celebration is given. Now the only thing left is to RSVP.

PRAYER

Dear Heavenly Father, I know You have a huge celebration planned for those who receive Your invitation. I accept it and look forward to the day when I attend the marriage supper with You. In Jesus' name I pray. Amen.

CAPITALIZE

(For he saith, I have heard thee in a time accepted, and in the day of salvation have I succoured thee: behold, now [is] the accepted time; behold, now [is] the day of salvation.)

2 Chronicles 6:2

"Carpe Diem" is Latin for "Seize the Day." The idea is that we are to take advantage of the opportunities before us on the current day, rather than living in the past or dwelling in the future. What all soldiers have before them is the current day to capitalize upon opportunities, and the one who squanders those opportunities lives only in regret on the morrow.

Salvation is that way. The Bible makes it very clear that there are opportunities for people to come to know Jesus Christ as their personal Savior. Some accept it and some do not, but they each have this in common—they experience the "accepted time" to receive Him. That day is today, and those who capitalize upon this, the greatest of opportunities, shall have all eternity to celebrate. Those who do not seize it when available will have all of eternity to remember how they failed to take advantage of life's greatest opportunity.

PRAYER

Dear Heavenly Father, thank You for the opportunity to receive Jesus as my Lord and Savior. Thank You for helping me capitalize upon Your offering, and may the rest of my life be spent following after You. In Jesus' name I pray. Amen.

COMPASSION

*But a Samaritan, as he journeyed, came to where he was, and
when he saw him, he had compassion.*

Luke 10:33

One of the unfortunate outcomes of instant news reporting is that
we see so much suffering in the world that we're in danger of becoming
desensitized. It seems that multiple times a day, we see live reports
of massive disasters around the world. How can one individual
respond to all this pain and suffering? The danger I see is that we not
only become desensitized, but paralyzed. We're feeling, *What can we
do in the face of so many needs?*

Jesus was asked: "What must I do to inherit eternal life?" The questioner,
in this case, wasn't really interested in eternal life, but in appearing
to be justified by his own standard. The lesson of this parable
was that compassion for those in need is more important to
God than keeping our religious rules. The example of compassion is
seen in the Samaritan, who sees someone hurting, goes to where he
is, and attends to his wounds.

The attitude of the questioner was, "What's in it for me?" (For example,
what must I do to inherit eternal life? and "Not my problem.")
The Samaritan's attitude was, "What can I do to help?" It is true we
can't help everybody, but we can help somebody. Compassion begins
with one person going to where one person is and asking, "How can I
help?" Jesus looked upon our need and was moved with compassion.

PRAYER

*Dear Heavenly Father, when I see the terrible results of
earthquakes and tsunamis, I am overwhelmed by the
suffering of those people. I don't want to turn away from the
pain because I can't help them all. Help me to respond with
the resources You've given me. In Jesus' name I pray. Amen.*

February 26
COMMUNICATE

But be doers of the word, and not hearers only, deceiving
yourselves. For if anyone is a hearer of the word and not a doer,
he is like a man who looks intently at his natural face in a mirror.
For he looks at himself and goes away and at once forgets
what he was like.

James 1:22-24

The world has more tools with which to communicate than at any previous time (for example, email, cell phone, instant messaging, and teleconferencing). Does that mean we are better communicators than our predecessors? If we look at the alarming number of divorces where "poor or lack of communication" is cited as grounds for the breakup, the answer is no. I recently observed a young couple having dinner in a restaurant. Each had cell phone and was texting someone else. No words were being spoken between them.

A very dear friend shared this definition: "The secret of a good memory is the art of attention." Giving someone our total attention increases the quality of communication. When someone or something is important to us, the impact on both of us will be lasting. How often do we fail to remember a new acquaintance's name because we didn't think we would ever see them again?

The eastern shepherds valued their flocks and often gave them names. The sheep learned their shepherd's voice and followed him because of the care provided by their shepherd. Jesus called Himself a Shepherd, and said, *My sheep know my voice and another they will not follow.* (John 10:3-5) People respond positively when we show that we really care. We communicate more by our actions than with just words.

PRAYER

Dear Heavenly Father, I don't want to neglect showing by my actions that I care for my family, and I thank You for being the good shepherd of my soul. In Jesus' name I pray. Amen.

February 27
CHOICE

... Do not look on his appearance or on the height of his stature, because I have rejected him. For the Lord sees not as man sees: man looks of the outward appearance, but the Lord looks on the heart.

1 Samuel 16:7b

A sign in our high school gym reads, "It's not the size of the dog in the fight, but the size of the fight in the dog." Coach Fowler stressed repeatedly that we were not to measure our chances of winning on the size of our opponents. Winning would be determined by desire, preparation and execution.

The nation of Israel asked the prophet, Samuel, to provide the people a king. Saul was anointed to be the nation's first king. He was tall and appeared to be a wise choice. However, Saul's leadership soon deteriorated as a result of pride and rebellion. The prophet is given the assignment of finding another king. God sends him to the house of Jesse to anoint David, the youngest son, as the new king. It is there that God makes an unlikely choice as the next leader of Israel.

Samuel looked for qualities that reflect physical strength, experience and appearance. Jesse's sons who matched these desirable qualities were all rejected by God. The prophet is given the most essential quality in making a wise choice. Outward appearance is not the deciding factor but the heart. Man looks on the outward appearance, but God looks on the heart.

PRAYER

Dear Heavenly Father, search my heart and create in me a right spirit. Forgive my quickness to judge by the outward size, gift and appearance. In Jesus' name I pray. Amen.

_____

_____

COMRADE

Share in suffering as a good soldier of Christ Jesus.
No soldier gets entangled in civilian pursuits, since his aim
is to please the one who enlisted him.

2 Timothy 2:3-4

Migration of the monarch butterfly is one of nature's most amazing feats. Each autumn millions of monarchs from eastern United States and Canada migrate thousands of miles to a small handful of sites in Mexico, where they rest for the winter. Then in the spring, they begin their return trip north. The amazing thing, in addition to the distance they travel, is that no individual monarch ever makes the trip to Mexico and back.

A butterfly that leaves the Adirondack Mountains in New York will fly all the way to Mexico. But in the spring, it begins the trip northward. After laying eggs in the milkweed of Texas and Florida, it will die. Those who make it back to the mountains of New York may be three or four generations removed from the original monarch that migrated south. The monarch's survival is dependent upon the community of their comrades.

The Bible calls us to live in community as soldiers of Jesus Christ. Like the monarch butterfly, our survival depends on the performance of others. A common expression says, "A chain is only as strong as its weakness link." We may not be the general who deploys the unit, but our job is equally important. As Christian soldiers, we must guard against any distractions that hinder our service to God.

PRAYER

Dear Heavenly Father, thank You for reminding me that my life has been enriched by the faithfulness of family and friends. Their prayers have watched over me and prompted me to seek You. I want to contribute to the success of my fellow soldiers. In Jesus' name I pray. Amen.

February 29

LOSSES

Whoever finds his life will lose it, and whoever loses his life for my sake will find it.

Matthew 10:39

As a member of the world's best trained and best equipped military, our soldiers today will very likely be deployed to one of the hot spots of the world. It is also probable that they will be in combat and their lives will be in danger. They may face the tough, but necessary, decision to take another person's life as a part of their duty. It's likely that each soldier wrestled with this possibility as they chose to join the military. Even so, this is not a decision to be treated lightly.

Some will not only face the choice to take another person's life but will also experience the death of a fellow soldier. They will see someone with whom they have shared good times and tough times make the ultimate sacrifice for their country. Perhaps a chaplain will bring the news that a comrade has been lost or family members or friends back home may die. It is common for death to be described as a loss. What is meant is *not* that our friend or family's life has been wasted or obliterated. Christians view the death of a believer as merely a separation. The loss is that they are absent from our presence, but not forever.

Jesus died and resurrected out of death. He promises that all who believe in Him will be resurrected, also. Believing in Him means "putting our trust" in His death, burial and resurrection. His death paid the debt for our sins, and His resurrection gave us the ability to live a new life by faith. Losing our lives means giving up the right to live independent of God, but finding our lives means living a new life in Him.

PRAYER

Dear Heavenly Father, life is a precious gift. I do not take lightly the death of anyone, whether friend or foe. Thank You for giving me the gift of salvation through Jesus Christ. In Jesus' name I pray. Amen.

FINISH

But I do not account my life of any value nor as precious to
myself, if only I may finish my course and the ministry
that I received from the Lord Jesus, to testify to
the gospel of grace of God.

Acts 20:24

"March Madness" brings 68 teams together all with dreams of ending the season as number one. The basketball season begins with 20 to 25 teams who have a reasonable chance to earn this prestigious title. Each year at least one team, not considered a favorite, will surprise or upset a favored team. In basketball, football, racing or life, it's not how well competitors begin, but how they finish the race that determines the winner.

The title of number one goes to the team or individual who finishes the race ahead of all other competitors. In sports for every winner, there is a loser. For our military, winning means protecting the lives and property of the people. To do so, they must win the battle and secure the peace.

In life in order for us to win, someone else doesn't have to lose. The prize is not a trophy proclaiming our superiority over all other individuals or teams, but a way of living in grace. Our victories declare that we have walked as children of God obtaining righteousness by our faith, not any works we have done. Paul the Apostle testified that his victory was due to God's grace.

PRAYER

Dear Heavenly Father You have provided grace that I
may finish this race of life successfully. There are times my
assignment requires that I confront my enemies, even those
You died to save. I pray that they will come to know Your
grace. In Jesus' name I pray. Amen.

MATURE

*Not that I have already obtained this or am already perfect,
but I press on to make it my own, because Christ Jesus
has made me his own.*

Philippians 3:12

It is obvious that we aren't born physically mature. Babies have to learn how to eat, talk, and walk. Maturity doesn't come automatically with physical growth or age. We can grow old and still not be wise.

An old preacher once said, "You can run off and leave more than you overtake." What he was saying is that growth is possible—but not inevitable. Our attitude will position us for growth or keep us from it. Growth (maturity) requires effort. We must press toward the goal, and have a desire to grow. Maturity requires us to align our behavior and attitude with our goal. Healthy growth requires proper food. What we feed our bodies facilitates or limits our growth. Maturity requires that we discipline our thoughts, because what we think shapes our attitude and our behavior.

What will maturity look like in us? First, we admit that we need to grow. Our motivation for life is driven by love not rules. Our ambition and goals are to serve others and not to gain position or power.

PRAYER

Dear Heavenly Father, I want to grow in my knowledge of You. You have been generous and gracious toward me. Help me to live generously toward others. In Jesus' name I pray. Amen.

_____

_____

_____

_____

_____

March 3
WALK

Look carefully then how You walk, not as unwise but as wise,

Ephesians 5:15

Walking is learned so early in our development that we don't even think about the effort required until something interrupts its function. We walk in our homes without the lights, because we're accustomed to walking and are familiar with the location of the furniture. But, let someone rearrange the furniture and our habitual pattern can be painfully interrupted.

Life can also be lived in a pattern of routine and repetitive traditions in which we aren't aware of our destination. All of us have at some time experienced driving the car and later realizing that we didn't remember the details of the journey. Habits are helpful in performing tasks that we perform every day.

We need to ask ourselves; what will we allow to dominate? Each of us live in a body and we also have a spirit. The Bible teaches us that our body gravitates toward the flesh. The Spirit resists the control of the flesh and seeks to steer us to God. The apostle, Paul, admonishes us to ... *walk by the Spirit, and you will not gratify the desires of the flesh.* (Galatians 5:16b)

PRAYER

Dear Heavenly Father I want to be awake and wise in my walk. Teach me the word so that I will not stumble. In Jesus' name I pray. Amen.

_____

_____

_____

_____

_____

March 4

WIN

*Have this mind among yourselves, which is yours in Christ Jesus,
who , though he was in the form of God, did not count equality
with God a thing to be grasped, but made himself nothing, taking
the form of a servant, being born in the likeness of men.*

Philippians 2:5-7

Corporations and universities are teaching that self-preservation and
self-expression are valuable, if not essential, to success. Assertiveness
training is prized and frequently required in our success-dominated
culture. For many people, winning is everything, and success is measured by achievement and position.

At the same time, there's a counterrevolution in children's recreation.
I recently attended my eight-year-old grandson's baseball game.
There I observed rules that countered the self-assertiveness emphasis in the marketplace. In children's recreation, there was a "no competition movement." Those in charge were saying, "We don't keep
score," but the kids were all asking, "Who's winning?" The win-at-
all-cost philosophy can be harmful, but children also need to know
when they're being successful.

Teamwork and sportsmanship have been the hallmark of athletic
participation. Young boys and girls have learned to win and lose with
humility and grace. We see an example of a healthy balance between
winning and losing in the life of Jesus. On one occasion, Jesus in the
role of a servant washed the feet of his disciples, but he also proclaimed to Thomas, *I am the way, the truth, and the life.* The apostle,
Paul, wrote that while He was equal with God, Jesus humbled himself to identify with man.

PRAYER

*Dear Heavenly Father, I don't have to push and shove to
make a place for myself. You came to show me the love that
God has freely given to me and the whole world. In Jesus'
name I pray. Amen.*

STEP

But I say, walk by the Spirit, and you will not gratify the desires of the flesh.

Galatians 5:16

George never learned to keep time with the music. He was in the middle school band for two years. He played the trumpet, but he was always a beat behind everyone else. Everyone tried to help him stay with the rest of the band. You could see him counting the beats. His head would be bobbing and his foot tapping, but he would come in early or late. The band director suggested that he watch the baton. He just didn't have a sense of timing.

Some think we are to imitate the life of Christ. However, keeping in step in the Christian life is not done through imitation, but by identification. We don't live the Christian life by trying to imitate the lifestyle of Christ. Rather, He lives His resurrected life through us because we have received Him by faith!

The beat wasn't inside of George, and imitating the other members of the band was impossible. The key was for the music to fill George until he and the music became one. Paul tells us in Galatians 5:25, *If we live by the Spirit, let us also walk by the Spirit.* We are to abide in Him, and then fruit grows out of His life in us.

PRAYER

Dear Heavenly Father I have often been out of step even when I've tried to do good things. I need to be filled with Your Holy Spirit. In Jesus' name I pray. Amen.

TALL

Which of you by taking thought can add one cubit
unto his stature?

Matthew 6:27

There was once a man who was so tall that he could hold a four by twelve piece of sheet rock on the ceiling of a room while he screwed it in place. Others were on stilts and ladders, but he had no problem holding the massive walling in place at all. Most of the men around him were jealous and desired to have his natural ability, but none were so lucky.

Later in the day, there was an opportunity afforded to drive a small sports car. All of the men working on the job site were allowed to test drive this special automobile. However, when the tall man tried to fit inside, his legs were too long, his neck couldn't bend down far enough, and his feet would barely fit into the floor compartment. Because of his height, he didn't get to drive.

The Heavenly Father knows exactly how each person should be physically. Although some traits might like to be changed, more than likely, the major ones won't be. The key is not to have anxious thoughts over such things, but to rely fully upon God's infinite wisdom that He knows how to create with His purposes in mind.

PRAYER

Dear Heavenly Father, I accept the way that You made me physically. Please help me to keep this perspective as I use this body to serve You in Your kingdom. In Jesus' name I pray. Amen.

_____
_____
_____
_____

March 7

PERSEVERANCE

Thou therefore endure hardness, as a good soldier of Jesus Christ.

2 Timothy 2:3

Mount Everest is the highest mountain in the world. Those who seek to climb it train for months to endure the hardships that await their venture. The grueling pain, the lack of oxygen, and the bitter cold combine to make that climb one of the most arduous tasks on earth. There must be endurance and there must be perseverance, if one is ever to stand upon the top of Everest's peak.

One of the most difficult tasks in life is to push past adversity. There is a tendency in most people to quit when situations and circumstances become hard, taxing, and resistant. There is a tendency to desire the path of least resistance, no matter what occasion presents itself. Those who are able to push past the desire to bail out are those who find themselves victors, champions and winners. Those who quit never see the glory.

As a Christian, trials and tribulations will come, hardships will avail themselves, and places of endurance shall be required. The nature of life and living brings these plights, but the wise one will hold fast to the Savior Jesus when these times come. The glory He has prepared will not be worthy to be compared to the sufferings of this present time.

PRAYER

Dear Heavenly Father, with all my heart I desire to persevere through the hardships and hold to Your mighty hand. Please help me to do so. In Jesus' name I pray. Amen.

March 8
PAIN

And God shall wipe away all tears from their eyes; and there shall be no more death, neither sorrow, nor crying, neither shall there be any more pain: for the former things are passed away.

Revelation 21:4

Pain is a God-given blessing to the human body. Pain indicates that something is wrong, out of order, and misplaced. Through pain, awareness is made that correction must be made, alteration is essential, and treatment is imperative. Yet, there are pains that must be.

Soldiers within bootcamps must endure pain. Football, baseball and other sports activists must push through pain to succeed. Women who have babies must endure pain both before and after birth. There is a benefit to pushing past the pain. Endurance is built, victories are won, and children exist because people endure pain.

The Bible promises one day *neither shall there be any more pain*, and those who are wise will realize that pain, no matter how difficult, no matter how long, no matter how life-changing, will someday be gone. Until then, as Jesus demonstrated upon the cross, endure the pain, for salvation is on the other side.

PRAYER

Dear Heavenly Father, as I go through painful times in this life, help me to rely upon You to carry me through whatever comes my way. In Jesus' name I pray. Amen.

March 9
PRIDE

Pride goeth before destruction, and an haughty spirit before a fall.

Proverbs 16:18

How many people have seen the punt returner carry the ball back in a speedy fashion toward the goal-line, get very close to crossing it, and then start "hot dogging it," only to drop the ball just before he finishes? Or who hasn't see the boxer who wins one match easily, begins mouthing off about it and gets knocked out within the first minute of the next match? There is something daunting about the fate of pride.

Being a proud person is doable, as long as one knows the source of accomplishment. Rather than giving accolades to one's own abilities, the wise person knows that gifts are given by God. When those gifts result in great achievement, the glory must go to God alone.

Most people get into trouble with pride when the source of their strengths and abilities is forgotten. Jesus said, *without me you can do nothing.* Paul the Apostle added, *I can do all things through Christ which strengtheneth me.* The key is to know and acknowledge the source.

PRAYER

Dear Heavenly Father, please keep me mindful that You are the source for all my abilities and achievements. May I always give glory to You for the great things You have done. In Jesus' name I pray. Amen.

PREDESTINED

*For whom he did foreknow, he also did predestinate [to be]
conformed to the image of his Son, that he might be the firstborn
among many brethren.*

Romans 8:29

What if there was a way to know in advance which horse would
win the famous Kentucky Derby? What if a person knew all of the
winning numbers to the lottery before they were selected? What if
the next greatest stock was already known before the opening bell?
What if the soldiers knew where the enemy would be before the
battle began? How would a person choose from these great winners?
Would it be foolish not to bet on the winning horse, the winning
numbers, the winning stock, and the strategic position? This is very
similar to God's foreknowledge as to who will accept Him and who
will not.

God knows everything and everyone. He is omniscient—all knowing. Since He is already aware of who makes it to heaven and who
doesn't, He *predestinates them to be conformed to the image of his Son.*
Some might think this is unfair, but for those who do choose to follow Him today, He will not deny us. However, if someone decides
not to choose Him, then that person is not chosen. One might complain, "But that's not fair!" Then choose Him and to be among the
chosen and be conformed to His Son's image.

For those who have chosen Him, or better yet, realized that He has
chosen them, their lives are to be molded and shaped so that the
world will know that they are "little Christs," which is what the term
"Christian" really means.

PRAYER

*Dear Heavenly Father, thank You for choosing me. May my
life be conformed to the image of Your Son Jesus today. In
Jesus' name I pray. Amen.*

POPULARITY

*And the multitudes that went before, and that followed,
cried, saying, Hosanna to the Son of David: Blessed [is] he that
cometh in the name of the Lord; Hosanna in the highest.*

Matthew 21:9

Being famous and well-known is a drive that many have in Hollywood today, but it not only registers there—being popular is a drive within most of the schools in America. There is a God-given inner drive for love and acceptance that is in every human being. Since people often do not realize this drive can only be filled by a relationship with God through Jesus Christ, they try to fill it with other relationships that fall short. That's the problem with fame—it is fleeting.

Jesus was popular with the crowds who cried, "Hosanna to the Son of David," on the day of the triumphal entry. However, only a few short days they were crying, "Crucify Him!" In other words, the fame was fleeting and Jesus' popularity fell in a totally opposite direction.

A wise person knows that popularity and fame are here today and gone tomorrow. The very people who praise one day will castigate the next. Wisdom from the Lord Jesus keeps in mind that there is only one with whom a person wants to be popular, the Heavenly Father. Popularity does not have to be earned—it must only be believed.

PRAYER

Dear Heavenly Father, please help me not to seek the fleeting popularity of man. May I always be in the arena of popularity with You. In Jesus' name I pray. Amen.

CHASE

Know ye not that they which run in a race run all, but one receiveth the prize? So run, that ye may obtain.

1 Corinthians 9:24

When there is a mission to be accomplished and a goal to be reached, there is in effect a sort of chase that is moved upon. The pursuit of the goal is more than half the battle. Reaching the goal is the motivating force that moves soldiers to follow orders, take action and move as directed. Delay compromises, and obstacles must be moved, for the chase is on and any opposing force will only inhibit the goal.

We Christians who closely follow Jesus Christ know that a chase is on. We rely upon the fact that there is only so much time allotted each person on this earth. The space we are allowed will determine our outcome for eternity. Faithfulness for whatever time is given is the goal, and to be racing toward the prize must be the constant motion. As with a mission, Christians must chase the goal with all their hearts.

Remember, there is a prize at the end of this chase. Through the Scriptures, we know that we will obtain it. Praise be to God!

PRAYER

Dear Heavenly Father, thank You for the time You have given me on this earth. I pray I shall use it to chase the prize that You have for me with all my spirit, body, soul, and mind. In Jesus' name I pray. Amen.

_____

_____

_____

_____

_____

AUTHORITY

What then shall we say to these things? If God be for us,
who can be against us?

Romans 8:31

An umpire named Babe Pirelli once called Babe Ruth out on strikes. The crowd booed the call, and Ruth turned to the umpire and said, "There's 40,000 people here who know that the last pitch was a ball." All the coaches and players expected the umpire to eject Ruth from the game. However, the umpire replied, "Maybe so, Babe, but mine is the only opinion that counts."

Life is similar to a baseball game in some ways. For example, there are boundaries that define whether the play is in fair or foul territory. Like baseball, there are rules that determine whether a player is safe or out. Baseball has umpires that have a responsibility to apply and enforce the rules of the game. But, unlike baseball, the Umpire of Life is not subject to a mistaken judgment or call.

In fact, the good news is that God is on our side. God, Who has every right to condemn us, chooses not to—rather, He provides us forgiveness. All we need to do is call upon the name of the Lord. (Romans 10:13) *For everyone who calls on the name of the Lord will be saved.*

PRAYER

Dear Heavenly Father, I was condemned by my own guilt and shame. I call upon Your mercy and ask that You cleanse my life from all sin. In Jesus' name I pray. Amen.

APTITUDE

Every good gift and every perfect gift is from above, and cometh down from the Father of lights, with whom is no variableness, neither shadow of turning.

James 1:17

How is it that one person seems to take to a project very naturally, whereas another doesn't even seem to know where to start? Some play piano with seemingly-less effort, while others cannot put two or three notes together. Some throw a ball for what seems to be a mile and another cannot even so much as play catch. The difference is aptitude.

If we have certain gifts and talents toward a particular function, we are naturally inclined to perform that function with ease. For those who are not gifted or talented in certain areas, those areas become a struggle. James knew from where the source of every gifting and talent came—*from the Father of lights*. If we are wise enough to realize that our aptitude comes from God above, we are more likely to discover that aptitude early and use it to its fullest.

The wise individual knows where the glory for the aptitude should shine. If there is talent, if there is ability, if there is gifting, then to God be the glory for the great things He has done.

PRAYER

Dear Heavenly Father, please help me to know the gifts that You have given to me. Give me today the opportunities to share that talent that You may be glorified. In Jesus' name I pray. Amen.

_____

_____

_____

_____

ABOUND

And God [is] able to make all grace abound toward you;
that ye, always having all sufficiency in all [things],
may abound to every good work:

2 Corinthians 9:8

There is mediocrity, and there is abounding. Some settle and others thrive. The difference comes in results. Those who choose to abound will find themselves advanced, ranked higher, and recipients of greater reward and honor than those who just get by.

The United States was formed by those who sought to abound. The principles they fought for were far beyond their individual preferences, but rather an idea and ideal that would penetrate an entire society and culture. Those who brandish the military badge know the fruit of abounding.

Paul the Apostle knew the benefit to abounding. His directive in writing was that the Christians at Corinth would abound *to every good work*—no work was excluded or exempt. Those who adopt that regiment will find the grace of God always toward them.

PRAYER

Dear Heavenly Father, I desire to abound in whatever work You have placed before me today. May Your grace be with me as I live before Your eyes. In Jesus' name I pray. Amen.

ABSORBED

And Jesus said unto him, No man, having put his hand to the plough, and looking back, is fit for the kingdom of God.

Luke 9:62

Sometimes our focus can be so intense that we regard no distraction around us, no matter how loud those distractions may be. Video game players and sportsmen are like this. When thousands of fans scream and yell, people playing soccer, baseball or football block them out. When video game experts concentrate, even a shouting parent is hard to get their attention. People become absorbed in their activities.

Jesus refers to absorption, but His attention is directed toward those who desire to be *fit for the kingdom of God*. Those who are distracted by the world and its offerings are not deemed fit. Only those who put their hands to the plough in the first place are addressed. The Christian must charge forward, and not look behind. The Christian must continue and not dwell in the past. The Christian must recon the path ahead and prioritize. That which is past must be left in the past. Those who absorb themselves in these attentions will find themselves within the kingdom of God.

PRAYER

Dear Heavenly Father, help me to keep my hand to the plough and look forward—not behind. In Jesus' name I pray. Amen.

March 17

ZEAL

The slothful [man] saith, [There is] a lion without,
I shall be slain in the streets.

Proverbs 22:13

Self-starters are rare to find. Those who take themselves up by the seat of their pants and get going without external stimulus are considered ambitious. Those who avoid, delay, procrastinate, and put off are considered slothful. A lot can be said about the person who is self-motivated.

Many people use excuses, and sometimes ridiculous excuses, for not performing a duty. They will devise all sorts of wild reasons as to why a particular task cannot be performed. They may say, "A lion is without," or "I might fall or get in trouble or break a leg or get eaten by a huge Gila monster," or whatever other beg-off might be conjured up.

Ambition comes from within and is mobilized by a relationship with the Heavenly Father. Ambition is predicated on living for His pleasure. Once we have settled that purpose in our minds, ambition follows without regard to escape.

PRAYER

Dear Heavenly Father, help me to know that my ambition comes from relating to You. May my day be motivated by my willingness to be pleasing before Your eyes. In Jesus' name I pray. Amen.

March 18
FAILURE

Simon, Simon, behold, Satan demanded to have you, that he might sift you like wheat, but I have prayed for you that your faith may not fail...

Luke 22:31-32a

Webster's definition of failure: "a failing to perform a duty or expected action." Colin Powell, U.S. Joint Chief of Staff and former Secretary of State said, "There are no secrets to success. It is the result of preparation, hard work, and learning from failure." Learning from failure is what separates losers from winners.

The Bible records the failure of Simon Peter, a disciple of Jesus, who vowed to remain loyal, even if it meant his death. When Jesus was arrested, Simon, along with the other disciples ran away in fear. Peter's failure was magnified, because of his boastful pledge of solidarity. Under the threat of his own arrest, he cursed and denied ever knowing Jesus. Adding to Simon's own anguish was Jesus' warning that he would, in fact, deny the Lord.

A tattoo artist was asked, "What is the strangest tattoo you've ever been asked to render?" He replied, "A man once asked me to tattoo the word, *failure*, across his chest." He was asked, "Why would anyone want failure tattooed on their body?" His answer, "Failure was in his heart before it was tattooed on his body." Everybody will fail at some point in their life, but failure doesn't have to become our lifestyle. Simon Peter's failure wasn't fatal. He learned the lesson and became a leading spokesman and a primary author of the Christian faith.

PRAYER

Dear Heavenly Father, I want to learn from my failures and grow in my dependence on Your strength. I am weakest when I boast in my own abilities. In Jesus' name I pray. Amen.

COWARD

My flesh and my heart may fail, but God is the strength of my heart and my portion forever.

Psalm 73:26

There will be times when all our training, fitness and courage will be tested to the max. We may even find ourselves gripped by fear. It has been said that fear can make cowards of the strongest person. Does having fear mean that we're weak? I don't think so. In fact, admitting that we're afraid can be the beginning of our victory.

We see that in Psalm 73, where the writer at first focuses on his enemies and is envious of their success. At that point, he realizes that he has a resource that the wicked lack: God is with him. This knowledge directs him to a new understanding and confidence. His strength is not in his training, fitness or courage, but in his faith in God. God will give strength to the weak.

PRAYER

Dear Heavenly Father, when I am afraid I will trust in You. You give me strength and will never leave me. In Jesus' name I pray. Amen.

FITNESS

You therefore must endure hardship as a good soldier of Jesus Christ.

2 Timothy 2:3

What are the qualities of physical fitness? Some have suggested the following: endurance, stamina, strength, power, speed and coordination. You might add others, but these most likely would be included in any list of necessary qualities of a good soldier.

A dad taught his son the value of endurance when the son wanted to quit his after-school job. The son wanted the paper route until he realized it meant early-morning deliveries on rainy, cold days. His dad refused to let him quit just because the job was more difficult than expected.

Life will bring us unexpected difficulties that will require endurance, stamina, and strength. We will be tested and our fitness questioned. Will we quit or will we endure?

PRAYER

Dear Heavenly Father, You know that I need Your strength. I'm going to endure. In Jesus' name I pray. Amen.

March 21

FIVE AND FLY

If you faint in the day of adversity, your strength is small.

Proverbs 24:10

Baseball has an expression for the pitcher who goes five innings and looks to the bullpen to preserve the win as a "five and fly." Modern pitchers rarely go the distance any more. Relievers who can come into the game and shut down the opposition are highly valued. The military gives this name to those who enlist, pursue educational opportunities, and bail after five years.

I ran in a 10K event and learned the value of a strong finish. I had trained for the race and when the day came, I felt exceptionally strong. So strong, in fact, that I ran the first 3K in my best time. However, the next 3K was torture. I ran out of gas and struggled to finish the race. I lost the time gained by my fast pace, because I failed to train properly.

Life is more like a marathon than a sprint. It is important to train, so that we can finish strong. The baseball team that turns the game over to someone who repeatedly surrenders the lead will soon find another closer. The runner who sprints out of the starting blocks but stumbles to the finish line will never win the medal. Soldiers who excel on the shooting range but go AWOL in the battle will disgrace themselves and fail in their mission.

PRAYER

Dear Heavenly Father, there are times when I feel like giving up. I need Your strength to finish my assignment honorably, and I want to run the race of life successfully. In Jesus' name I pray. Amen.

_____

_____

_____

FLEE

Flee also youthful lusts: but follow righteousness, faith, charity, peace, with them that call on the Lord out of a pure heart.

2 Timothy 2:22

Retreating is an important part of warfare. Wise soldiers know the advantages of moving their positions back and regrouping for another attack. Those who use retreating properly are advantaged by it.

There are some places in life where the best policy is to flee. Prayer, discussion, hoping, and giving some time to it are not sufficient for avoiding great troubles. Joseph knew what to do when Potiphar's wife continued her seduction of him. Although his running away cost him because of her lies, it did not cost him before God.

When the battle is hot and the enemy is winning, retreat. Flee and watch righteousness, faith, charity, and peace come into being like never before.

PRAYER

Dear Heavenly Father, help me to know when I should just flee. I desire a pure heart before You no matter what the temptation may be. In Jesus' name I pray. Amen.

_____

_____

_____

_____

_____

_____

_____

_____

_____

_____

FAN

Woe unto you, when all men shall speak well of you! For so did their fathers to the false prophets.

Luke 6:26

Some people become one of these every week. Some even dress in team colors, while others will paint their faces and alter their bodies to reflect their passion. These are none other than fans. They support their teams and root them on. There is no team like their team—all other teams are foes and enemies.

Isn't it interesting, however, how there seem to be more fans in the stands when the team is winning? What if their team lost a few games? What if they didn't win at all during the entire season? What happens then? Who and where are the fans at that point?

Jesus knew that His disciples would have fans: *people who shall speak well of you.* There is warning here. His words were that these "fans" even spoke well of false prophets. In other words, their attention was given to themselves and their own benefit. If they were benefited, they were fans. If there were no benefits, they were not fans. This warning from the King of Kings and the Lord of Lords is so important that He began these words with, "Woe unto you." Those who are wise will heed the One who knows all things, both true and false.

PRAYER

Dear Heavenly Father, help me to discern the accolades of people around me. Let my life be a reflection of circumspection that You give charge to be included in my life. In Jesus' name I pray. Amen.

_____

_____

_____

_____

March 24
FANATIC

For I could wish that myself were accursed from Christ for my brethren, my kinsmen according to the flesh.

Romans 9:3

There is a difference between a fan and a fanatic. It is usually measured by the amount of time, effort and commitment that fans have for their team. With regard to outerwear, attendance, expenditure and revelry, a fanatic is easily identified.

Paul the Apostle was a fanatic toward Jesus Christ and His plan for salvation. Oh, not in the weird sense of the word, but in the "all-out" attitude of his life. His passion was for everyone everywhere to know Jesus Christ as their Lord and Savior. He had a particular passion toward those of his own brethren and kinsmen in the flesh. His words were basically that if he could be eternally damned that they might be saved, he would do it. Now that's a fanatic.

Warriors know the idea of fanaticism. Commitment to the mission above all else is the mantra of very few. However, those who are fanatics on behalf of others, rather than themselves, are the greatest fanatics of all.

PRAYER

Dear Heavenly Father, I want to be a fanatic for You, not in a foolish way, but in a way that is committed to Your cause and Your Gospel, no matter what it costs me in this life. In Jesus' name I pray. Amen.

FAULT

And the man said, "The woman whom thou gavest [to be] with me, she gave me of the tree, and I did eat".

Genesis 3:12

Admission of guilt is about as hard to find as a Hope Diamond in the middle of a landfill. There seems to be a huge amount of blame game going around. It's never anyone's fault except for someone else, who isn't directly related. Even Adam knew this as he began the blame game in the beginning.

When asked by the Heavenly Father if he had eaten from the tree, Adam essentially blamed the woman and by doing so, blamed God. When a failure occurs, most people look for reasons other than themselves to charge. "It's someone else's fault," is usually the phrase spoken in defense. However, the Heavenly Father knows, and blaming another does not dismiss our involvement.

When wrong is done, admission is necessary. From honest response comes natural forgiveness and alteration. Otherwise, we remain in the same state and continued blaming will occur. Sometimes the best medicine is to just look in the mirror, take responsibility, and say, "It's my fault."

PRAYER

Dear Heavenly Father, I know there are things that are none other than my fault. I ask for Your forgiveness, and I pray that You will help me from making future mistakes like these ever again. In Jesus' name I pray. Amen.

_____

_____

_____

_____

_____

FEDERAL

Behold, how good and how pleasant [it is] for brethren to dwell together in unity!

Psalm 133:1

If a 90-pound weakling tries to block a 350-pound lineman in a football game, more than likely there had better be an ambulance nearby. However, if fifty 90-pound weaklings unite together against the large foe, the ambulance will be carting the big man off the field. The difference is the fifty are united in effort. The fifty are federal.

The idea of federation is to have a group of people or entities that unite under one common agreement or government. Troops who unite together are federate in nature. The power of the many will be much stronger than one or a few. When the battles arise, those who are greatly united usually are the victors, while those who separate and divide become the victims.

The Bible is clear as to what it means to be united. The Psalmist called it "good" and "pleasant" when brothers unite. When the principle of being together formulates in minds, the onslaught of the enemy is much less potent. When unity with the Father is of utmost importance, every foe that rises up against shall fall. The federate with the Father wins.

PRAYER

Dear Heavenly Father, I choose to unite with You today. May every move I make and every foe I face be in light of my federation with You. In Jesus' name I pray. Amen.

_____

_____

_____

_____

_____

March 27
FEW

Because strait [is] the gate, and narrow [is] the way, which leadeth unto life, and few there be that find it.

Matthew 7:14

Top secret information is an important portion of the protection of the country. The need-to-know basis is formulated to resist enemies and keep them at bay. There are just a few who have access to some data that must be kept quiet.

The interesting part to following Jesus Christ is that the way to follow Him is unlike Top Secret initiatives, since it is well-known. The difference is that although people know the narrow way, hardly anyone ever takes it. Few people find the way, because they do not take the first step.

Here is the secret: Jesus is the way, the truth and the life. No man comes to the Father but by Him. Those who choose this narrow way, find it. Those who do not are left out on the greatest need-to-know basis idea ever presented to man.

PRAYER

Dear Heavenly Father, thank You for showing me Your narrow way. I desire to follow it every day until I see You face to face. In Jesus' name I pray. Amen.

FINISH

I have fought a good fight, I have finished [my] course,
I have kept the faith:

2 Timothy 4:7

The big race was on! The tortoise versus the hare was to be the race of the century. "On your mark, get set, go!" screamed the race starter, and off the hare ran at blazing speed. Along the way, since he was so far ahead, the hare decided to take a nap. Step by step, the slow little tortoise plodded along until he passed the sleeping hare. Once the tortoise was about to cross the finish line, the hare awoke. Although he used every bit of speed within him to catch up, it was too late. The tortoise had already crossed the finish line.

The famous children's story about the tortoise and the hare is worthy of every soldier's reminding. The moral within the story aligns with the Bible's idea about how we should live our lives. Many people start out quite strong. However, after an allotment of time passes, they feel that they no longer have to run—they can rest, or even worse, not be concerned about the race at all.

It really is not how we start our race, but how we finish it. The mode of running is not nearly as important as the fact that there must be running. Those who follow after Christ must keep themselves in the race and finish well. Any other alternative only hurts the one who regards the race a waste of time.

PRAYER

Dear Heavenly Father, please keep me on track that I will run this race You have set before me with all my heart all the days of my life. In Jesus' name I pray. Amen.

_____

_____

_____

FITNESS

For bodily exercise profiteth little: but godliness is profitable unto all things, having promise of the life that now is, and of that which is to come.

1 Timothy 4:8

Obstacle courses, 20-mile runs with full gear, mountain climbing, and physical training of any sort can be taxing upon a body. Those who endure the physical pains of getting into shape know exactly of that which this writer speaks. There is a price for fitness, but the events of the future may require fitness as regiment.

Even the Bible says that bodily exercise profits. Even though it says that it "profits little," at least it does profit some. However, there is another quality that exceeds bodily fitness and that is "godliness." Being like God is one of the most profitable pursuits a person can have. Adding to the qualities in our lives that are more and more like God will benefit long after physical fitness is no longer obtainable.

The body slowly, but surely, wears out, and those activities that we involves ourselves in while young will not be available later in life. However, godliness will continue to profit long after the body doesn't function as well anymore.

PRAYER

Dear Heavenly Father, thank You for my physical body. Help me to remember to keep it fit, but also to work toward godliness that will profit beyond this temporary body made for the earth. In Jesus' name I pray. Amen.

FLOGGED

Then Pilate therefore took Jesus, and scourged [him].

John 19:1

When a 20- or 30-mile hike with a full pack is completed, only the soldier who has endured such flogging can tell of the pain. The agony within the body is deep, causing many soldiers to wonder if they can ever make it another step. Somehow this torture of being flogged is to make the weakest of persons a stronger soldier who is ready for battle.

Jesus, however, was flogged, scourged for no reason of His own. With a "cat of nine tails," a whiplike device that had nine strands of leather with pieces of bone and metal attached to the end of each strand, a soldier beat Jesus time after time after time. The usual amount was 40 lashes minus one, or 39 times that they beat a prisoner. The idea was that any prisoner had committed a crime would confess to it early in the scourging process. However, Jesus had nothing to confess, so He took the entire beating.

The Bible says, "And by His stripes we are healed." There was purpose in His flogging. However, the flogging was taken for the benefit of those who follow Him and not for Himself. Once again the endurance required for the long hike ahead pushed Jesus to do for others what they could not do for themselves.

PRAYER

Dear Heavenly Father, thank You for the flogging that You took for me. I do not take it for granted. May I take every flogging in my life be in the same spirit in which You took Your beating for me. In Jesus' name I pray. Amen.

_____

_____

_____

March 31
FRACTION

By little and little I will drive them out from before thee, until thou be increased, and inherit the land.

Exodus 23:30

Battles usually are never won in a day. Operations and directives are given with an overall plan in mind that may last days, months or even years. Those who meet in such planning sessions do their best to accomplish the goals with as little loss as possible. Fraction by fraction, they conquer until the whole is fulfilled.

Those who know the history of Israel when they marched into the promised land know about the way the Lord gave them success over their enemies. It was little by little. The reasons were, *Lest the land become desolate, and the beast of the field multiply against thee,* according to Exodus 23:29. In other words, the Heavenly Father knew the timing and reasons for fulfilling His will.

In one's own life, God may fulfill His will fractionally or a little at a time. When this occurs, the key is to understand that He has His reasons, and the reasons are only meant to protect people from damages that they cannot see.

PRAYER

Dear Heavenly Father, I trust You with my future and with the fulfilling of Your will. Help me to keep the perspective that when You fulfill it in pieces, You have Your reasons why. In Jesus' name I pray. Amen.

_____

_____

_____

_____

_____

April 1

INVASION

Behold, I stand at the door and knock. If anyone hears my voice and open the door, I will come in to him and eat with him, and he with me.

Revelation 3:20

There are many famous military invasions in our nation and the world's history. The invasion of Poland by Germany in September 1939 brought the USSR into the war and led to the division and annexing of Poland by Russia and Germany. A significant turning point in WWII was the invasion of Normandy by the Allied armies led by General Dwight Eisenhower. The most recent invasion occurred May 1, 2011 when a team of U.S. Navy Seals stormed the compound hiding the head of the Al Qaida network and killed Osama Bin Laden. Will this be the turning point in the ongoing struggle against terrorist? That is still to be determined.

Each invasion wrote a new chapter in the history of nations. Those who have benefited from the sacrifice and bravery of those who fought the battles are left to evaluate the lessons of their struggle. Hopefully, we can clearly see the evil our generation was spared by the defeat of Nazi Germany, and our children will better understand the terror that will be stopped by the defeat of Al Qaeda.

However, the most significant invasion occurred over two thousand years ago. Without fanfare or force, a child miraculously was born to a virgin and changed the course of history. He came as a shepherd, not as a soldier, and he spoke rather than fought. Instead of blasting His way into human hearts, He stands outside knocking, waiting to be invited in. Everyone who recognizes His voice and invites Him in receives the gift of eternal life and He gives them the power to become sons of God. (John 1:12)

PRAYER

Dear Heavenly Father, I invite You to enter my heart and enable me to live as a son of God. I have heard Your knock and Your voice. I welcome Your presence. In Jesus' name I pray. Amen.

April 2

OTHERS

Greater love has no one than this, that someone lay down his life for his friends.

John 15:13

September 11, 2001 (to all U.S. citizens, simply 911) a generation of brave men and women ran into the twin towers while thousands were fleeing. There's no criticism of those who fled for their lives as those towers fell in New York City. However, it is certainly appropriate to honor those courageous fire and police officers who willingly sacrificed themselves attempting to save others.

This example of selflessness is the spirit of the United States of America military. Interviews with the survivors of 911 were quoted as saying, "I was just doing my job." Similarly, veterans of World War II, who endured and survived Omaha Beach deflected any praise saying, "We had a job to do." These are the qualities that have made this nation a world power.

The notion of laying down our life for a friend or for our country is at the heart of Christianity. Granted, not every soldier or every firefighter or policeman past or present was a Christian. However, the greatest example of this quality is when Jesus Christ, who was sinless, died for sinners. *For our sake he made him to be sin who knew no sin, so that in him we might become the righteousness of God.* (2 Corinthians 5:21)

PRAYER

Dear Heavenly Father, I am thankful for those men and women who have sacrificed their lives for my freedom! Thank you Jesus for dying, so that I can be free from the guilt of sin. In Jesus' name I pray. Amen.

April 3
CHIEF OF SINNERS

*This [is] a faithful saying, and worthy of all acceptation,
that Christ Jesus came into the world to save sinners;
of whom I am chief.*

1 Timothy 1:15

Mistakes are made often in soldier training. Part of the process is to work through those mistakes and learn how to avoid them in the future. Those who make mistakes miss the mark and realignment is necessary, if they are to become effective soldiers.

Sin, at it's basic meaning, is to "miss the mark." It is an archery term, where participants would place a hoop or target on a tree, pull back the bow, and let an arrow fly. If the arrow missed the mark, they called it a sin. The mark is perfection and, therefore, everyone has missed the mark. Everyone has sinned.

Paul the Apostle called himself the "Chief" of sinners, and if he so named himself, what does that mean for the rest of the population? Simply this—all are sinners, and it was for sinners that Jesus came to die and be resurrected. Those who believe that He came to deliver them from their sins shall be saved. Those who do not believe will remain in their sins and mistakes to repeat them over and over again.

PRAYER

Dear Heavenly Father, I know that I have missed the mark and am a sinner. I come to You today asking for forgiveness and that Jesus Christ will come into my heart and life. Wash away my sin I pray. In Jesus' name I pray. Amen.

CHEAT

*The thief cometh not, but for to steal, and to kill, and to destroy:
I am come that they might have life, and that they might
have [it] more abundantly.*

John 10:10

Although many know and have employed the idea of cheating, not many enjoy being cheated against. Some who are in the armed forces know what it is like to feel cheated out of a job, position, assignment, or location. Anger often sets in and revenge is a primary motivator.

Jesus makes it known who is the greatest cheater of all—Satan. His entire mission is to steal, kill and destroy as many people as he can before he meets his final destination in the lake, which burns with fire. He constantly uses other people to cheat others so they will react in ungodly ways, which end up cheating themselves. His devices are devious and his ways are unscrupulous. He has great hatred toward everyone who loves the Lord Jesus.

Whenever a person feels cheated, even if very wrongfully so, remember, Jesus came to give life, and life more abundantly. That supersedes any onslaught of cheating the enemy may have in mind.

PRAYER

Dear Heavenly Father, please help me not to cheat anyone, especially You. For those who have cheated me, I place them in your hands to do with as You will. In Jesus' name I pray. Amen.

_____

_____

_____

_____

_____

April 5
CRUCIFY

And it was he third hour, and they crucified him.

Mark 15:25

Wars have seen some of the most horrific of deaths. The devastation and destruction left by battles and engagements of armies are many times too much for any human being to digest. Many who have fought in those intense battles know what it means to crucify the flesh, and the image of these things doesn't easily disappear.

Jesus was crucified, and for those who study such things, the Crucifixion of the body is one of the most horrible deaths that a person can endure. Suffocation occurs and the excruciating pain is like no other as the body cries out for relief from every nerve ending. There was a greater purpose in mind when Jesus subjected Himself to this painful death, which was to save mankind. Without the crucifixion of Jesus, no one would be saved. There had to be a perfect sacrifice for the sins of mankind, and no one else has the qualifications of perfection.

Jesus was crucified for everyone, but not all receive Him. Those who do will have eternal life. Those who do not will suffer carnage that will last forever and ever and ever.

PRAYER

Dear Heavenly Father, thank You for Jesus being crucified for me. I know that I am a sinner and am perfect in no way. I accept and receive the sacrifice that You have made for me. In Jesus' name I pray. Amen.

_____

_____

_____

_____

April 6

CLEANSE

Since we have these promises, beloved, let us cleanse ourselves from every defilement of body and spirit, bringing holiness to completion in the fear of God.

2 Corinthians 7:1

I saw an individual suffering from a severe obsession with guilt. During one episode, this individual went to the refrigerator, emptied all the ice into the kitchen sink, and turned on the hot water. While the steaming hot water melted the ice, this suffering man began washing his hands in the mixture of hot and cold water.

The man's actions reminded me of the account of Pilate who sought to be free of any responsibility in Jesus' trial ... *He took water and washed his hands before the crowd, saying, I am innocent of this man's blood, ...* (Matthew 27:24b) Pilate didn't absolve his guilt regarding the death of Jesus any more than the hot/cold water washed the disturbed man's depression and guilt away.

Psalm 119:9 asks, *How can a young man cleanse his way?* The answer follows in the same verse, *By taking heed according to Your word.* We should examine ourselves and honestly face the areas where we fail to live ethically and morally. Clearly, the Scriptures teach us that nobody can forgive sin and none of us can wash away guilt. God's Word gives us the answer: *If we confess our sins, He is faithful and just to forgive us our sins and to cleanse us from all unrighteousness.* 1 John 1:9

PRAYER

Dear Heavenly Father, thank You for providing cleansing for my sin and guilt. I confess my sin and believe in Jesus Christ as my Savior. Cleanse me from all sin. In Jesus' name I pray. Amen.

April 7

CONNECTED

I am the vine; you are the branches. Whoever abides in me and I in him, he it is that bears much fruit, for apart from me you can do nothing.

John 15:5

Most of us live in cities. We travel on asphalt or concrete streets, live in homes that are air-conditioned and centrally heated. We buy food from stores and only a few people get dirt under their fingernails. I've never tended a vineyard, but I've grown tomatoes and peas and picked some cotton. I know a little about planting and reaping, and I know, good fruit requires effort.

What grows without any effort? Weeds! But if we want sweet, juicy grapes or tomatoes, we will need to plant, weed and prune. Jesus uses the illustration of the vineyard to teach us the principle of a healthy life. As a branch must be connected to the vine to produce grapes, we must be connected to Jesus.

Jesus is not saying everyone who is not a Christian will die immediately—we do have a choice. To abide in Him is to have His life and bear good fruit. Choosing to go our own way will also result in fruit. The fruit of Jesus is love, joy, peace, patience, kindness, goodness, faithfulness, gentleness, and self-control. And the fruit of self or the flesh is immorality, impurity, sensuality, idolatry, sorcery, enmity, strife, jealousy, fits of anger, rivalries, dissensions, divisions, envy, drunkenness, orgies and the like. (Galatians 5:19-22a) Stay connected to Jesus!

PRAYER

Dear Heavenly Father, I want to stay connected to the true vine. Without You, I am nothing. In Jesus' name I pray. Amen.

CLOSE

Since all these things are thus to be dissolved, what sort of people ought you to be in lives of holiness and godliness, waiting for and hastening the coming of the day of God, because of which the heavens will be set on fire and dissolved, and the heavenly bodies will melt as they burn!

2 Peter 3: 11-12

Where were we ten years ago? Is our memory clear or distant? How do we view time? It is easy to be caught up in the here and now. Upon graduating from high school, three members of that class made a pact to meet on the tenth anniversary of their graduation. All three would become a pastor of a church. Despite their common interests and sincere desire to stay in touch, the meeting never happened.

The apostle, Peter, reminds us God views time differently than we. In fact, he notes that with the Lord one day is as a thousand years... What does that mean? One explanation says, "No delay that occurs is long to God: God's eternal-ages measure differs wholly from man's hourglass." The here and now are important, but we need to see the big picture. Our life is very brief from the perspective of eternity.

What happens now has eternal significance. Since everything we see and use is temporary, including our lives, shouldn't that impact how we live? If I embrace God's view of time, will it change my behavior or set new priorities? Peter's question is worth considering: "What sort of people ought we to be?"

PRAYER

Dear Heavenly Father, I need to remember that the physical world is temporary at best. Help me use the things in my world, while not allowing them to become my master. I want to live a holy and godly life. In Jesus' name I pray. Amen.

CLOCK

For everything there is a season, and a time for every matter
under heaven:

Ecclesiastes 3:1

I once lived five miles from the eastern and central time zone boundary. Many of our neighbors lived in the central time zone but worked in the eastern time zone. The frequently asked question was, "What time is it?" And the reply was, "Fast time? Or slow time?" (Eastern time was called fast time and Central time was called slow time). Many households kept two clocks, one for each zone. One they lived by and the other they used for work.

Living so close to the time zone boundary required adjustments to every activity. It also required careful communication when planning an event. You could never assume the time of a service, party or meeting. "What time is it?" became a very relevant and necessary question.

Think about our life. What time is it? When we're young, we are too busy living to waste time thinking about dying, but we do grow old and even young people die. Psalm 90:10 tells us, *The years of our life are seventy, or even by reason of strength eighty; yet their span is but toil and trouble; they are soon gone, and we fly away.* It is good that we ask ourselves the question, "What time is it?" Or as the psalmist prayed: *So teach us to number our days that we may get a heart of wisdom.*

The clock reminds us we have the gift of time, twenty-four hours each day. Each movement of the clock measures the time and opportunity God has given to every individual. They will soon be gone. Have we used our time to gain wisdom? What are we doing with our lives?

PRAYER

Dear Heavenly Father, I've been guilty of thinking only about today. Teach me to examine my life in light of eternity. In Jesus' name I pray. Amen.

April 10
FESTIVE

*And he saith unto me, "Write, 'Blessed [are] they which are called
unto the marriage supper of the Lamb.' And he saith unto me,"
These are the true sayings of God."*

Revelation 19:9

There are times in life when the event calls for festivity, celebration,
and jubilation. Graduations, retirements, birthdays, and anniversaries are a few of those events. People love to join together in activities
that speak of reward, accomplishment, and the end of an era. Those
who graduate bootcamp know what this means.

The Bible promises a festivity of festivities one day. It is called the
"marriage supper of the lamb." At the time when the world is going
through the worst seven years of tribulation that it has ever seen,
those who are Christians will be at the marriage supper. The apostle,
John, wanted readers to know this so emphatically that he wrote,
"These are the true sayings of God."

At the end of this life, there will be a celebration like no other, and
Jesus will be the host. Those who have a relationship with Him are
invited, and they shall attend. Those who do not know Him will face
the greatest terror ever known to man. Know Him today.

PRAYER

*Dear Heavenly Father, I know you have great plans for me
some day, and I desire to be with You in those festivities.
Help me to live my life in such a manner that others will
be drawn to eat with You there, too. In Jesus' name I pray.
Amen.*

FERTILIZE

*But grow in grace, and [in] the knowledge of our Lord
and Saviour Jesus Christ. To him [be] glory both
now and forever. Amen.*

2 Peter 3:18

An older woman, who was an expert at domestic plants, explained to a young man the importance of fertilizing. "Healthy and abundant growth is promoted by fertilizing," she would say and then warn against overfertilizing. "If too much fertilizing is done, the plant will die. Fertilizing must be done at the right time and in the right amount for it to endure the storms or harsh elements that come against it."

Just a short time before Peter's was crucified upside down, he wrote his second letter that includes today's verse. Peter knew the importance of growing in both the grace and the knowledge of the Lord Jesus. Jesus was and is gracious, and Jesus is worth growing to know. Fertilizing our lives with the Word of God, studying His Word, and increasing in the ways of grace and in the knowledge of Jesus gives us many advantages beyond those who never see its importance.

One of the main reasons for dwarfed plants is lack of fertilization. Those Christians who do not continue in Scriptures are like dwarf plants, tiny in their ways, in their walk, and in their ability to weather the storms of life.

PRAYER

Dear Heavenly Father, help me to fertilize my life today by being in Your Word. Please remind me to stay in Your Word that I might grow. In Jesus' name I pray. Amen.

_____
_____
_____
_____

April 12
FEED

Give us this day our daily bread.

Matthew 6:11

One of the simplest parts of living is eating food. As long as one has the capacity to do so, bringing oneself to the dinner table never seems to be a problem. The body requires nourishment, and function within the body depends upon it. The physical body simply needs to feed. Those who know the bugle sounds for "chow time" find it to be one of the greatest sounds of the day.

There is, however, another type of feeding that must occur within the Christian's life. The Christian must feed upon the Word of God. Bible reading is essential to the healthy walk of Christians who put their trust in the Lord. Malnutrition within the spirit makes us subject to temptation, depression and fears. A weak constitution spiritually makes us an easy target for the enemy of the soul. As the Scripture says, *Be sober, be vigilant; because your adversary the devil, as a roaring lion, walketh about, seeking whom he may devour.*

In other words, either eat or be eaten. Even if it is a small portion every day, feeding upon the Word of God has no substitute. Those who know the value of the Bread of the Word are strong in the battles that come their way.

PRAYER

Dear Heavenly Father, please give me a desire to feed upon Your Word. I know that the nourishment I receive from Your Word will make me strong in the battles of this world. In Jesus' name I pray. Amen.

_____

_____

_____

_____

April 13
FED

I have fed you with milk, and not with meat: for hitherto ye were not able [to bear it], neither yet now are ye able.

1 Corinthians 3:2

People have different levels and tolerances for foods. Babies do not usually feed on steak, but are fed with milk. Adults are not fed out of baby food jars, but rather enjoy a large plate of meats, vegetables, and starches. The level of maturity determines the food.

Some people are new to the Christian faith and should be fed with the Milk of the Word. These are basic principles, such as the love of God, salvation through Jesus Christ, and baptism—both physical and spiritual. Those who have walked a little longer search for the deeper truths, such as justification, sanctification, and the return of Jesus Christ.

The key is to be fed. No matter whether the content is as milk or meat, the Christian must be fed. As we grow, so does our faith. As we mature, the depths of the knowledge and the grace of our Lord Jesus Christ are limitless. No one will ever over-gorge to the ends of it.

PRAYER

Dear Heavenly Father, I desire to be fed by Your Word. Help me today to understand what I can. Give me a desire to grow in grace and the knowledge of You. In Jesus' name I pray. Amen.

REST

And on the seventh day God ended his work which he had made; and he rested on the seventh day from all his work which he had made.

Genesis 2:2

Everyone gets tired. Whether it is from an exhausting day of marching or running a marathon with an 80-pound pack, weariness comes and fatigue arrives.

Although the Scripture states that God rested on the seventh day from all his work, it doesn't denote exhaustion. Rather it means he stopped creating. He doesn't grow tired like human beings, but He knows that the human body needs rest. Rest is a necessary part of recuperation. Those who find rest will find themselves able to perform at a better pace than those who are not well rested.

Fatigue is normal, but if we are wise, we will observe the words of the Heavenly Father who knows best as our Creator exactly what His creation needs—rest.

PRAYER

Dear Heavenly Father, I know my need for rest. Help me to find rest when rest is available to me. In Jesus' name I pray. Amen.

April 15
FEES

Peter saith unto him, Of strangers. Jesus saith unto him,
Then are the children free.

Matthew 17:26

Taxes and fees are demanded from citizens all the time. Tag fees here, permit fees there, taxes here, sales tax there—it seems there is a never-ending trend to those who collect taxes from people. Even Jesus Himself wasn't exempt from tax collection.

In this passage, Jesus was engaged by Peter, because someone had challenged him as to whether Jesus, his master, paid taxes. Jesus offers a wonderful response to the question, "Then are the children free?" However, he also sends Peter on a fishing trip, where he finds a coin in a fish's mouth to pay the required tariff.

The old saying is that no matter who a person is, there are two certainties in life, death and taxes. In some form or another, we all will have fees and taxes. There is a way out of paying taxes though—just die. Either way, there is a price to pay.

PRAYER

Dear Heavenly Father, please help me to be able to pay my fees and taxes. May everything I do, whether it be paying taxes or other works, be to Your glory all the days of my life. In Jesus' name I pray. Amen.

FARMER

*The husbandman that laboureth must be first
partaker of the fruits.*

2 Timothy 2:6

When society moved from an agrarian to an industrial state and then further on, to an informational one, people moved away from the idea of farming. Many people do not even know how to take care of simple flowers, whereas the labor of a farmer provides sustenance for life.

However, each of us is a farmer in our own right, for we sow seeds in our own and the lives of others. Oh, these seeds are often not visible, although some may be. Usually, they come in the form of comments, attitudes and modus operandi, the method by which we operate.

These seeds bear fruit. If we sow good seed, good fruit arises, but if it's bad seed we sow, bad fruit arises. The difference depends on who the farmer is. Scriptures warn us, "Whatsoever a man soweth, that shall he also reap." Those who hear Paul's teaching know that the farmer will "be first partaker of the fruit" that is harvested.

PRAYER

Dear Heavenly Father, help me today to sow good seed. If any bad seed is sown, please let it fall upon fallow ground and not bear fruit at all. In Jesus' name I pray. Amen.

_____

_____

_____

_____

_____

_____

_____

April 17
FAIR

Behold, the days come, saith the LORD, that I will raise unto David a righteous Branch, and a King shall reign and prosper, and shall execute judgment and justice in the earth.

Jeremiah 23:5

The little boy screamed at his playmate, "You are not being fair," as he bantered back and forth over the last piece of candy in a bag of treats. From childhood, most people have heard that "life is not fair." Those who have lived long enough know exactly what that means. It seems for most, "fair" means that as long as we get exactly what we want, when we want it, and how we want it, and, of course, where we want it, that's fair. Anything else would be unacceptable.

Justice and equity are usually desired when we are wronged, even if it is not acceptable to someone else. As long as it is acceptable to us as the ones being advantaged, we don't complain. Sounding off is reserved for those who feel wronged.

There will be times when others are advanced, given a greater portion, or are elevated for no fair reason found. In those times, we must put our trust in the Heavenly Father, who sets one up and pulls another down. He will indeed raise up the righteous branch, Jesus, who will execute proper justice in due time. The key is to align ourselves with Him and His desires well before He comes.

PRAYER

Dear Heavenly Father, thank You for Jesus, who though He was treated unfairly has come to be a comforting guide in this life, which is often oh so unfair. In Jesus name I pray. Amen.

_____

_____

_____

FUTILE

... but they became futile in their thinking, and their foolish hearts were darkened.

Romans 1:21b

Military wisdom says, "If your attack is going too well, you're walking into an ambush." The ability to hear and process information accurately is essential to our survival as a soldier. How many like to experience pain? Most of us do not, but is pain to be avoided at all costs?

Would our bodies remain healthy if we didn't have the capacity to feel pain? Not for long—for example, leprosy is a disease that damages the nerves and interrupts the transmission of the message to the brain that injury has occurred. People suffering from leprosy may keep injuring the affected limb until infection and disease result in amputation.

When we aren't thinking clearly, we don't respond appropriately. The Bible warns of the danger of rejecting the truth of God and becoming ineffective or of no use. What a waste it is to our comrades when we refuse to carry out our assignment. Even more serious is the waste of the prospect of not carrying out God's mission for our lives.

PRAYER

Dear Heavenly Father, You have provided the Bible for my instruction. Teach me Your ways so that I will not become foolish in my thinking. In Jesus' name I pray, Amen.

April 19
AMBITION

And Paul said, I would to God, that not only thou, but also all that hear me this day, were both almost, and altogether such as I am, except these bonds.

Acts 26:29

Paul, the apostle, thought big. His desire was that everyone who heard him on the day that he gave testimony before King Agrippa would come to know Jesus Christ as their personal Savior. Now that is ambition.

Those who are ambitious are motivated from within. There is a drive that no one has to start, and it doesn't need to be told what to do. It looks for opportunity and is constantly on the lookout for ways to be fulfilled. Every job is a new venture, and every task is a conquest ready to be realized.

Ambitious people align with the purposes of God when they seek that everyone should be saved. The key is to have the correct directive, for without the proper ambition, we can be like the proverbial hamster on the wheel with much activity and very little progress.

PRAYER

Dear Heavenly Father, please help me to be ambitious for the things for which You are ambitious. I commit my life anew and afresh to follow after Your ways. In Jesus' name I pray, Amen.

_____
_____
_____
_____
_____
_____

April 20

DECISION

*I know that you can do all things, and that no purpose
of yours can be thwarted.*

Job 42:2

The presence of evil in the universe is an undeniable fact. Good men
have often wrestled with the idea that if there is a God who is all
powerful, then why does He allow evil to exist? The book of Job
records the struggle of men to understand this paradox.

God has brought Job full cycle to the issue of evil in the universe.
He permits evil in order to reveal His grace. God has revealed the
character of Satan—fearing no one on earth, lording it over the high
of the earth, and presiding over the pride in human hearts.

Job is left with a decision—can he affirm his faith in God, knowing
that Satan is still permitted to work evil in the world? Can he put
his trust in God who will not answer his question of "why"? Even
more personally, can he believe in God who will give him no promise
of immunity from the mysterious accidents of nature or from the
deliberate actions of Satan, whose intent is to make him curse God
and die?

Job's conclusion is that he has asked the wrong question. The
question is not, "Why?" but "Who?" And he confesses that he has
relied on himself and possessed limited knowledge. Now Job af-
firms a faith in a God bigger than himself and *things too wonderful for me* (Job 42:3b).

PRAYER

*Dear Heavenly Father, I confess that I don't understand
why, but I trust You! Your love for me gives me faith to
leave the judgment of evil in Your hands. In Jesus' name
I pray. Amen.*

BLESS

Finally, all of you, have unity of mind, sympathy, brotherly love, a tender heart, and a humble mind. Do not repay evil for evil or reviling for reviling, but on the contrary, bless, for to this you were called, that you may obtain a blessing.

1 Peter 3:8-9

Recently a student athlete at a major private university was dismissed from the basketball team for violating the school's code of conduct. It seems that this university requires all students to sign a covenant in which they agree to abide by a code of conduct. That violation cost the athlete the opportunity to play in the post season, but it cost the team a valuable player.

Increasingly, we have technology that provides access to information that can be both good and bad. The internet may offer helpful information, but it also introduces areas of great temptation. Internet gambling and pornography are easily available in the privacy of our homes. Some maintain that this privacy is our right and nobody's business. Yet, the tragic results can be devastating to individuals, as well as their families.

Peter offers helpful principles of personal conduct. Live as a person of faith. Be agreeable, sympathetic, courteous, and positive. We have the opportunity to bless those we live and work around. We Christians are people blessed by God, thus we can live by a higher standard. Instead of thinking about our own privacy, we ask, "How will this choice affect others?"

PRAYER

Dear Heavenly Father, You have called me to a higher code of conduct than others in this world. Let Your Word guard my mind and keep me true to it in my private time. In Jesus' name I pray. Amen.

April 22

AFTERWARD

*A fool uttereth all his mind: but a wise [man] keepeth
it in till afterwards.*

Proverbs 29:11

Many a person has spoken everything they know about a matter to
the point that they do not even know all they have said. They have a
tendency to not allow for silence and listening, but just blurt everything out at once, like a vomiting of proverbial thoughts.

God, the Father, uses Proverbs to show there is a place for silence.
There is a place for listening and for keeping thoughts and judgments
within until afterward. Gather facts. Hear the opinions. Listen to
the stories, and only then conclude and add input. Keep the idea of
afterward in mind as the conversations roll.

Only a fool continues speaking until all the resources of his thoughts
are vanished. Those who would be wise understand that the principle of keeping thoughts under strict regard pleases the Heavenly
Father and provides huge benefits to those who obey His Word.

PRAYER

*Dear Heavenly Father, thank You for the wisdom that
is provided for me in the book of Proverbs. May my lips
refrain from spilling all I know, and may my thoughts and
judgments be reserved until a matter is fully known. In Jesus'
name I pray. Amen.*

ALLOCATION

And unto one he gave five talents, to another two, and to another one; to every man according to his several ability; and straightway took his journey.

Matthew 25:15

The Master of the Universe gives gifts unto men and women. Some tasks come much easier to some people than to others. Some run faster, jump farther, shoot better, and command better than others. Some have talents in office areas, while some have talents in the field. Some people do better at hands-on undertakings and others do better in the planning. Gifts are allocated differently and abundantly so that the collectivity of the whole is completed.

Those who are wise enough observe the combined gifts of everyone involved and understand their importance to the team. Not all are quarterbacks, lest their be no blockers. Not all are wide receivers, lest there be no running backs. To be successful, players or soldiers alike must perform their duty. Solo superstars never win all by themselves. There must be a combination of the allocations of gifts of the entire team.

PRAYER

Dear Heavenly Father, I know you have allocated certain gifts to me and to others. Help me to recognize my own talents and those of others that I may please you with reaching forward to the prize that is set before me. In Jesus' name I pray. Amen.

April 24
ALIVE DAY

If the Spirit of him who raised Jesus from the dead dwells in you, he who raised Christ Jesus from the dead will also give life to your mortal bodies through his Spirit who dwells in you.

Romans 8:11

When I was a high school senior, a friend and I were out raising funds for our class trip to Washington D.C. Driving home we topped a slight hill and a car pulled out from a side road. My friend slammed on the brakes, and we skidded several feet, narrowly missing a collision. We were speeding and narrowly escaped our own death and the death or serious injury of those in the other vehicle.

Every time I drive that road, even though its been over 50 years, I celebrate an "alive day." What is an alive day? It is the anniversary of a close escape from death or serious injury. Service in the military may present a soldier with one or more of these special anniversaries, but hopefully, they'll be times to laugh about with family and friends.

God's Word tells us that we all were dead in the trespasses and sins. (Ephesians 2:1) *Jesus taught, unless one is born again,* we remain dead in our sins. (John 3:3) Our sinful condition will result in eternal separation from God unless we accept the gift of eternal life. *For the wages of sin is death, but the free gift of God is eternal life in Christ Jesus our Lord.* (Romans 6:23) If we accept God's free gift, we can celebrate a new "alive day."

PRAYER

Dear Heavenly Father, because of Your great mercies I am alive today. I have been spared death so that I could accept Your gift of eternal life by faith. Thank You. In Jesus' name I pray. Amen.

ALIENATE

*And You, who once were alienated and hostile in mind,
doing evil deeds, he has now reconciled in his body of flesh
by his death, in order to present You holy and blameless
and above reproach before him,*

Colossians 1:21-22

No single word captures more accurately the emotion of rage than alienation. We see it in the news about the tormented perpetrators of mass killings so prevalent in our cities. Explanations often cite a long list of slights, taunts and rejection both perceived and actual. The common description of almost every one of those who carry out this violence is that they are "loners," and "angry."

The definition of "alienation" from Webster's dictionary is "a withdrawing or separation of a person of his affections from an object or position of former attachment." The root word, "alienate," is defined as "to make unfriendly, hostile, or indifferent."

Many people react to family problems, sickness, increasing violence in our society and social injustices with frustration. Feelings of powerlessness leads to anger and rage. "Road rage" is common on our highways. All of us feel angry and powerless at times. So, what will we do with hostility, anger and loss of control?

The Scriptures identify that the root problem is our alienation from God. Our hostile behavior reflects a need to make peace with our inner self and our Creator. Accepting Jesus' sacrifice for our sins cancels our debt and takes away our guilt. He restores our relationship with God and, through forgiveness, our relationship with others.

PRAYER

Dear Heavenly Father, while I serve my country, there are times I feel alienated from my family and those I love. When I see injustices all around me, I also feel angry. Your word says that I can be reconciled through Jesus Christ. I thank You for that promise. In Jesus' name I pray. Amen.

REHAT

I have been crucified with Christ. It is no longer I who live, but Christ who lives in me. And the life I now live in the flesh I live by faith in the Son of God, who loved me and gave himself for me.

Galatians 2:20

I love this definition from military double-speak: rehat - "to outfit military personnel in different uniforms in order to show a change of allegiance or authority." A soldier may be required to transfer from one branch to another to accept a new assignment or enter a different elite squad. I understand that marines are sometimes invited to join the navy seals.

Paul, the apostle of Jesus who is responsible for most of the New Testament, was first known as Saul of Tarsus. As Saul, he was a fierce enemy of Jesus who persecuted anyone professing faith in the Christian teaching. While actively tracking down followers of Jesus, Paul had a vision that altered his life totally. He was transformed in a matter of hours from persecutor into the church's greatest apologist.

Saul was transformed into Paul the Apostle and into a bond servant of the Lord Jesus Christ. His testimony was that, *I have been crucified with Christ. It is no longer I who live, but Christ who lives in me.* That's the invitation available to all who will accept it. No matter what hat we've worn to this point, Christ offers us a "makeover." In Christ we have the opportunity to change our allegiance and accept a new assignment. *Therefore, if anyone is in Christ, he is a new creation.* (2 Corinthians 5:17)

PRAYER

Dear Heavenly Father, I have served my own desires long enough. I want to give You total allegiance. I invite Jesus to reign in my heart. In Jesus' name I pray. Amen.

PASSION

Greater love hath no man than this, that a man lay down his life for his friends.

John 15:13

No matter what we do, it is done trying to protect something we love. Every sin is born out of love not hate. One might ask, "Well, what about jealousy?" That is love threatened from without. In other words, someone tries to take something we love and is willing to kill for it. Another might ask, "Well, what about envy?" Envy is love threatened within. We have something that someone else does not have, so the envious one, out of love for self, wants it, too.

Love, and what one has passion for, is a determinate for direction, path and purpose. If we love the right thing, we have it made. However, if we love the wrong thing, we don't have it made. The key is to know what to love. Because Jesus loves mankind so greatly, He fulfilled the very words that came out of His mouth, *...that a man lay down his life for his friends.*

Those who expend their lives daily in the military fulfill the purpose and statement of Jesus. The passion they exhibit is of the utmost honor, respect, and giving known to man. If we have passion that is directed by the Lord Jesus, we have fulfilled the highest calling of no greater love.

PRAYER

Dear Heavenly Father, help me to be passionate for that which You are passionate, and remove passions from my life that are not in keeping with You. In Jesus' name I pray. Amen.

_____

_____

_____

PRINCIPLE

And the LORD said unto Moses, Come up to me into the mount, and be there: and I will give thee tables of stone, and a law, and commandments which I have written; that thou mayest teach them.

Exodus 24:12

When the Lord God gave the commandments to Moses, He knew there was a need for an order. Without laws, society would be chaos. Social, interactive, health and medicinal laws are in place to keep people from going out of control. Sometimes a person knows why the rules are in place, but other times, the meaning behind the law is hidden. Those who make the laws are supposedly superior in knowledge and thus implement them.

God has principles within His kingdom to follow. He has supreme knowledge in that He knows the past, present and future of lives everywhere. He does not give laws and principles to live by in vain. His principles are direct, with purpose, and driven by love. His compassion for mankind drives Him to put in limits, a call to duty, and restrictions.

Whenever principles are put before wise men, their knowledge that understanding does not always have to be present is a key component to obedience. Sometimes principles must simply be obeyed.

PRAYER

Dear Heavenly Father, please help to recognize when principles are given that I must simply obey. In Jesus' name I pray. Amen.

April 29

TRANSFORM

Do not be conformed to this world, but be transformed by the renewal of your mind...

Romans 12:2a

The film, *The Elephant Man*, tells the inspiring story of the power of kindness to change another human being. In the movie we meet a man who has been treated like an animal and is the attraction of circus goers, but shunned like a leper. It was little wonder that he was withdrawn and perceived to be unintelligent. A young doctor was the first to discover that beneath this suffering and horribly deformed creature was a human being.

Under the compassionate care of this doctor, the Elephant Man whose name was Joseph Merrick, was given a new life. Once he was treated no better than an animal, but due to the efforts of the doctor and many others, he became a celebrity. He was far from being ignorant and soon gained his own self-respect. Instead of being isolated, he was visited by many important people. It is said that a smile from a pretty young woman signaled the beginning of his amazing transformation.

This story teaches us the negative impact people's treatment can have on an individual. In this case, Mr. Merrick had severe physical abnormalities, but don't we all have imperfections that can be exploited? Think about the positive power of a simple act, like a smile, to give hope and open new opportunities. We have the potential to have just such an impact on someone in our lives. We can change the way we look at someone who is suffering from their some imperfection.

God's declaration of unconditional love provides fuel for a transformation of how we view ourselves. *For God so loved the world, that he gave his only Son, that whoever believes in him should not perish but have eternal life.* (John 3:16)

PRAYER

Dear Heavenly Father, I have been conformed to the opinions and expectations of people. You have called me Your beloved, I pray that You will renew my mind and change my life to Your image. In Jesus' name I pray. Amen.

April 30
EASTER

For I delivered to you as of first importance what I also received:
that Christ died for our sins in accordance with the Scriptures,
that he was buried, that he was raised on the third day in
accordance with the Scriptures,

1 Corinthians 15:3-4

Easter commemorates the resurrection of Jesus from the grave and signals the beginning of the Christian faith. This holy day is the most significant in the Christian church. Hiding eggs and wearing new clothes have become traditions observed by many on this holiday. However, its purest meaning lies in the life, death, burial and resurrection of Jesus.

Two men portray the clearest picture of Jesus' impact on his followers. Judas was a disciple who became disillusioned and agreed to betray him to those who wanted Jesus' influence curtailed. After seeing Jesus arrested and crucified, he was filled with remorse and returned the money he was given for his betrayal. His remorse led him to take his own life. Peter also betrayed Jesus, swearing on three occasions that he never knew the man, Jesus. Both Judas and Peter denied their relationship with Jesus. Judas took his life, but Peter repented and became a great leader in the Christian church.

One of the most persuasive arguments for the credibility of the resurrection of Jesus is the willingness of those early disciples to die for their faith. History records that all the original disciples except Judas and John died a martyr's death. Jesus' resurrection guarantees the same for all who believe in Him.

PRAYER

Dear Heavenly Father I am thankful for the testimony of those who were eye witnesses of Jesus' death and resurrection. I join with all those around the world in celebrating life in Christ. In Jesus' name I pray. Amen.

FUTURE

For I know the thoughts that I think toward you, saith the LORD, thoughts of peace, and not of evil, to give you an expected end.

Jeremiah 29:11

Every mission has an idea of the future in mind. There are certain expectations that are derived in advance of the way things should look at the end of the engagement. Securing the site will be secured, freeing the people, and preparing the location all have to do with the way the future should look once the mission is over. Most of the time the future is fulfilled, but in battles, sometimes they are not.

The Lord of the Universe has a plan for every person. Some realize this and some do not. Some fulfill this, and others do not. When we take the time to know that Jesus Christ came to this world to save those who were lost, rescue those who needed saving, and direct those who wander, we will realize that His thoughts toward us are of peace, not of evil, and for the purpose of the future—the expected end.

Whenever life results in a Christian veering off-path, misalignment or backward thinking occurs. When that occurs in our lives, we only have to remember that God Almighty has a great plan for us and that He will work out our future.

PRAYER

Dear Heavenly Father, thank You for way You think about me. I know that You have great plans for my life, and I desire to live every day to the fullest to bring about the future that You have for me. In Jesus' name I pray. Amen.

_____

_____

_____

May 2
FUNERAL

Now when he came nigh to the gate of the city, behold, there was a dead man carried out, the only son of his mother, and she was a widow: and much people of the city was with her.

Luke 7:12

The experience of someone dying, especially if that person is close to us, is one of the most difficult experiences within life. Although it is very true that ten out of ten people die, the experience, whether it be on the battlefield or in a hospital, hurts to the core of our being.

The reason death is so difficult is because originally people were created never to die. When sin entered into the world, death appeared. The Christian has the advantage of knowing that Jesus conquered death, even as He did for the widow and her son. Although the funeral march was being held, Jesus interrupted, and the boy was raised to life again.

When we know Jesus Christ as our personal Savior, we enter into a place where death will have no sting. The moment breath leaves our body, we will be present with the Lord, and so shall we ever remain with Him. Now that's a funeral interruption worth knowing!

PRAYER

Dear Heavenly Father, thank You for interrupting funerals. Although one day the breath shall leave this body, I know because of this interruption, I shall ever be with the Lord. In Jesus' name I pray. Amen.

_____

_____

_____

_____

_____

May 3
FRIGHTENING

What time I am afraid, I will trust in thee.

Psalm 56:3

Let's face it. There are times in the military that are very scary. In those times, it is very natural to be afraid. Some situations that threaten life and limb merit the highest caution, so the fear that is inside us is a mechanism to preserve.

The sweet Psalmist, David, knew about battle and fear. He knew combat, hand-to-hand and army-to-army. He faced the most fierce of enemies in Goliath, and although he obtained victory after victory, there were times when he was afraid. The key to his life was that he knew where to put that fear when it came. He didn't say, "If I am afraid," but he asked, "What time?" In other words, any time he was afraid, he put his trust in the Lord.

Frightening times come, and they make everyone who encounters them afraid. The difference between a person who knows Jesus Christ and one who doesn't is that Christians have a reliable place to put their fear. The trust the world offers is unreliable, so those who fall for it will be overcome by their own fears.

PRAYER

Dear Heavenly Father, there are times when frightening things come into my life. Help me to put my trust in You when they arrive. In Jesus' name I pray. Amen.

_____

_____

_____

_____

_____

_____

FORSAKEN

*He is despised and rejected of men; a man of sorrows, and
acquainted with grief: and we hid as it were [our] faces from him;
he was despised, and we esteemed him not.*

Isaiah 53:3

A soldier never leaves a man behind. In other words, no matter what
the danger or no matter what the cost, the soldier who has been
injured or killed in action is to be retrieved at all cost. Many have
given their own lives for the sake of others who could have been left
behind.

The interesting thing about what Jesus did when He came to the
earth is that He abandoned everything for the sake of those whom
He desires to save. He risks it all and yet, there continues to be those
who, in a sense, leave Him behind. Isaiah said although he was *despised and rejected of men*, still He came to save those very men.

The idea of being forsaken runs deep into the soul of mankind. As a
soldier does not desire to be forsaken on the battlefield, neither does
the Lord Jesus want to be left out of our daily lives—invite him in
today. Rather than abandon Him, receive Him.

PRAYER

*Dear Heavenly Father, I realize that You sent Jesus into a
Christ-rejecting world. I desire to receive Your gift of Jesus
every day of my life. Please remind me daily to not forsake
Him. In Jesus' name I pray. Amen.*

_____

_____

_____

_____

_____

FIXATED

Thou wilt keep [him] in perfect peace, [whose] mind [is] stayed
[on thee]: because he trusteth in thee.

Isaiah 26:3

How do soldiers in the midst of the battle keep their minds at peace? Whenever a drill sergeant is yelling and everything seems to be going wrong, how can we stay quiet within our souls? When heartbreak comes or disappointment appears—when things do not go the way we expected—how do we make it through without going insane? The answer is found where we focus our minds.

God Almighty knew there would be difficult situations. He knows there will be disappointments, worries and circumstances that are beyond our ability to handle, so He included the answer to those times: *Keep your mind stayed on Me.* Rather than looking at the situations, above all the worries and anxiety, keep looking toward the Lord Jesus. Do not be distracted. Do not look any other place. Just be mindful of the things of God, His promises and magnitude. All problems will pale in comparison to His greatness.

God is not called Almighty without reason. He is greater, stronger, and mightier than any raging problem, any difficult situation or any trouble that we might encounter in our lives. Focus on Him, and peace of mind is ready to be found.

PRAYER

Dear Heavenly Father, I desire to keep my mind upon You.
When the troubles in life appear, help me to keep my focus
on You and give me the peace that You have promised within
Your word. In Jesus' name I pray. Amen.

_____

_____

_____

_____

FAR

*Wherefore the Lord said, Forasmuch as this people draw near
[me] with their mouth, and with their lips do honour me, but
have removed their heart far from me, and their fear toward me is
taught by the precept of men.*

Isaiah 29:13

There is such a thing as "foxhole religion". When soldiers are in the
heat of battle and the situation is very dangerous—even life-threatening—we tend to look toward the other side of life and the possibilities there. Many souls draw close to God when their lives are
at stake.

People use various statements to try to show their closeness to God.
However, when an examination of their lives is made, their actions
do not correspond to their words. As one person said it, "Your actions are speaking so loudly that I cannot hear a word you are saying."
There is more to Christianity than just verbalizing it. There must be
"fruit" that reveals true repentance and the following of Jesus Christ.

The condition of our hearts is shown greatest when we are not in
danger and don't have the perceived threat of death over our heads.
Whether we are far or near to the Lord is determined by our behavior. Those who align themselves with the Heavenly Father will
manifest the behavior of His Son.

PRAYER

*Dear Heavenly Father, if my heart is far from You, I draw
close to You today. Help me to stay near to You at all times
no matter what situation comes before me. In Jesus' name I
pray. Amen.*

BATTLE

*And David said to Saul, "Let no man's heart fail because of him;
thy servant will go and fight with this Philistine."*

1 Samuel 17:32

One of the greatest battle stories ever told is the battle between David the shepherd boy, and Goliath, the Philistine warrior. Against huge odds, David defeated the raging enemy of Israel that day with just a flying stone and lopping off the giant's head. What was it within David that made the difference, and how does that difference apply today?

David had a boldness to fight the enemy. David knew the enemy was not just against the people of Israel, but against the Lord God Almighty. There were other soldiers, including David's own brothers at the battlesite, but David was the only one to recognize what the battle was all about and who the battle was against. He felt that no man's heart should fail or be afraid of this raging ungodly Philistine.

When warriors gain a proper perspective, they know the purpose for which they fight. The purposes of God Almighty include nobility, notoriety, and recognition. Those who know the life of David know that he received all three for his boldness in trusting in the Lord when the fight ensued.

PRAYER

Dear Heavenly Father, I know there are battles that You desire to win. I make myself available today to boldly fight any time You have a cause. In Jesus' name I pray. Amen.

_____

_____

_____

_____

_____

_____

May 8
FOE

Thy right hand, O LORD, is become glorious in power: thy right hand, O LORD, hath dashed in pieces the enemy.

Exodus 15:6

There is what is called, "The Law of First Mention" in the Bible. Basically, it is that when a word is first used in the Bible, the idea of that word continues throughout the remainder of the Bible any time it appears. Exodus 15:6 is the first mention of the word, "enemies." The meaning has beneficial aspects that transfer not only throughout the rest of the Bible, but also in a soldier's everyday life.

Every foe and every enemy the Lord Jesus knows in advance. Alignment with Him and His power is crucial and wise as He has the definite advantage. No foe can stand against Him. All who rise up against Him shall fall. When we realize that real power is with the Lord, we only advantage ourselves as we face the enemies ahead.

Whether foes be physical or spiritual, those who stay with the right hand of the Almighty will find every enemy dashed in pieces.

PRAYER

Dear Heavenly Father, help me to stay under the power of Your mighty right hand. I know there is no help and protection greater than Yours. In Jesus' name I pray. Amen.

_____

_____

_____

_____

_____

_____

_____

_____

FIGHT

...Do not be afraid of them. Remember the Lord, who is great and awesome, and fight for your brothers, your sons, your daughters, your wives, and your homes.

Nehemiah 4:14b

The words, "afraid" and "fear," illustrate the necessity of defining our terms. There is a fear that is good. We are told to fear the Lord (a wise precaution), but there is also a fear that is evil. The fear of the Lord speaks of awe and reverence. We may encounter fear that would paralyze us or even cause us to flee when we should fight.

Nehemiah has taken on the task of rebuilding the walls of the city of Jerusalem. Those who opposed this project had made the workers afraid. The work had ceased and the people were paralyzed by their fear. These consequences affected not only the security of the city, but every son, daughter, wife and home.

The encouragement was, *Remember the Lord!* He cares for us. If he sees the sparrow that falls, feeds the birds and clothes the flowers, He will take care of us and *fight for our sons, daughters, wives and houses!* The battle is not just for our safety, but we stand on behalf of all who are threatened by fear and evil.

PRAYER

Dear Heavenly Father, I will fight the fear that tells me to give up. You are faithful! In Jesus' name I pray. Amen.

AMMUNITION

*And take the helmet of salvation, and the sword of the Spirit,
which is the word of God: Praying always with all prayer and
supplication in the Spirit, and watching thereunto with all
perseverance and supplication for all saints.*

Ephesians 6:17,18

Soldiers know the importance of their weapons. Weapons can be
the difference between life or death of self or of others around them.
Those weapons need ammunition, for a rifle without ammunition
never fulfills its deadliest potential.

We who walk with Jesus Christ also have weapons. These weapons are not physical, as in this world, but are mighty in the spiritual realm. The Word of God and prayer are the greatest weapons available to man. Yet, so few take up arms or realize their potential. Therefore, very few survive the onslaught of the enemy against their souls.

Bear arms, dear Christians. Read and study God's Word. Pray, and watch the kingdoms of darkness and enemies fall to the left and the right of us.

PRAYER

*Dear Heavenly Father, help me to know the power of the
weapons available to me. Please give me a desire to use them
more and more. In Jesus' name I pray. Amen.*

_____

_____

_____

_____

_____

_____

AMBIVALENCE

And Jesus answering said, A certain [man] went down from Jerusalem to Jericho, and fell among thieves, which stripped him of his raiment, and wounded [him], and departed, leaving [him] half dead. And by chance there came down a certain priest that way: and when he saw him, he passed by on the other side.

Luke 10:30,31

A woman is being attacked by a man in the middle of a crowd, but no one stops to help. A little boy is being beaten by his mother and no one tries to stop her. A country makes decisions that violate the Word of God, and no one reacts. All these are prime examples of ambivalence. There is motivation within to get involved, but conflict says, "Do not waste time."

Jesus knew the tendency for people to not get involved in lives of others, especially of those who are hurting. The man who fell among thieves was overlooked ambivalently by a priest and a Levite. These men should have been involved—they saw the condition of the man and still passed by. Their ambivalence was regarded by Jesus, but not in a favorable way.

As we travel through life, we will happen upon injustice, injury, and inappropriate behavior. A choice will be made—will we be ambivalent or will we get involved? If we are among those who choose to help, we are commended by Jesus—He will reward our compassion.

PRAYER

Dear Heavenly Father, please remove areas of ambivalence from my life. May I live my life today as a sacrifice for others who are hurting in this world. In Jesus' name I pray. Amen.

ABUSE

Then said Saul unto his armourbearer, "Draw thy sword,
and thrust me through therewith; lest these uncircumcised
come and thrust me through, and abuse me."
But his armourbearer would not; for he was sore afraid.
Therefore Saul took a sword, and fell upon it.

1 Samuel 31:4

The warrior, King Saul, was at the end of his life and now lay wounded upon the battlefield. He knew he didn't have long to live and if the enemy found him, he would be abused. Even at the point of death, Saul knew enough about that abuse and wanted no part of it. No one who was sane would ever want to experience it.

Abuse comes in many forms. It can be war-related or domestic, civil or familial. Sometimes it is related to alcohol, drugs or sexual or physical behaviors. At other times, it reveals itself emotionally, and the soul of a person is damaged. Whatever form it takes is harmful and shameful to man.

Jesus came to save people and yet, He knew what abuse was like in every form known to man. In fact, He was abused for the sake of all who ever abused. The prudent person becomes like Jesus, who knew the effects of abuse, but did not abuse others Himself. Jesus' model of living, unlike King Saul's, is the manner unto which all who are wise will subscribe.

PRAYER

Dear Heavenly Father, please help me to never abuse myself
or others. May my life be fashioned like Jesus who came to
save and not to abuse. In Jesus' name I pray. Amen.

_____

_____

_____

_____

May 13
CENSOR

For then must he often have suffered since the foundation of the world: but now once in the end of the world hath he appeared to put away sin by the sacrifice of himself.

Acts 9:26

Top-secret classified information is available only to certain individuals within the military. Operations and procedures for managing life-threatening acts must not fall into the wrong hands. The reason for this censorship is valid, and those who hold such information must be compliant with not speaking about such matters. Compromise in this censorship may cost lives.

Christians understand one aspect of censorship. When it comes to our sins, Jesus has managed them in such a way that He knows them all, but doesn't tell everyone about them. His purpose for coming to the earth was motivated by the information that He alone censored. The classified information available to Him about every man and woman was enough to move Him from heaven, wrap Himself in human flesh, suffer a horrendous death, rise again and return to the place from which He came.

His purpose was to eradicate sin, and make a way for us to live with Him forever, where censorship will never be needed again.

PRAYER

Dear Heavenly Father, thank you for the way that you censor my sin. I am so grateful for your sacrifice of coming to the earth to die for that which you know. In Jesus' name I pray. Amen.

ARMOR

Finally, be strong in the Lord and in the strength of his might.
Put on the whole armor of God, that you may be able to stand
against the schemes of the devil.

Ephesians 6:10-11

Think about the news that confronts the current generation of young people. They have grown up with the images of the twin towers burning and crumpling into a massive heap, while terrified men and women fled for their lives. Repeatedly we're shown images of suicide bombers destroying themselves and hundreds of their fellow citizens. Homeland security now dominates our travel and complicates every major activity.

Personal safety is a high priority for civilians and the military. Soldiers are accustomed to the necessity of protecting themselves from attacks. Civilians are not so accustomed to thinking about needing protection. The military has a term for personal armor, calling it, "battle rattle." In the day of smart bombs, suicide bombers and drones, the necessity for extreme alertness cannot be overemphasized.

We live in an extremely dangerous world. Do we ignore these threats to our safety and just take our chances? Or, do we lock ourselves behind fortified walls while forfeiting our precious freedom? The answer is "No" to both questions! It would be foolish to pretend that the danger doesn't exist, but we must never surrender to the enemy's threats. The Bible gives us another option, that is, to be strong in the Lord! God is our source of protection and He provides armor that empowers us to live boldly and freely.

PRAYER

Dear Heavenly Father, I cannot escape the dangers in our world. I choose to live my life in faith, trusting You to keep me safe. I want to keep on the armor You provide at all times. In Jesus' name I pray. Amen.

May 15

VICTORY

*For everyone who has been born of God overcomes the world.
And this is the victory that has overcome the world—our faith.*

1 John 5:4

The definition of victory is, "the overcoming of an enemy or antagonist." So, for soldiers, what does it mean to win the victory? In combat, it means that the enemy dies and we live, doesn't it? It may mean that the enemy has relinquished a claim on property or assets in dispute. Another meaning of this word is the achievement of mastery or success in a struggle. What about in the arena of our personal life? How do we define victory in our relationships, thoughts, and emotions?

Movies portray victory coming with decisive, superior firepower. The bad guys are routed and the good guys take control. Order is restored. In life, the battles are often fought within our own conflicting desires. One writer in the Scriptures described it as, *For I do not understand my own actions. For I do not do what I want, but I do the very thing I hate.* (Romans 7:15) The enemy that frustrates our intentions to do the right thing cannot be conquered by physical strength. In combat, we smash the enemy until they are overcome.

However, there is a victory that is only won by faith. The absence of war doesn't mean we have peace. Realizing peace with God is the most important battle anyone will encounter. Jesus promised to give us a peace that will remain even when our world is in conflict. The Scriptures tell us, *For where jealousy and selfish ambition exist, there will be disorder and every vile practice. But the wisdom from above is first pure, then peaceable, gentle, open to reason, full of mercy and good fruits, impartial and sincere.* (James 3:16-17) *The victory of faith is the peace of Jesus living within you.* (John 14:27)

PRAYER

Dear Heavenly Father, I have struggled to master my thoughts and failed many times to contain my emotions. I invite Jesus to live in me and His peace to rule my heart. In Jesus' name I pray. Amen.

CELL

And when they had laid many stripes upon them, they cast [them] into prison, charging the jailor to keep them safely. Who, having received such a charge, thrust them into the inner prison, and made their feet fast in the stocks.

Acts 16:23, 24

Remarkable men and women have been captured and made prisoners of war. Procedures for giving name, rank and serial number only have been drilled into the minds of anyone who is in danger of this horrific fate. The mere thought of enduring the suffering of being a POW is enough to challenge the greatest of soldiers. Sitting in a cell overseen by the enemy would be the desire of none.

When Paul and Silas were put into a jail cell for sharing the Gospel of Jesus Christ, there are many actions they could have taken. Their backs had been beaten with many stripes and now they sat in stockades and treated like cattle. They could have complained. They could have moped and cried. They could have yelled in defiance or wrestled and thought of escape. But rather, they sang praises unto God. Other prisoners heard them and an earthquake ensued. That must have been some powerful singing!

Whenever the world places us into a prison cell so to speak, a choice will be made as to how we react. The wise person knows that there is no greater break from the troubles of a cell than to just give praise to the Creator above who knows exactly where we are located.

PRAYER

Dear Heavenly Father, no matter where this world takes me, I desire to sing praises to You. Help me to have a great attitude toward You, no matter what cell I may be in. In Jesus' name I pray. Amen.

May 17

CAVITY

It shall even be as when an hungry [man] dreameth, and, behold, he eateth; but he awaketh, and his soul is empty: or as when a thirsty man dreameth, and, behold, he drinketh; but he awaketh, and, behold, [he is] faint, and his soul hath appetite: so shall the multitude of all the nations be, that fight against mount Zion.

Isaiah 29:8

"Fill that cavity, soldier!" and the private goes to the hole. "Run to that hole, soldier" and the order is fulfilled. Whether the cavity is in the ground or in a vacancy left by another troop, there is advantage to filling in the gaps and closing the holes.

There is a gap within every person who lives. This cavity is left for none other than God Almighty Himself to fill. The soul of every man and woman is empty, but those who try to fill it with any other substitute than a relationship with Jesus Christ find themselves going from one venture to another, one person to another, one job to another, and on and on, until they finally find the only answer to complete the filling.

The appetite of the soul searches for one thing and one thing only, a relationship with Jesus, and this satisfaction is just a simple prayer away.

PRAYER

Dear Heavenly Father, I turn my heart's desire completely over to You. Please come and fill this longing within my empty soul, and satisfy the cavity within my heart. In Jesus' name I pray. Amen.

CELESTIAL

[There are] also celestial bodies, and bodies terrestrial:
but the glory of the celestial [is] one, and the [glory]
of the terrestrial [is] another.

1 Corinthians 15:40

When soldiers are in foxholes, surrounded by the enemy with bullets flying and bombs threatening everywhere, they begin to think about the afterlife. Knowing that they are giving their lives as a sacrifice for others is extremely honorable and their thoughts generally are projected into the next life.

The Bible is very clear about earthly or terrestrial bodies and celestial or heavenly bodies. In advance, the words of Paul the Apostle gives assurance that this life is not all there is. There are heavenly bodies awaiting us. Those who follow Jesus Christ have the promise that our new bodies will be with Jesus some day. Our outward bodies will die, but will be replaced with new bodies that are made without hands by God, designed for Heavenly living.

The key for those who find interest in the afterlife is in knowing the Author of this eternal plan. Jesus made it, designed it, died for it, and will assuredly implement it for all who willingly surrender to Him.

PRAYER

Dear Heavenly Father, I know there are celestial bodies, and that You have one waiting for me. I pray that I shall live in such a manner that when I receive it, I shall give glory to You all the days of my eternal life. In Jesus' name I pray. Amen.

CATEGORICAL

Then Agrippa said unto Paul, "Almost thou persuadest me to be a Christian."

Acts 26:28

A supply sergeant manages supplies by categorizing items according to their use, size, venue, and function—each item has a place. The organization of those tasks, although sometimes daunting, is an important function of military operations. Without the supply squad, soldiers are ill-equipped.

There are those who look at Christianity in a categorical manner. They generally believe some of what Christianity says. However, they also believe the other views in the world. Their position is that one is as good at the other. When King Agrippa said to Paul the word, "almost," he immediately placed himself in the arena of saying no to Christianity. There is no place for uncertainty. Without being fully persuaded, unbelievers place themselves into the Denial category.

Jesus stands in a category all by Himself. There is no other means for knowing the Father and no individual will have entrance into fellowship with God unless it comes through Jesus. Any other way immediately puts us in a category of trying to save ourselves, which cannot be done.

PRAYER

Dear Heavenly Father, thank You for Jesus who stands in a category all by Himself. I choose to make Him Lord and Savior of my life. I am fully persuaded that He will equip me no matter where I go. In Jesus' name I pray. Amen.

_____

_____

_____

CAPITULATE

And when he had called the people [unto him] with his disciples also, he said unto them, Whosoever will come after me, let him deny himself, and take up his cross, and follow me.

Mark 8:34

Surrender is one of the last resorts of a soldier. To give up one's weapon, place, security and ambition is almost as bad as giving one's life. In fact, for some individuals, it is worse. People do not like to capitulate, so any effort to resist this type of yielding is met with great challenge.

Followers of Jesus Christ must capitulate. Absolute surrender of one's self must occur. Otherwise, there is no need for a Savior. If we could save ourselves, there would be no need for Jesus to intervene. The very fact that He came to pay such a great price for this redemption verifies the importance of capitulation. Jesus capitulated to a horrific death that He might save many.

Surrender, capitulation, and absolve are imperative if we are to know the fullness of a relationship with God. Without denial of self, the throne belongs to one who cannot and will not be able to save.

PRAYER

Dear Heavenly Father, I surrender and capitulate, to You. I give You my all as You have given Your all to me. Thank You for Your sacrifice that I may be able to follow after You. In Jesus' name I pray. Amen.

_____

_____

_____

_____

_____

CALAMITY

Therefore the LORD God sent him forth from the garden of Eden, to till the ground from whence he was taken. So he drove out the man; and he placed at the east of the garden of Eden Cherubims, and a flaming sword which turned every way, to keep the way of the tree of life.

Genesis 3:24,25

When battles rage, and missions fail, calamity is either among the troops or not far behind. There is no feeling like losing, especially when the stakes are extremely high. Regrouping must occur and motivation must be restored.

When Adam and Eve fell in the garden, it marked one of the greatest calamities ever known to man. That which was perfect, in a perfect environment, with a perfect God, was now tragically off-limits, and even angels guarded the entrance. There are some things at which a person only has one chance. After that opportunity has been squandered, missed or failed, there are no second chances. Life is altered, and things will never be the same again.

Christians must guard against such missed opportunities that lead to calamity. As much as possible, rely upon the Lord God Almighty to protect, warn and help in times where calamity lies on the other side. Reliance upon One greater than ourselves is the only remedy to the calamities yet to come.

PRAYER

Dear Heavenly Father, please help me to be aware of my opportunities, and to make judgments in them wisely. I know that calamities are certain should I decide to ignore You and Your ways. In Jesus' name I pray. Amen.

CEASE

Cease from anger, and forsake wrath: fret not thyself
in any wise to do evil.

Psalm 37:8

Whenever activities are to be halted, the word, "cease," may be employed. Military personnel know the importance of ceasing an operation or mission. Those in higher command give orders to stop activities at certain points because directives or plans have changed, the mission is accomplished or a perimeter has been secured. In other words, the need to continue is trumped by the need to stop.

Christian are given charge to cease from certain activities when they are detrimental to their witness and unbecoming a likeness to Christ. Those who are constantly watching Christians delight to see them fall. Errors Christians make often relieve their own inward flaws, because with someone else to blame, there is no need to blame themselves.

When Christians cease from anger, forsake wrath, and turn in every way from evil, not only are they observed with interest, but Jesus shines through and becomes an attraction rather than a distraction to which no one has interest.

PRAYER

Dear Heavenly Father, I desire to be a witness for You. Help me to cease from anger, forsake wrath, and stay away from evil. In Jesus' name I pray. Amen.

May 23
CAPTIVE

Wherefore he saith, When he ascended up on high, he led captivity captive, and gave gifts unto men.

Ephesians 4:8

In order for there to be captives, there must be those who capture them. The very idea of one capturing another implies the dominance of one who is superior over one who is inferior. Those who have been taken as POWs know the feeling of being dominated and wondering when a superior rescuer will bring them out.

So it is in the case of sin, which captures every human. It has no preference for color or creed, nor does it discriminate according to race, culture or background. All have sinned and come short of the glory of God. This fact implies the need for rescue from this captivity.

Jesus is more powerful than any sin. The only sin that can make us captive for all eternity is the rejection of His rescue, otherwise known as the blasphemy against the Holy Spirit. The only way for us to remain a captive to sin is to reject the rescue that Jesus paid for when He died on the cross. Receive, o' captive one, the rescue from the Lord Jesus on High!

PRAYER

Dear Heavenly Father, I receive Your rescue from my captivity to sin. Thank You for Jesus who made it possible to be free from that which I am too inferior to overcome. In Jesus' name I pray. Amen.

_____
_____
_____
_____
_____

CANNOT

So then they that are in the flesh cannot please God.

Romans 8:8

Although soldiers are trained to discover how they can or cannot do something, there are certain activities that must not be done. Resignation to limitations is imperative. Recognition of this early in the process will lead one to alternative solutions.

There are things that the Christian cannot do. One is to please God in the flesh. No matter how hard one tries, fleshly pursuits always fall short. This is why it becomes necessary to worship in spirit and in truth. All the fleshly efforts in the world work to no avail, but those who find fellowship with the Father in the Spirit know what it means to please God. Only that which is done with the direction of the Spirit will suffice. Those who find this path are those who are able to lift the countenance of God.

PRAYER

Dear Heavenly Father, I desire to walk in the spirit with You. I realize I cannot please You with my flesh. Help me to walk in the spirit every day, and may my life be pleasing to Your eyes. In Jesus' name I pray. Amen.

May 25

CAN

I can do all things through Christ which strengtheneth me.

Philippians 4:13

"Can't never could and it never would because it never tried," is a popular saying from years gone by. Soldiers soon learn during basic training that they need to find a way to accomplish something, rather than think about how that task cannot be done. Overcoming obstacles and removing impediments is symbolically manifested during the obstacle course. Those who endure that pain realize they can do things they never thought possible.

Those who follow Jesus know there is a tendency to do things within one's own sufficiency. The need for Jesus and His help is best realized in trials that go beyond a person's ability to manage. Whenever times become so difficult that no human can possibly succeed, Jesus is there to help us be successful. With the addition of His power, all things can be accomplished. With the addition of His strength, even that which seems unmovable is pushed aside with ease.

PRAYER

Dear Heavenly Father, I need Your strength. I need Your power, and without Your help, I am nothing. Please help me to remember You in the times when I think there is no way possible for me. In Jesus' name I pray. Amen.

FOUNDERS

*Moreover he said, I [am] the God of thy father, the God of
Abraham, the God of Isaac, and the God of Jacob. And Moses
hid his face; for he was afraid to look upon God.*

Exodus 3:6

The founders of our country knew that the opportunity for freedom would come at an expensive price. Some would give their lives physically, while others would give their livelihoods to manage and care for an ideal that was greater than their own pursuits. The drive for protection of this freedom inspired the beginning of the armed forces, a force that is alive and well today.

Some faithful people are known as the founders of the belief in God and the plan of salvation and freedom from sin that He offers were men of great faith. Yet they were men of great humanness, too. Although they had their flaws, they kept faithful to one ideal; They trusted in God. Above all the other failings, misgivings, misunderstandings and hardships lay a faithfulness that penetrated even the strongest onslaught against them.

Founders are like pillars in a grand building. The stronger they are, the greater the structure can be. The ideals laid down by founders of the United States of America and the founders of Christianity account for the freedom we enjoy today. May all who benefit from these freedoms be ever grateful for the founders.

PRAYER

*Dear Heavenly Father, thank You for the founders of our
faith both in the United States, and in Christianity. May my
life be lived in gratitude for the sacrifices they have made. In
Jesus' name I pray. Amen.*

CHANCE

*The wicked flee when no one pursues, but the righteous are bold
as a lion.*

Proverbs 28:1

The fear of failure keeps many people from attempting anything great. The apostle, Peter and the other disciples of Jesus were crossing the Sea of Galilee in a boat. Jesus appears to them walking on the water, causing fear in all the disciples. Peter, who always seemed to act before he thought, asked the Lord to confirm His identity by giving him permission to walk on the water.

Peter is both bold and fearful. First, he did walk on the water, but his fear returned and he had to be rescued by the Savior. The other disciples, safe in the boat, didn't sink, but they never walked in Peter's daring faith either. Peter failed other tests, but probably because of his willingness to risk failure, he demonstrated qualities that made him one of the great leaders of Christianity.

Knowing that we are walking in the truth gives us boldness. The first century believers suffered great persecution for their faith, yet their boldness won many converts to Christianity. Our mission in life is not to seek safety and comfort at the expense of truth. Jesus said, *"You shall know the truth and the truth will set you free."* (John 8:32)

PRAYER

Dear Heavenly Father, grant me the boldness of knowing that I am walking and living in the truth. Guard my heart from the fear of failing. In Jesus' name I pray. Amen.

_____

_____

_____

_____

MEMORIAL DAY

*...When it passed over the Jordan, the waters of Jordan were
cut off. So these stones shall be to the people of Israel a memorial
forever.*

Joshua 4:7b

Memorial Day is observed on the last Monday of May. It was formally known as Decoration Day and commemorates all men and women who died in military service for the United States. Many people visit cemeteries and memorial parks on Memorial Day. It is traditionally seen as the start of the summer season.

In some, mainly rural communities of the Carolinas, Decoration Day is still observed by visiting cemeteries. Family and friends clean around the graves of their loved ones and place flowers in their honor. These rituals serve to maintain the appearance of the cemetery and honor the lives of the deceased.

The nation of Israel was instructed by Joshua on the occasion of their entrance into the promised land to erect memorial stones to commemorate the event. Future generations would ask the meaning of these stones and would receive the oral history of their people's journey from slavery to freedom. In the United States of America, we pay tribute to the men and women who have paid the ultimate price for our freedom.

PRAYER

Dear Heavenly Father, we are indebted to the many service men and women who have given their lives for our nation. Thank You, Father, for putting the ideals of freedom in the hearts of brave men and women. In Jesus' name I pray. Amen.

_____

_____

BITTER

*For all the promises of God in Him are Yes, and in Him Amen,
to the glory of God through us.*

2 Corinthians 1:20

Several years ago, I was part of a team that went to Guatemala to build a church. We spent ten days partnering with the local believers to construct a new house of worship. At night we visited several small villages in the area sharing in their church services. Two things impressed me. First, they were very friendly and second, they had so little of the stuff we North Americans think important to our happiness. One pastor proudly showed us his home, which consisted of a combination kitchen-living room, dirt floors and a bedroom with cardboard for the walls. Yet, they were enthusiastic about life and God.

The book of Ruth records a family in Israel who left their homeland in search of a better future. Either a period of hardship had brought fear of famine to this previously prosperous family or it might have been a fear of death that prompted them to seek a better life in Moab. Whatever their motive, the results were tragic. The husband and two sons died as strangers in a foreign land. The wife, Naomi, was left a widow with two widowed daughters-in-law and no means to support them. Bitterly, she sought to send them back to their own families. Ruth, for whom this book was named, refused to leave her mother-in-law and accompanied Naomi to her homeland.

The lessons of the book of Ruth are many, but here are five: One, decisions made under pressure can have long-term consequences. Two, tough times come to all of us. Three, build into our life values that will survive tough times. Four, it's never too late to go home. Five, having lots of stuff won't guarantee contentment.

PRAYER

Dear Heavenly Father, You are all I really need! My tendency to take for granted my many, many blessings is wrong. I want to be more thankful and more generous! In Jesus' name I pray. Amen.

DESTRUCTION

Enter by the narrow gate. For the gate is wide and the way is easy that leads to destruction, and those who enter by it are many. For the gate is narrow and the way is hard that leads to life, and those who find it are few.

Matthew 7: 13-14

I read a compelling account of two unemployed young men who while trying to make a living entered a partly demolished medical clinic in Brazil. They discovered and then dismantled a cancer therapy machine and peddled parts of it to various junk dealers. One such dealer purchased a stainless steel cylinder about the size of a gallon paint can. Inside was a cake of crumbly powder that emitted a mysterious blue light.

The junk dealer took the seemingly magical material home and distributed it to his family and friends. His six-year-old niece rubbed the glowing dust on her body. The dust was cesium, a highly radioactive substance. You can guess the rest of the story. The girl died and others died or became very sick. More than 200 were contaminated.

We live in a world where healing instruments can become death machines in split seconds; A world where the best and the worst are only a hair's breadth distance apart, and a world where airliners can become deadly bombs. We live in a world that rejects the authority of the church to tell us that sin is deadly and that the way to life is to deny ourselves, take up our cross and follow Jesus!

PRAYER

Dear Heavenly Father, the majority is not always right. And the right way is not always easy. I want to choose life—not destruction. In Jesus' name I pray. Amen.

_____

_____

_____

DEATH

He will swallow up death forever; and the Lord God will wipe away tears from all faces, and the reproach of his people he will take away from all the earth, for the Lord has spoken.

Isaiah 25:8

A lifetime can be short or long. In a cemetery, there are markers for children, youth and adults. While we're young, we're not likely to think about dying, but as we get older, the thoughts of our death are more common.

Will I die? The answer is yes! There are two deaths spoken of in the Scriptures: one is separation from God, the result of sin, and the other is physical death. All of us will die physically, but none of us need to be separated from God. Jesus died on the cross to take our punishment for sin. The *wages of sin is death.* (Romans 6:23) He was raised from death to make possible our new life in Him.

What will this new life be like? The Bible tells us that the death due to our sin will be removed by Jesus' resurrection and we will be given a new body like unto His glorified body.

PRAYER

Dear Heavenly Father, I accept my new life through faith in Jesus' resurrection. In Jesus' name I pray. Amen.

June 1

COMBAT

Put on the whole armor of God, that you may be able to stand against the schemes of the devil. For we do not wrestle against flesh and blood...

Ephesians 6:11,12a

The Vietnam War remains a painful period in the United States of America military history. One valuable lesson from that conflict was the difficulty of identifying the enemy. The combatants weren't always adults, nor did they wear uniforms. Both sides suffered unnecessary casualties as a result.

The ability to identify and target the enemy is a crucial strategy in warfare. Every person born into this world soon recognizes that life is precious and vulnerable. Wise soldiers train their minds and bodies to be on the alert for the enemy.

Health is defined as mental, physical and social well being, not just the absence of disease. How do we protect ourselves from enemies that would attack our mental, physical and social health? Proper diet, exercise and wholesome information are helpful, but the Bible also alerts us to another enemy, the devil. To identify and target him, we need the armor of God.

PRAYER

Dear Heavenly Father, I need Your armor to stand against the strategy of Satan. I will put on the righteousness of Jesus Christ. In Jesus' name I pray. Amen.

_____

_____

_____

_____

_____

_____

June 2
CHILDISH

When I was a child, I spake as a child, I understood as a child,
I thought as a child: but when I became a man,
I put away childish things.

1 Corinthians 13:11

When soldiers have completed basic training or skill training, they are ready for a position that will utilize the skills they learned. There is a time where infancy and childlike behavior must be put away, and the "adult," highly trained individual appears. Until then, soldiers are not prepared for difficulties that will arise in missions.

The Bible is very clear about moving into maturity. Things that once were attractive as a child, should no longer have the same interest. People move from tricycles to motorcycles, from building blocks to cranes and from tiny pianos to symphony orchestras. Maturity sets in and childish things are put away.

There is a time when a person must move from childish activities to become an adult. So is it with Christianity. There must be a time of growth out of the basic ideas of the Christian faith and into maturity. Those who are wise grow in faith, hope and love. and There is no greater growth than a relationship with the Heavenly Father. Put away childish things.

PRAYER

Dear Heavenly Father, I submit my childish things and ways before You now. I ask that You help be to mature and be used in this world for Your glory and honor all the days of my life. In Jesus' name I pray. Amen.

_____

_____

_____

_____

June 3

CHILDREN

Lo, children [are] an heritage of the LORD:
[and] the fruit of the womb [is his] reward.

Psalm 127:3

When a drill sergeant receives new recruits, it's as if he has become their parents. Some of these new soldiers are weak, untrained, unskilled, and mentally and emotionally challenged. It is the sergeant's job to train them, work with them, and to mold them into soldiers that function properly on missions and military operations.

The Bible is very clear when it comes to children. People who are fortunate enough to have children must realize that the Lord God Almighty is the source of their coming into being. Children are actually the Lord's, but He places them in the care of parents to train, strengthen, and ready them for living in the world. Without parental training, children have a difficult time managing themselves in the sometimes hostile environment of this world.

The key to parenting children is to realize that the source from which they came is the source upon which parents should rely when it comes to their training. There is no better instructor than the Lord Himself and He is keenly interested in raising His children.

PRAYER

Dear Heavenly Father, thank You for children, and thank You for the skills to train them. I pray that I shall continually be aware that they are from You, and that I can rely upon You for wisdom in training them all the days of my life. In Jesus' name I pray. Amen.

_____

_____

_____

_____

CHATTER

Even so the tongue is a little member, and boasteth great things.
Behold, how great a matter a little fire kindleth!

James 3:5

There are times when soldiers must be totally quiet, and any compromised sound could be very dangerous. The smallest of sounds may be heard by the enemy, and lives could be lost. This is not a time for meaningless chatter—those who violate this principle may cost themselves and others.

James shares about the nature of the tongue. He states that it "boasts great things," and he likens it to a small fire, like a match that ignites an entire forest. There is reason to hold one's tongue, as disregard of doing so tends only to lead to great destruction. Many wars have begun simply because diplomacy broke down and the wrong words were selected to use.

Wise Christians know when to keep their tongues from meaningless chatter, Those who obey this simplest of proverbs understand, it is better to keep one's mouth shut and be thought to be a fool than to open one's mouth and remove all doubt.

PRAYER

Dear Heavenly Father, I submit to You my tongue. Help me
to keep it in a manner that is not with meaningless chatter.
May the words of my lips be always filled with Your wisdom.
In Jesus' name I pray. Amen.

_____

_____

_____

_____

_____

CHASTISE

For whom the Lord loveth he chasteneth, and scourgeth every son whom he receiveth.

Hebrews 12:6

There are times when disciplinary actions must be taken against a soldier. Sometimes the correction is to realign, but at other times, it is because an infraction occurred. Either chastisement is meant to keep people within accepted bounds and not allow for rebellion against authorities. A military without boundaries would be chaos and very little would be relied upon should such bedlam be allowed.

The Almighty God considers Christians to be His children. There are times where correction is necessary, even though sometimes the correction is painful. However, as with a child, without chastisement that child will become an embarrassment to his mother and father, and a nuisance to the rest of the world.

Chastisement is not fun, but it is important. Wise people are those who see the benefit later in life. Those who do not see it and do nothing will reap the results of their complacency.

PRAYER

Dear Heavenly Father, thank You for Your correction. I know that I do not necessarily enjoy chastisement, but I understand that You have my best long-term interest in mind. In Jesus' name I pray. Amen.

CAPACITY

And unto one he gave five talents, to another two, and to another one; to every man according to his several ability; and straightway took his journey.

Matthew 25:15

The rankings within the military are there for a reason. As people comply with requirements and standards equal to certain positions, advancement is obtained. From private to general, positions are given and earned according to one's capacity to handle the job. Those who have the capacity are effective, while those who do not have the capacity often fail.

So it is with the Christian. God Almighty gives and sorts out gifts according to a person's capacity. Some have higher profile positions and others maintain simplicity. Some are well-known, while others are barely known at all. Everyone serves according to their own ability to serve.

The requirement in the kingdom of God is not in advancement of position, but rather what we do with the capacities given to us. Faithfulness at whichever position far outweighs the notoriety or rank. That which is required is measured with whatever capacity we find ourselves.

PRAYER

Dear Heavenly Father, thank You for the capacity that You have given to me. I pray that I shall fulfill the standards for whatever is required within the place and rank I have been awarded. In Jesus' name I pray. Amen.

_____
_____
_____
_____

CEREBRAL

And be not conformed to this world: but be ye transformed by the renewing of Your mind, that ye may prove what [is] that good, and acceptable, and perfect, will of God.

Romans 12:2

There are those among military personnel who seem to have great gifts of "brains." Their intelligence supersedes others. Things that are normal to them are hardly seen by the remainder of the human race. The cerebral factor is a gift from God and those who use it properly benefit those who have no capacity to understand such things.

When we come to Jesus Christ and accept Him as our Lord and Savior, a cerebral change occurs. Christians begin to think differently, so the thoughts that used to be in place are removed to allow for alignment with God's thinking. The true gift of the cerebral is only recognized as we see it through the progressive revelation of God's will for our lives. Those who align themselves with the thoughts of God will know *what is that good, and acceptable, and perfect, will of God.*

PRAYER

Dear Heavenly Father, I desire to think as You think. Please help me to be transformed in my thinking so that my thoughts are like Your thoughts, and my ways are according to Your ways. In Jesus' name I pray. Amen.

_____

_____

_____

_____

_____

_____

_____

June 8

CAPTAIN

*And he said, "Nay; but [as] captain of the host of the
LORD am I now come." And Joshua fell on his face to the earth,
and did worship, and said unto him,
"What saith my lord unto his servant?"*

Joshua 5:14

Walt Whitman in his favored poem about Abraham Lincoln wrote, "O Captain, my Captain! our fearful trip is done." Thus lies an encapsulation of a President who lead through one of the greatest battles ever seen on American soil. When brothers were fighting against brothers and families against families, it was necessary to have many references to the captain of that day.

Christians have a captain, too, and when Joshua saw him, he fell down to worship him. In his fear, Joshua wanted to be sure that this warrior, this theophany (an early manifestation of Jesus), was on his side. Indeed Jesus deserves worship. Those who recognize Him as Lord of their lives will have no problem doing so, even when there are times where they wonder if this wonderful Captain is on their side. Indeed He is and the battles ahead are His to engage when we fall prostrate before Him and allow Him to lead.

PRAYER

*Dear Heavenly Father, thank You for being my Captain. I
desire to worship You and thank You for being on my side for
the battles ahead. In Jesus' name I pray. Amen.*

June 9,

CRUCIBLE

For the LORD thy God [is] a consuming fire,
[even] a jealous God.

Deuteronomy 4:24

Fire consumes, and the military personnel who use the weapons that cause fire, know the power of the removal of material that is undesirable. Whether it is clearing jungle vegetation or reducing a building to a pile of ash, soldiers use fire to manage obstacles that impede their mission.

When we come before God Almighty, the test of His consuming fire will be the measure of the value of our works. Like gold in a refiner's fire, heat and fire are used to burn away the dross within our lives. The works that have the proper motive will remain, while those works that were done for self-aggrandizement or personal acknowledgment will be burned away. The Divine crucible will distinguish between the two.

We would be wise to bow our heads and ask the Heavenly Father above to help in keeping every function and thought under the obedience of Jesus Christ. Every action we complete as unto the Lord Jesus, and none other, will remain through the crucible.

PRAYER

Dear Heavenly Father, I know that You have a Divine crucible by which You will judge all my works. May my life be lived in a manner that is pleasing to You, gives You all the glory, and remains through the crucible of Your Divine judgment. In Jesus' name I pray. Amen.

June 10

CANDOR

Neither is there any creature that is not manifest in his sight: but all things [are] naked and opened unto the eyes of him with whom we have to do.

Hebrews 4:13

Covert operations are an integral part of military operations. Top-secret security issues are given only on a need-to-know basis. Any compromise to this will jeopardize not only the mission, but also the lives of those involved. Candor must be among the elected elite and disregard for selective discretion is imperative.

When it comes to the Heavenly Father, nothing is secret with Him. He sees all and knows all things. He is an omniscient God with whom candor is the only choice. Regardless of the attempt to hide or disguise, the practice results in an exercise of futility. God sees. God knows, and God loves beyond all His vision and knowledge.

Since He already knows everyone and everything, the wise person realizes the best way to relate to the Heavenly Father is with candor. Agree, confess and comply, and the Father above Who sees all is ready and willing to forgive.

PRAYER

Dear Heavenly Father, I open my entire life to You. I realize that You see and know everything that is in my life. I ask You to forgive my shortcomings and sin that You are sure to see. In Jesus' name I pray. Amen.

_____

_____

_____

_____

_____

CITIZEN

So then you are no longer strangers and aliens, but you are fellow citizens with the saints and members of the household of God.

Ephesians 3:19

Very few people thrive in isolation. For example, babies who are cuddled and held prove to be healthier. In the judicial system, isolation is used as punishment for the inmate who refuses to abide by the rules. Picture a soldier in a room full of unknown people speaking a foreign language. Imagine this individual is perceived as a threat to these people so they are going to kill the soldier. How would that soldier respond if someone in that room quieted the crowd by saying, "Wait, stop what you're doing! My son will take your place!"

The apostle, Paul, records these pivotal words ... *you are no longer strangers and aliens…members of the household of God.* Why were they so vivid in his memory? A few years earlier Paul (known at that time as Saul) was on his way to kill and imprison anyone who identified with Jesus Christ. He heard words that invited him into the household of God. He came to know the reality of moving from alienation to citizenship.

We can be surrounded by people and yet feel like a stranger. Just because we're in a crowd, doesn't mean we feel accepted. The household of God is where we find our true identity, our eternal residence. People either encourage or hinder our development in this world, but only God gives us life and citizenship.

PRAYER

Dear Heavenly Father, You found me when I was alienated and a stranger. I know that by Your grace I am a saint and a citizen of God's kingdom. In Jesus' name I pray. Amen.

CONVINCE

He must hold firm to the trustworthy word as taught, so that
he may be able to give instruction in sound doctrine and also to
rebuke those who contradict it.

Titus 1:9

As a sixth grader, I remember going to the lunch room (that's what it was called in the fifties) with dread and excitement. Most of the food was delicious and nutritious! But there were some of the nutritious foods I didn't like, for example, English peas. One teacher I'll never forget, Mrs. Fowler, was determined to expand my appreciation for vegetables. She refused to let me leave the lunch room until I ate them or persuaded someone else to eat the peas. (As an adult, I have learned to love them!)

Instruction may at times seem like a disliked vegetable, but if we are to grow, someone must firmly point us to the higher level. Appreciation for the peas and the teacher, for me, came years later. Maturity will give us a clearer understanding of those teachers and instructors who confronted our ignorance.

But we all need to embark on a lifelong pursuit of truth. The simple definition of truth is found in the Gospel of John 14:6, *Jesus said to him [Thomas], "I am the way, and the truth, and the life."*

And again, in John 6:29, *Jesus answered them [disciples], 'This is the work of God, that you believe in him whom he [God] has sent.* If we are convinced of this truth then we can help others expand their appetite for truth.

PRAYER

Dear Heavenly Father, I am thankful that You sent people like Mrs. Fowler to help me grow physically. However, more importantly You have sent those who have introduced me to Jesus. In His name I pray. Amen.

ACCEPTABLE

Let the words of my mouth, and the meditation of my heart, be acceptable in thy sight, O LORD, my strength, and my redeemer.

Psalm 19:14

Speech can tell a lot about a person. The way one talks, the language used, communicates intelligence, awareness, frivolity, or filthiness. Words have a powerful way of unveiling what is in one's soul. Some people have mouths that are so dirty that a flush handle should be installed on their heads. Others have words that are so smooth, they sound like butter coming from their lips.

Most know of people whose meditations of their hearts are revealed through their language. The Christian has an incredible opportunity to reveal the Savior who resides within. In fact, acceptable language with God Almighty begins and ends with the meditation of the heart. Those who hear the sweet Psalmist's words know the importance of having acceptable meditation within the heart and words that match that meditation. Otherwise, the Son of God is reflected in a very poor manner, which should never happen.

PRAYER

Dear Heavenly Father, please allow the words that come from my lips to glorify You, and help any area of the meditation of my heart that is not pleasing to You to be corrected before I speak. In Jesus' name I pray. Amen.

ACADEMIC

And that ye study to be quiet, and to do Your own business, and to work with Your own hands, as we commanded You;

1 Thessalonians 4:11

Much studying can make us wise. However, what we choose to study must be more than studying itself. There are those who make themselves of no civil use by giving study to study itself. They are usually called professional students and their contributions are only to their own minds rather to than the betterment of society.

The Bible encourages us to study to be quiet and do our own business, to work with our own hands. This is productive, generative and successful study. Practical learning benefits others and allow soldiers to complete their mission without regard to personal accolades for how much they know.

PRAYER

Dear Heavenly Father, please help me to study quietness, doing my business, and working with my hands. May my academics always have Your plan in mind. In Jesus' name I pray. Amen.

ACHIEVEMENT

His lord said unto him, Well done, [thou] good and faithful servant: thou hast been faithful over a few things, I will make thee ruler over many things: enter thou into the joy of thy lord.

Matthew 25:21

Advancement comes from those who are in greater authority. Those who are beneath others are basically servants to those who are above them. There is a ranking of power and privilege, and those who achieve advance through the ranks.

The Lord Jesus, who is King of Kings and Lord of Lords, knows about achievement. Those who follow Him are His servants, and He is not a Lord who doesn't recognize others. The Bible states that every idle word that men shall speak, they shall give an account thereof. Those who are wise take note that the master is watching. He desires to give advancement and achievement through obedience is promised for those who do as He says.

PRAYER

Dear Heavenly Father, I desire to do well before Your eyes. Help and remind me to achieve as You give me opportunities to advance Your cause. In Jesus' name I pray. Amen.

June 16
ABORT

Flee also youthful lusts: but follow righteousness, faith, charity, peace, with them that call on the Lord out of a pure heart.

2 Timothy 2:22

Retreating is sometimes one of the best military moves. There are times where the enemy has produced a massive assault. Fleeing from the onslaught allows for redirecting, planning again, recomposing and restructuring to attempt the battle on another day.

The Bible is very clear about youthful lusts. The wise person flees from them. There are times where Satan will bring temptations that are very difficult to overcome. Sin is enticing and pleasurable for a season. However, sin always has a price and many times that price lasts for a lifetime—there is only one chance for some things. The lust that is indulged in today may be one that has a "no turning back" sign on it tomorrow.

Righteousness, faith, charity and peace are much better eternal pursuits. Those who abort lusts will enjoy lives that never have eternal regrets. Those who do not abort youthful lusts will find themselves trapped, with no retreat in sight.

PRAYER

Dear Heavenly Father, help me to flee youthful lusts and to be able to recognize them when they arise. I desire righteousness, faith, charity and peace. Please add them to my life today. In Jesus' name I pray. Amen.

June 17
SELFISH

For where jealousy and selfish ambition exist, there will be disorder and every vile practice. But the wisdom from above is first pure, then peaceable, gentle, open to reason, full of mercy and good fruits, impartial and sincere.

James 3:16-17

An old preacher said; "I am not in competition with any man; another's success does not diminish me whatsoever. God made a big world; there's room for everyone."

We should want to do our best, according to our ability, at whatever we are doing. Excellence in work and character makes our world a better place.

Seeking our own welfare at the expense of others is sowing seeds of our own destruction.

PRAYER

Dear Heavenly Father, I want to be the best I can be with Your help. And I want to encourage others to be at their best. In Jesus' name I pray. Amen.

_____
_____
_____
_____
_____
_____
_____
_____
_____
_____

EXAMPLE

*Let no one despise you for your youth, but set the believers an
example in speech, in conduct, in love, in faith, in purity.*

1 Timothy 4:12

Famous athletes are often called role models for the younger generation. Some have protested saying that they didn't want to be viewed as a role model. We don't have to be famous to influence someone's life. The question is, will our influence be positive or negative? The more visible we are, the greater our responsibility to those we influence.

Whether we're famous or not, we have an impact on someone. We may not be nationally known, but somebody looks up to us and strives to follow our example. Children look up to their parents and students take on mannerisms of their teacher—all of us are influenced by someone.

Like the unwilling athlete, we may not aspire to the position, but we have a responsibility to set a good example. The apostle charged his student, Timothy, to set a good example. Remember the story of the young man who complained to the preacher about his emphasis on the death of Christ. He thought more emphasis should be given to Christ as an example to follow. The preacher asked: "Are you ready to follow Christ's example of perfection." When the young man said, "No," the preacher replied, "Then what you need is a Savior—not an example."

PRAYER

*Dear Heavenly Father, You are perfect, but I am not. Help
me to point others to You. In Jesus' name I pray. Amen.*

June 19

ENDURANCE

Therefore, since we are surrounded by so great a cloud of witnesses, let us also lay aside every weight, and sin which clings so closely, and let us run with endurance the race that is set before us,

Hebrews 12:1

The first day of a workout is great and feels good. Endorphins, the body's natural anti-depressants, flow freely during exercise. The next day reacquaints us with "the agony of defeat." Endorphins are never around when we try rolling out of bed. Our sore muscles are screaming, "What were you thinking?"

Now the phrase, "feel the burn" doesn't sound so macho. The instructor who pushed us to the limit of our endurance has no sympathy for our new but sore muscles. The theory behind this suffering is that when our muscles are pushed beyond the usual, we start to build new muscles, acquire more endurance and enjoy a healthier body. If soldiers stop working out because of soreness, they will never realize the benefit of the exercise. They will only get perpetual soreness.

Standing still is our biggest hurdle. Accepting the fact that pain is a normal part of the price we must pay to become physically healthy keeps us in the race. Military instructors provide motivation to push through the inertia, and pain. Christians draw their motivation from the community of believers and the example of Jesus Christ. He endured the ultimate pain of crucifixion to secure our salvation.

PRAYER

Dear Heavenly Father, I am ready to quit when I face difficulty. I pray for renewed motivation to push through the pain and to increase my endurance. In Jesus' name I pray. Amen.

REBEL

*Let every person be subject to the governing authorities. For there
is no authority except from God, and those that exist have been
instituted by God. Therefore whoever resists the authorities resists
what God has appointed, and those who resist will incur judgment.*

Romans 13:1-2

Wikipedia gives the following definition: "Rebellion, or upris-
ing, is a refusal of obedience or order." It may be, therefore, seen
as encompassing a range of behaviors aimed at destroying or replacing an established authority such as a government or a head
of state. On the one hand, the forms of behavior can include
non-violent methods such as the (overlapping but not quite
identical) phenomena of civil disobedience, civil resistance and
nonviolent resistance. On the other hand, it may encompass
violent campaigns. Those who participate in rebellions, especially if they are armed rebellions, are known as "rebels."

In the military, rebellion is considered to be an act of insubordination and is not tolerated. There was a time when failure to obey an order was grounds for a court-martial. Today,
the individual who refuses to obey a command most certainly
will be discharged from service. While the penalty for rebel-
ling against authority may have changed, the consequences are
significant.

Our school systems are prime examples of the lack of discipline
and rebellion. The tragic results are that student achievement
has drastically declined, violence has increased, and dropout
rates are spirally upward. Society cannot survive when citizens
refuse to respect and obey authority. The environment for a
healthy and productive community, whether civil or religious,
is connected to that body's obedience to authority.

PRAYER

*Dear Heavenly Father, I want to guard my attitude against
rebellion. I may not agree with everything my leaders do, but
help me not to become a rebel. In Jesus' name I pray. Amen.*

PASSED

I have fought a good fight, I have finished [my] course, I have kept the faith:

2 Timothy 4:7

When accomplishment is recognized, a person feels appreciated. Sometimes that appreciation comes from others, and sometimes it comes from within. To finish a task, to have run a race, or to have completed a chore, test or goal is one of the greatest parts of being alive. There is nothing like making the passing grade.

For those who acknowledge Him, God the Heavenly Father has a task for everyone to complete. Some are given what men deem to be noble tasks, such as being a doctor, scientist or professor. Others are given duties that are less esteemed, like janitors, ditch diggers and garbage men. However, it is not the task that is measured for passing, but rather the attitude and motive by which the job is accomplished. In other words, it's not what the job is, but how the job is performed.

Today there may be some undesirable duty at hand. Buck up, dear soldier, the Almighty Creator is watching and waiting to award the passing grade.

PRAYER

Dear Heavenly Father, help me today to realize that all tasks come before Your eyes. May what You see as I perform them be a blessing to You and a passing grade for me. In Jesus' name I pray. Amen.

_____

_____

_____

_____

_____

June 22
PRODUCTIVE

Ye have not chosen me, but I have chosen You, and ordained You, that ye should go and bring forth fruit, and [that] Your fruit should remain: that whatsoever ye shall ask of the Father in my name, he may give it You.

John 15:16

Each person produces something every day. Some will produce activity, while others will produce inactivity. Some will accomplish certain tasks, and others will accomplish nothing. The choice, in most cases, is up to the individual. Most of the time, one's attitude determines how little or how effective a person is in producing.

Jesus uses the idea of producing "fruit" in His words. This illustration serves as an example of how truly effective a person may be when it comes to producing. The key is knowing the source of the production is the relationship with Jesus Christ, "Ye have not chosen me." Those who know Jesus are fruit producers of a different and superior sort. Their production remains and, rather than temporary achievement, eternal and lasting fruit is the result.

There are accomplishments that are like days on a calendar, "Here today and gone tomorrow." Those who are wise always keep the eternal in mind and produce fruit that shall never fade away.

PRAYER

Dear Heavenly Father, please help me to produce fruit that is eternal and not settle for the temporary. In Jesus' name I pray. Amen.

June 23

PURPOSE

For it is God which worketh in you both to will and to do of [his] good pleasure.

Philippians 2:13

There is a God given purpose for every individual who lives. Some people are businessmen and some are doctors. Others are lawyers or politicians, while still others are military personnel. The common denominator, no matter what the vocational position, is that people fulfill the purposes of the will of God.

There are those who step outside the will of God for their lives. The Heavenly Father has placed within each person the ability to choose. Sometimes those choices are outside His purposed best. Although the Lord Jesus will honor the decision, it doesn't mean that it is His perfect will.

The key for the one who follows Jesus is to remember to allow the Lord to work in the area of desire first and then realize that He also will work in the area of performance. Those who find God's desire and execution of His purposes within their lives will bring good pleasure to the Creator.

PRAYER

Dear Heavenly Father, place Your desires within me, and help me to execute them for Your good pleasure. In Jesus' name I pray. Amen.

_____

_____

_____

_____

_____

_____

June 24

PROFIT

*Count it all joy, my brothers, when you meet trials
of various kinds,*

James 1:2

Christianity is much more than philosophy, theology or religious teaching. It is a lifestyle based upon a vital relationship with God. He has invited us to love Him with all our hearts, with all our souls, with all our minds and with all our strength. (Mark 12:30) He desires for us to not only know about Him, but to know Him personally. (1John 4:7)

Normal people do not enjoy trials. Do we? Most of us attempt to avoid trials. James is writing to people familiar with severe trials. Many of them have lost their homes and their jobs. They have fled to avoid being killed and are separated from family and friends. It is to this audience he says, "... *count it all joy when you meet trials!*"

We can profit from trials, if we remember the helps mentioned in these Scriptures. First, consider the trial or adversity as training. Second, know that God is using this test to develop our faith. (As fire purifies precious metals, trials refine our faith.) Third, testing helps us become mature and complete. Basic training seemed to be punitive at times. Later, soldiers realize the value of those training exercises. So, God uses trials to remove impurities, strengthen and purify His followers.

PRAYER

Dear Heavenly Father, my first reaction is to complain when trials come my way. Teach me the value of the trials, and help me to grow in purity and in my relationship with You. In Jesus' name I pray. Amen.

WEAK

For the sake of Christ, then, I am content with weaknesses, insults, hardships, persecutions, and calamities. For when I am weak, then I am strong.

2 Corinthians 12:10

Strength is the goal that motivates us to endure the rigors of conditioning exercises. In every arena, weakness is considered an enemy that must be defeated if we are to achieve success. Even in the animal kingdom, the rule is "survival of the fittest." In the human kingdom, we have our own system of rewards for the strong. While humans don't kill their weak, there are definite consequences for those who don't keep pace with the rest.

Are there times when "being strong" is a liability or being "weak" is an asset? Granted, when it comes to defending our country from an attack, strength of our military is essential. However, in our personal life, where we cultivate faith and spiritual strength, maintaining a strong, self-reliance prevents us from admitting our need for a Savior. In this arena, weakness is definitely an asset, because we can ask for help.

Listen to the wisdom of Scripture: "*Therefore let anyone who thinks that he stands take heed lest he fall.*" (1 Corinthians 10:12) Again we read in the Scripture: ... *My grace is sufficient for you, for my power is made perfect in weakness.* (2 Corinthians 12:9a) The apostle, Paul, had asked for the removal of a situation in which he felt weak. God's answer to Paul was; *My power is made perfect in weakness.* When he understood this truth, Paul responded, "*When I am weak, then I am strong.*" This seems upside-down to our system that values strength over weakness, but for those who trust in Christ for eternal life, this is the nature of our faith.

PRAYER

Dear Heavenly Father, Your kingdom is upside down in relationship to the systems of this world. You said, "If I gain the whole world and lose my soul, what profit is it?" I gladly confess that when I'm weak, You are strong! In Jesus' name I pray. Amen.

WARFARE

This charge I entrust to you, Timothy, my child, in accordance with the prophecies previously made about you, that by them you may wage the good warfare, holding faith and a good conscience..

1 Timothy 1:18-19a

Life has injustices. People sometimes are too busy to care. Some will prove to be self-righteous, while others will prove to be proud. People we trusted may disappoint or even betray us. The idealism that prompted us to join the military may now appear to be misplaced. What will we do? Will we lose heart? Will we give up? Will we become bitter?

My dad experienced disappointment in someone he respected as a spiritual leader. For many years, he allowed that man's action to prevent him from benefiting from any fellowship with the church. His bitterness toward one man's wrong isolated him from the opportunity to see that not all leaders are the same. Late in his life, he realized that he had allowed one man's failure to hinder his growth.

The apostle, Paul, calls Timothy to a remembrance of his purpose. He charges him not to deviate from the mission to which he was called, and to give attention to his own standard of conduct, while being guided by faith and a good conscience. Paul's words to Timothy are appropriate for our warfare.

PRAYER

Dear Heavenly Father, help me to keep my heart free of bitterness. People will disappoint me, but help me to keep my eyes on the goal. In Jesus' name I pray. Amen.

_____

_____

June 27

SAFETY

He who dwells in the shelter of the Most High will abide in the shadow of the Almighty. I will say to the Lord, 'My refuge and my fortress, my God, in whom I trust.

Psalm 91:1-2

This Scripture has been called the "service man's Psalm." We will find encouragement to trust God to guide us through the evils of life. Also, we'll find great promises of protection from the dangers and perils that accompany warfare.

In addition to the encouragement and promises, these Scriptures challenge us. On the one hand we read, *You will not fear the terror of the night, nor the arrow that flies by day, nor the pestilence that stalks in darkness, nor the destruction that wastes at noonday.* (Psalm 91:5-6) But does that mean we will never be injured? Obviously, we do see colleagues injured and killed. We are not promised protection from all suffering and danger.

So what does it mean to live in the secret place of the Most High? He is telling us that if we set our love on Him, He will deliver us when we're in trouble and when we call, He will answer. We will know His presence, receive His power, experience His protection and enjoy His provision.

PRAYER

Dear Heavenly Father, I make You my dwelling place. When I face danger, I will remember Your promise to be with me and protect me from evil. In Jesus' name I pray. Amen.

_____

_____

_____

_____

June 28

TANDEM

A friend loveth at all times, and a brother is born for adversity.

Proverbs 17:17

Troubles and problems occur all throughout a person's life. One mission will lead to another mission, and as one fellow said it, "You'll create a new problem trying to fix the one you have now." So true, and yet so disparaging.

When troubles come, real friends are discovered. When a person's life is on the line or marriage is difficult or when financial hardship comes, acquaintances stand afar off, but friends and brothers come near. In other words, friends love no matter what. Brothers are there when times of adversity come. Those who know the depths of this love know that they work in tandem with one another. Therefore, trials, troubles and problems only serve to draw us closer together.

Those who realize the benefits of true friendship and the comfort of having someone beside them. They realize a divine characteristic as the Holy Spirit of God who is called by Jesus, the "Comforter, one who comes along side," without regard to troubles, problems or any such difficulties.

PRAYER

Dear Heavenly Father, Thank You for the Holy Spirit. May I realize the benefits of friends and brothers by the comfort that the Holy Spirit affords to me. In Jesus' name I pray. Amen.

_____

_____

_____

_____

_____

June 29

TREASURE

Do not lay up for yourselves treasures on earth, where moth and rust destroy and where thieves break in and steal, but lay up for yourselves treasures in heaven, where neither moth nor rust destroys and where thieves do not break in and steal.

Matthew 6:19-20

I once owned a reliable, clean, and importantly, paid for car. It had 168,000 miles on it and was in great mechanical condition. I was anticipating another couple of years of no car payments and minimum repairs. I had stopped at a traffic light when I glanced in my rear view mirror and saw an approaching vehicle.

In a blink of an eye, I was in the middle of a big bang. Quickly my dependable, payment-free transportation landed in the junk heap—my dream of 200,000 plus miles was gone. Cars don't make the list of treasures that survive the bump and grind of this temporary world. Everybody is interested in things that last. Our cars wear out and so do clothes, shoes and everything about us. Even the faces on Mount Rushmore have to be repaired occasionally.

Where do we find treasures that will endure? Jesus warned against investing our lives in treasures that are, at best, temporary. *Do not lay up for yourselves treasures on earth ...* (Matthew 6:19a) And Solomon wrote, *Whoever trusts in his riches will fall, ...* (Proverbs 11:28a) Why? At best, earthly treasures are temporary and, at worst, they become our master, robbing us of true treasures.

Our soul is more valuable than earthly riches. A Scripture from Paul's letter to Timothy identifies true treasures. *Now godliness with contentment is great gain. For we brought nothing into this world, and it is certain we can carry nothing out. And having food and clothing, with these we shall be content.* (1 Timothy 6:6-8)

PRAYER

Dear Heavenly Father, show me the value of laying up treasures in heaven. I confess that the temptation to seek earthy riches tempts me. In Jesus' name I pray. Amen.

OWNERSHIP

Pride goes before destruction, and a haughty spirit before a fall.

Proverbs 16:18

The dictionary defines pride as a "high or inordinate opinion of one's own dignity, importance, merit, or superiority, whether as cherished in the mind or as displayed in bearing, conduct." How many times a day do we use the word, "my"? Commonly we refer to my life, my church, my time, my children and my money. Could this, unwittingly, be taking ownership of things that belong to God?

Where is the line where we cross over from healthy self-worth to unhealthy self-worship? The definition uses the term inordinate opinion of self-meaning "excessive and unregulated." Baseball's hall of fame pitcher, Dizzy Dean is quoted as saying, "It's not bragging if you can back it up," but if people are so absorbed with themselves that they talk about nothing else, they're in need of some balance.

Excessive and unregulated self-exaltation leads to pride. Pride that takes ownership of things and people that, in truth, belong to someone else will not prosper and will lead to destruction. People who are excessive in their opinion of self, overestimate their own strength and underestimate the contribution of others. The unit is more important than any individual.

PRAYER

Dear Heavenly Father, help me to examine my attitude. Have I taken ownership of things that belong to You? Search my heart and create in me a right spirit. In Jesus' name I pray. Amen.

_____

_____

July 1

VALOR

*And the angel of the Lord appeared to him and said to him,
'The Lord is with you, O mighty man of valor.*

Judges 6:12

Early in our marriage, my wife and I lived in a small framed house in rural Florida. During the summer, it was not uncommon for us to leave the doors unlocked at night. The summers were hot, and since we had no air conditioning, our cooling system was open windows and doors. One night I was awakened by my wife telling me that she heard a noise at the door. It sounded like someone or something opened the screen door. She was insisting that I get out of bed and confront whatever or whoever was now is the kitchen! Honestly, I didn't feel as brave as she apparently assumed or expected.

My experience reminded me of a man in the Scriptures hiding while he threshed out some grain for his family. His people were harassed by neighboring bullies who came at harvest time and stole their food. He was trying to survive, and nothing in him said, "Stand up" or "Enough is enough!" He was acting more like a coward than a patriot. An angel appeared at that moment and said, "The Lord is with you, O mighty man of valor." God saw something in Gideon he could not see in himself.

We don't always act courageous nor do we always respond to a crisis with bravery. Gideon was given an assignment that would require courage and skill. It wasn't apparent that he possessed either, but God knew what he needed to become a mighty man of valor. My wife's prodding persuaded me to act brave, when I didn't feel brave. I was relieved to discover the prowler was our cat! God knows the potential buried beneath our timidity and fear.

PRAYER

Dear Heavenly Father, You are speaking to me and calling me to a mission that intimidates me. I need reassurance that You will give me victory. In Jesus' name I pray. Amen.

FEAR

*And the fear of God was on all the kingdoms of [those]
countries, when they had heard that the LORD fought against
the enemies of Israel.*

2 Chronicles 20:29

There is no greater fear than the fear of God. To stand before the
Almighty Creator and deem oneself to be any sort of challenge is not
only ridiculous but absurd. There is no power greater, and within a
moment's time, that person could literally vanish from existence.

When fear comes upon us, usually one of two things happens:
we either fight or take flight—war or run. Sometimes one action
is better than the other, but both can be defensive mechanisms.
However, when it comes to the Heavenly Father, submission is best
in fearful situations. Running, even in fear, will never help us get
away—just ask Jonah.

The best posture for the one in the fear of the Lord is obedience and
humility. By these traits, we will find ourselves friends of God, but
His enemies will be the ones who have fear.

PRAYER

*Dear Heavenly Father, I humbly submit before You today,
and I put my enemies before You to deal with in Your
powerful way. In Jesus' name I pray. Amen.*

FAITH

Faith cometh by hearing, and hearing by the word of God.

Romans 10:17

Trust is a quality that must be shared by comrades. Those who have been in the heat of the battle know the importance of having faith in a fellow soldier. Lives depend upon it, and the life that is saved may be one's own.

But how does one acquire faith or a greater measure of faith in this life? What is the key element involved and can anyone have more faith? The answer is yes, and it is found in this phrase, *Faith cometh by hearing, and hearing by the word of God.* Put it this way: faith comes by hearing, and hearing, and hearing, and hearing, and hearing, and more hearing the Word of God. There must be a continual hearing of the Word of God for our faith to increase.

As we get to know others better, trust and faith increase. Even more so, when we read the Word of God, allow it to sink into our spirit, and come to know God more and more, our faith increases. When that happens, the problems of life shrink in their ability to overwhelm our lives.

PRAYER

Dear Heavenly Father, please give me a passion for Your word, so that my faith and trust will be in You no matter what I must endure. In Jesus' name I pray. Amen.

INDEPENDENCE

*And you, who were dead in your trespasses and the
uncircumcision of your flesh, God made alive together with him,
having forgiven us all our trespasses, by the canceling the record
of debt that stood against us with its legal demands. This he set
aside, nailing it to the cross.*

Colossians 2:13-14

Known as the Fourth of July and Independence Day, July 4th has
been a federal holiday in the United States since 1941. However, the
tradition of Independence Day celebrations goes back to the 18th
century and the American Revolution (1775-83). In June 1776,
representatives of the 13 colonies then fighting in the revolutionary struggle weighed a resolution that would declare their independence from Great Britain. On July 2nd, the Continental Congress
voted in favor of independence. Two days later, its delegates adopted
the Declaration of Independence, a historic document drafted by
Thomas Jefferson. From 1776 until the present day, July 4th has
been celebrated as the birth of American independence, with typi-
cal festivities ranging from fireworks, parades and concerts to more
casual family gatherings and barbecues.

The ideal of independence was born in the hearts of men and wom-
en who sought a place to be free from the tyranny of political oppression. Those who signed the Declaration of Independence pledged
their lives and their fortunes to see this ideal become a reality. Many
of the original signers, in fact, lost their homes in the Revolutionary
War. It has been said, "Freedom is not free." The Fourth of July reminds us to remember and celebrate the birthday of our nation.

The Bible announces the declaration of our freedom from the power
of sin. All of us are born owing a debt that we could not pay. Jesus
Christ came to satisfy the holy demand of the law through paying
the debt for us. If we believe in Him and call upon His name, we can
be free from sin.

PRAYER

*Dear Heavenly Father, I have lived as though I didn't need
You. Forgive all my sin and cancel the debt I owed. In Jesus'
name I pray. Amen.*

FUSIBLE

Art thou bound unto a wife? seek not to be loosed.
Art thou loosed from a wife? seek not a wife.

1 Corinthians 7:17

Unity is imperative for soldiers accomplishing a mission. There is indeed power in numbers. Those who take advantage of the team advance far greater than they could if they performed alone. The ability to be fusible with others is imperative. Without the support of the group, greater exposure to difficulties arise.

When a man marries a woman, they become fusible together. In God's eyes, He sees them as one. They are unified, together, and inseparable. The value of being together brings great advancement, not only in this life, but also in one's relationship with God. A Christian marriage is where two Christians help each other to be a greater Christians than if they were alone. Fusibility allows for and promotes this growth.

The advantage of being fusible is shown by results. We do not have to go far to find tragedies that prevail by going it alone.

PRAYER

Dear Heavenly Father, I desire to be fusible with You, my spouse, and with others around me. I know that You will use others to help me to grow in my walk with You. In Jesus' name I pray. Amen.

_____

_____

_____

_____

_____

_____

July 6

FLAG

Render therefore to all their dues: tribute to whom tribute [is due]; custom to whom custom; fear to whom fear; honour to whom honour.

Romans 13:7

Those who hear and know the *Star Spangled Banner*, the national anthem of the United States, know the pride that comes with the commitment behind that flag. The flag is a symbol of the ideals that many have given their lives for to defend. With such a great price, there must be honor.

The Bible is very clear on how powers of government are set up and torn down. The Almighty God has His input on the elected, and each of them are participants in the governing He chooses for a country. In the past, the Heavenly Father has chosen people both good and evil to rule, but all of them were working His divine purposes.

Flags are symbolic of our beliefs. However, even if our beliefs are strong, our lives may not be spared. When considering the kingdom of God, what price are we willing to pay to raise the flag of the Christian faith throughout the world?

PRAYER

Dear Heavenly Father, help me today to bear the flag of a Christian in such a manner that everyone with whom I come into contact will see the ideals that are portrayed by a relationship with You. In Jesus' name I pray. Amen.

July 7

UNDERDOG

...and that all this assembly may know that the Lord saves not with sword and spear. For the battle is the Lord's, and he will give you into our hand.

1 Samuel 17:47

The 2007 Appalachian State-University of Michigan college football game was held on September 1 at Michigan Stadium on the campus of the University of Michigan in Ann Arbor, Michigan. It pitted the #5 ranked Michigan Wolverines against the two-time defending champions of the Division I FCS (I-AA), the Appalachian State Mountaineers. In what was hailed as one of the biggest upsets in the history of American sports, the Mountaineers shocked the fifth-ranked Wolverines 34–32. In the world of sports, Appalachian State was a underdog and not supposed to win.

The Jewish people pulled off a military upset in what is called the Six Day War, June 5 through June 10, 1967. This conflict was between Israel and the neighboring states of Egypt, Jordan and Syria. The outcome was a swift and decisive Israeli victory. Israel took control of the Gaza Strip and Golan Heights from Syria. Israel appeared to be a huge underdog, with no chance of defeating the well-equipped armies of her neighbors. This battle epitomized the term, "underdog," which is applied to a perceived loser or predicted loser in a struggle or contest.

Goliath was a nine-foot, one inch tall giant and was covered front and back with a coat of mail made of brass. David was not considered mature enough to fight in the army. Logically, there was no way for David to defeat Goliath.

The lesson for us in these examples is that the outcome of the battle isn't always predictable. Upsets do occur and the underdog does win! Another important factor is that God's favor is more important than weapons or strength.

PRAYER

Dear Heavenly Father, You give strength to the weak, and those who wait on You will mount up on wings of eagles. In Jesus' name I pray. Amen.

KOREAN WAR (1950-1953)

CHEER

A merry heart doeth good [like] a medicine:
but a broken spirit drieth the bones.

Proverbs 17:22

Victory! Success! Winner! Attainment! All of these have to do with being victorious over challenges. Whether the challenge be succeeding over an obstacle course or defeating a foe, the venue for celebration and cheer is at hand. Soldiers know the excitement that accompanies a great victory and their cheer can be heard from great distances away.

The Bible denotes the importance of cheer and merriness in a person's life. In fact, the Bible likens a merry heart to taking medicine. Indeed, a good cheer or laugh does make the soul feel much better. However, those with broken spirits find themselves downcast, troubled, and often sad or depressed.

The wise person realizes the importance of cheer and laughter. Finding humor is a necessity for functioning with a good attitude in the world. Both those who enjoy laughter and those around those joyful people will be affected by their inner spirit that is filled with cheer.

PRAYER

Dear Heavenly Father, I know there are times where cheer is not going to be a part in my life, but I ask You today to help me to have a merry heart that will draw others to You as their Savior, no matter what I go through. In Jesus' name I pray. Amen.

MATURE

But the fruit of the Spirit is love, joy, peace, longsuffering, gentleness, goodness, faith, meekness, temperance: against such there is no law.

Galatians 5:22-23

When a mission is accomplished and a battle is won, the victory often explodes into cheer. Soldiers who overcome obstacles, resist resignation, and purpose resolve deserve a time of celebration when their feat is finished and their triumph is fulfilled.

Within all Christians is accomplishment that deserves cheer. This celebration, however, is not that we may accomplish on our own. This victory is won by the Holy Spirit of God. Christians who continue to grow in maturity find themselves managed by the Holy Spirit from victories gained within their own souls. The fruit of the Spirit, when in full fruition, has victory after victory over works of the flesh. When we manifest the fruit of the Spirit, we have reason to cheer and give glory to the One who works in areas that never before have been seen. The flesh submits and the Spirit of the Living God dwells victoriously within them.

Glory be to God!

PRAYER

Dear Heavenly Father, I desire that Your Holy Spirit work within me to drive out all the works of the flesh. I give glory and honor to You as I celebrate in advance what You will do in my life. In Jesus' name I pray. Amen.

July 10
CAMP

And the LORD shall utter his voice before his army: for his camp [is] very great: for [he is] strong that executeth his word: for the day of the LORD [is] great and very terrible; and who can abide it?

Joel 2:11

Armies set up camp for strategic purposes and planning. The gathering together of soldiers for the purpose of equipping them for service is part of the military routine. Those who have camped in war zones know the importance of the intelligence they receive within campsites.

Christians are also in a war. Daily trials, both personal and among other Christians, formulate every day. The onslaughts of the enemy of the soul never stop. Those who come together realize the importance of having the Captain of our army as the sole instructor for the battles ahead. When Jesus is placed in the proper position and in the proper place, plans unfold, details are revealed, and defenses are strengthened. The gathering together of the saints of Jesus Christ readies each participant for whatever the enemy throws their way.

PRAYER

Dear Heavenly Father, I know that You know the future, and our coming together to the camp is so important to knowing Your plans. Help me today to realize the impact of camping with Your people. In Jesus' name I pray. Amen.

July 11
CALM

He calms the storm, so that its waves are still.

Psalm 107:29

The news brought reports of an earthquake in Japan, which caused a giant tidal wave called a tsunami. A huge wall of water raced out from the epicenter of the quake, threatening life and property in the Pacific and the west coast of the USA. Watching homes, businesses and vehicles swept away like sand castles on the beach demonstrates the power of nature.

There is a power greater than the energy found in the tsunami or the earthquake. Storms are a frequent occurrence in some regions of the world. In the Bible, the most frequent storms happened on the Sea of Galilee. Fishing was a common way of life. In fact, several of the disciples were fisherman. On more than one occasion, Jesus rescued his friends from a violent storm.

Jesus spoke to the storm and calmed the wind. The soon-to-be fishers of men were amazed at this demonstration of God's power over nature. Jesus pointed them to God's desire to calm the storm inside the hearts of men. It would require massive energy to calm a tsunami or negate the destruction of an earthquake. A greater miracle is the saving of a soul.

PRAYER

Dear Heavenly Father, Jesus came to seek and to save the lost. When He calmed the storm on the Sea of Galilee, He demonstrated that with God nothing is impossible. You give me calm when I face a storm. In Jesus' name I pray. Amen.

_____

_____

_____

_____

July 12
COMPETE

Again I saw that under the sun the race is not to the swift, nor the battle to the strong, nor bread to the wise, nor riches to the intelligent, nor favor to those with knowledge, but time and chance happen to them all.

Ecclesiastes 9:11

Much of the time the outcome of a race, battle, or contest is predictable. Good causes work good effects. Speed does win the race and strength wins the battle. Diligence and intelligence do result in security and wealth.

However, there are additional factors that determine the outcome of the battle. In addition to speed, effort and strength, time and chance also affect the outcome of events. Superior diligence and intelligence, along with effort and strength, are important and should not be neglected.

The arena of competition reminds us that chance often brings about an upset. Lesser armies have defeated forces with greater resources, numbers and training. What we call chance may be God's unpredictable influence in human behavior. It is wise to put our trust in God rather in our own strength. Psalm 20:7 has a good word to remember: *Some trust in chariots and some in horses, but we trust in the name of the Lord our God.*

PRAYER

Dear Heavenly Father, I will prepare to be a good soldier ready to do my best. I commit the battle to You and ask that You will take care of the outcome. In Jesus' name I pray. Amen.

_____

_____

_____

ACCOMPLISH

But none of these things move me, neither count I my life dear unto myself, so that I might finish my course with joy, and the ministry, which I have received of the Lord Jesus, to testify the gospel of the grace of God.

Acts 20:24

There is nothing like accomplishing a task or mission that has been set forth to do. When commands are given and a work is undertaken, therein lies intestinal fortitude to see that hill taken or that building secured or that foe defeated. When soldiers set their minds to accomplish these undertakings, nothing will stop them. The goal must be reached.

Paul, the apostle, understood this. Though he endured great hardship for the Gospel of Jesus, he continued to pursue finishing his course. The side events that masked themselves in beatings, shipwrecks and the like didn't deter him from testifying about the Gospel of the grace of God.

Set and firm determination helps us accomplish our goals. Setbacks are only fuel for continuing until the labor is finished. Those who keep their eyes on the goal will not be affected by the onslaught of deterrents, which are sure to raise their ugly heads.

PRAYER

Dear Heavenly Father, thank You for the goals You have set before me to accomplish. Please help me to keep on task as I push toward completing the missions You have for me. In Jesus' name I pray. Amen.

_____

_____

_____

_____

FRIVOLOUS

My son, if sinners entice thee, consent thou not.

Proverbs 1:10

Disciplines are added to a soldier's life as preparation for real engagements. Without it, soldiers are ill-equipped and their lives are in danger. There is no time for frivolous activity when such importance is on the line. Although the pressure may seem unsustainable, wise soldiers know not to involve themselves with those who participate in wasteful ventures.

So also is it true for the Christian. There are situations where the enemy of the soul will use people try to persuade one into frivolous activity. The invitation may be enticing, and the venture or function seems like fun, but the end incurs penalty, loss, and pain.

Be careful. Frivolity and meaningless activity can lead to a life-altering circumstance. When we are caught within the web of enemy ploys, we may never have another chance to undo what has been done.

PRAYER

Dear Heavenly Father, I know the tendency to bend toward frivolous activity. Please help me to easily identify when these activities arise and give me the strength to resist when they do. In Jesus' name I pray. Amen.

July 15
FORTIFY

Watch ye, stand fast in the faith, quit you like men, be strong.

1 Corinthians 16:13

Those who fortify a city or village know the importance of securing every aspect to the area. Even the smallest of openings can be an opportunity for the enemy to get in and do damage. The harm that is caused through the weakest link may be enough to destroy the entire place.

Paul, the apostle, encouraged the church at Corinth to "quit you like men," which is essentially being men of courage. Courageous people work hard to fortify, take great measures to assure security, and are willing to give their lives for the safety of others. The price for fortifying may be expensive, but the price for leaving a place without fortification will be far greater.

To fortify our own lives, stay within the fortress of the Word of God and prayer. Safety, peace and security are within those walls that no person on earth can provide and no man will ever perform.

PRAYER

Dear Heavenly Father, please fortify me within the bounds of Your words. I desire to stay under the shadow of Your wings all the days of my life. In Jesus' name I pray. Amen.

FEROCIOUS

Because that he had been often bound with fetters and chains,
and the chains had been plucked asunder by him, and the fetters
broken in pieces: neither could any [man] tame him.

Mark 5:4

Terror and terrorist are one of the most vicious parts of living. Those who have no regard or value for others' lives and who will kill innocent people shall have their meeting with the Heavenly Father above, by Whom vengeance shall come. Make no mistake about it, this God Almighty of great grace is also a God of great justice. Those who perpetrate against others as terrorist shall have their day.

Jesus shows His superior power over both human and spiritual beings when he faces the man filled with terror from Gadara. As soon as this vicious-acting wild man saw Jesus, he fell at His feet. Though man had tried to bind and tame him, only the eyes of Jesus brought him to his knees. Now that's power! Ferocious power! Jesus' power was stronger and more mighty than anything anyone could throw at Him. His meekness restrained that ferocious power as He gave Himself willingly on the cross for every person.

The soldier who understands power, whether it be in position, rank, equipment or command, realizes that there is no power given but that which has been given by God, and the ferociousness of His power is greater than all the other powers combined.

PRAYER

Dear Heavenly Father, I realize that You have absolute power and that the ferociousness of that power can overcome every foe. Help me today to rely upon You for every foe I come against, whether physical or spiritual. In Jesus' name I pray. Amen.

_____

_____

July 17
FIERCE

Because thou obeyedst not the voice of the LORD, nor executedst his fierce wrath upon Amalek, therefore hath the LORD done this thing unto thee this day.

1 Samuel 28:18

Enemies surround those who would be right every day. Soldiers know when they engage the enemy, their lives are threatened. Without proper execution, the soldier and his fellow troops may incur injury or death. When enemies mean to kill and destroy, they must be treated in a fierce and prompt attitude. The enemy is not one to be underestimated, nor is the enemy to be treated in an aloof manner.

God Almighty faced enemies and He continues to face them today. Although at any time, all enemies could be eliminated under His fierce power, God allows them to survive to aid in His mission to save. Some will convert, while others will not. Those who do not will be dealt with fiercely when the time comes.

Make no mistake about it, the Heavenly Father is a gracious and loving God. However, at the same time, He is a fierce foe to any of His enemies. God understands enemies, and His opposition to them is greater than any that man could ever inspire. No one, and let the writer repeat, no one should want to be the enemy of God.

PRAYER

Dear Heavenly Father, thank You for calling me Your friend. I know that You will deal with the enemies in the world, so please help me to know Your ways before them. In Jesus' name I pray. Amen.

July 18
FALTER

Only be thou strong and very courageous, that thou mayest observe to do according to all the law, which Moses my servant commanded thee: turn not from it [to] the right hand or [to] the left, that thou mayest prosper whithersoever thou goest.

Joshua 1:7

Bravery and courage are not easily mustered in some situations. When the odds do not seem in our favor or when the battle seems to be going to the other side, it's easy for these traits to falter. What are we to do when faltering replaces courage or when cowardice replaces bravery? Hear the words of the Heavenly Father once again.

There is no resource for redirection like the Bible. In God's Words, we find strength and faith like no other source can provide. Hearing the Father's words by reading His instructions moves a person to different ideas, different thoughts and different directions. Note the bravery of David who fought Goliath! His boldness came from knowing the Great Shepherd, and He knew him by His Word.

The next time the tide of fear is threatening and a wave of faltering is on the horizon, sit with the Word and meditate on it. Allow the Word of God to penetrate the soul to the point of being strong and very courageous again.

PRAYER

Dear Heavenly Father, help me to find Your word as the resource for when my heart and soul begin to falter. I choose to have You in control of my life. In Jesus' name I pray. Amen.

July 19

FAINTHEARTED

*Only be thou strong and very courageous, that thou mayest
observe to do according to all the law, which Moses my servant
commanded thee: turn not from it [to] the right hand or [to] the
left, that thou mayest prosper whithersoever thou goest.*

Joshua 1:7

One of the greatest soldiers of all times was Joshua. He was faithful
to his leader, Moses, and his loyalty was beyond that of any in the
army of Israel. Now, his opportunity to lead was before him. Moses
was dead, and now Joshua was in charge. This was not a time to be
fainthearted. This was a time for courage and strength, and his help
must come from a source greater than he.

There are times of advancement in life. These times call for courage, strength, and quite possibly, endurance that does not come
from within. Fainthearted people cower in light of danger, and
like the Cowardly Lion in *The Wizard of Oz*, they run in the face
of opposition.

When advancement comes and challenge arises, remember that
there is a source Who causes elevation. The Heavenly Father doesn't
call anyone to a task to which He does not stand ready to equip.
If we realize the source of true courage and strength, we will bow
before Him and be ready to perform exploits that are beyond our
wildest imagination.

PRAYER

*Dear Heavenly Father, I need courage and strength that
come from You alone. Help me today to not be fainthearted,
and give me boldness to be all that I can be before Your eyes.
In Jesus' name I pray. Amen.*

_____

_____

GHOST SOLDIER

*You hypocrites! Well did Isaiah prophesy of you, when he said:
'This people honors me with their lips, but their heart
is far from me;*

Matthew 15:7-8

Ghost soldier is the term in the military for someone who is active in name only. They are soldiers who are enlisted or placed on active duty but do not serve—fake names listed as active-duty soldiers. Sadly, there have been those who sought to have a record of military service, but evaded active duty.

Jesus encountered religious people who relished the title of piety, but whose daily life betrayed their deceit. They were described as hypocrites, a term for those who pretend or act religious but are, in fact, wicked. In the military, they would wear the uniform, but be a no-show in battle. Jesus said of the hypocrites that they were clean outwardly, but inwardly were greedy and wicked.

In Arlington National Cemetery, a grave is marked, "The Unknown Soldier." In honor of the service and memory of this unknown patriot, guards keep a round-the-clock vigil. Whoever is buried in that tomb gave the ultimate sacrifice for our nation. It is appropriate that a grateful nation salutes the nameless soldiers who have showed up for every battle in our history.

PRAYER

Dear Heavenly Father, I don't want to be among those who serve in name only. Search my heart, try my thoughts and remove every evil way from me. In Jesus' name I pray. Amen.

_____

_____

_____

July 21
HONOR

When they saw the star, they rejoiced exceedingly with great joy. And going into the house they saw the child with Mary his mother, and they fell down and worshiped him.

Matthew 2:10-11

Parents of military sons and daughters deployed on a mission often display in their front window a small, white vertical banner bordered in red. In the center of the banner is a simple blue star. It calls attention to the fact they have given a loved one to the cause of freedom, justice and peace in the world.

If a soldier is killed in combat, the grieving parents display another banner in their front window. This time the star in the center is gold. This star indicates that they have a son or daughter who has made the ultimate sacrifice in service to their country. Both the parents and the serviceman or woman are worthy of our gratitude.

In the Gospel of Matthew, we read of the appearance of a single star that led the Magi to Bethlehem. They discovered the Christ child and worshiped Him. The Christ child came to lay down His life for everyone. Thus, the Magi worshiped, anticipating His supreme sacrifice.

PRAYER

Dear Heavenly Father, thank You for sending the Christ child to lead me to the truth. I bow in recognition of Your love and mercy to me. In Jesus' name I pray. Amen.

_____

_____

_____

_____

_____

DISCIPLINE

All Scripture is breathed out by God and profitable for teaching, for reproof, for correction, and for training in righteousness, that the man of God may be competent, equipped for every good work.

2 Timothy 3:16-17

It is a well-established fact that discipline is essential in every area of life. However, most people think that when we talk about discipline, we're talking about absence of freedom. Freedom was one of the foundational principles in the founding of this nation. However, freedom without restraint leads to chaos and anarchy.

Think about a major traffic intersection in, say, New York City. Picture no traffic lights or cops and everyone is free to drive without any restrictions. Traffic jams and fatal accidents would soon bring the freedom to drive to a stop. Nobody would be able to drive! We all benefit from the discipline of traffic lights and the laws that define their function.

Freedom is a basic human value. No one likes to be controlled by others, but absolute freedom is not always good. Self-control restores order to the chaos of a traffic jam. When we practice self-control, we find that rules and regulations actually give us more freedom. The intersection with traffic lights provides us with the freedom of movement, whereas, the absence of traffic lights stops all movement.

PRAYER

Dear Heavenly Father, Your word defines the boundaries for my life. I am learning that when You restrict my freedom, You are protecting me from a danger or a sin. Thank You for Your Word! In Jesus' name I pray. Amen.

July 23
SALT

You are the salt of the earth, but if salt has lost its taste, how shall its saltiness be restored? It is no longer good for anything except to be thrown out and trampled under people's feet.

Matthew 5:13

Today we think of salt as cheap and plentiful, but before modern mining methods, salt was rare and valuable—even worth fighting a war. In India there was plenty of salt, but the British colonial law dictated that only the government could mine and disperse salt. The Indian people were forced to pay for something they could have gotten free at the seashore.

Mahatma Gandhi led a march to the sea in protest, which became known as the Salt Wars, thus beginning India's struggle for independence. India's tropical climate made salt indispensable to the diet of her people. During the pre-refrigeration era in our country, salt was vital in the preservation of food, especially meats.

The world doesn't need another flavor in their religious choices. They need a person whose life has been cleansed and preserved by the incorruptible Word of God. Jesus calls *whosoever will* to become a follower and sends them into the world to be salt and light. Any nation or individual without Christ is like food without the preserving properties of salt.

PRAYER

Dear Heavenly Father the corruption in the world cries out for healing. You have called us to be disciples who have been changed by Your Word. Let Your light shine through me to those in darkness. In Jesus' name I pray. Amen.

_____

_____

_____

_____

July 24
THREATENED

What time I am afraid, I will trust in thee.

Psalm 56:3

Even the bravest of soldiers is afraid when they are threatened by something greater than their capacity to handle it. The overwhelming thoughts of defeat and demise can demobilize anyone. Everyone is threatened from time to time in this life. Whether it be bullets or bombs, disease or cancer, life has frightening aspects to it.

God Almighty knew there would be times when people are afraid. He knows man's abilities, and He knows that many times those abilities are limited. In those limited situations, God has designed man so that in a moment, we can call upon Him. The Creator will be the hero. The Creator has capacity indeed and will receive the full glory for the victory.

The next time huge opposition arrives or the enemy threatens, remember where to put confidence and trust. Rely upon the resources of one who is greater than all the problems, resistance, and threats that we will ever face.

PRAYER

Dear Heavenly Father, I put my trust in You, and I place all the threats within my life at the foot of Your throne. May You receive all the glory for the victory I shall enjoy. In Jesus' name I pray. Amen.

July 25

THOUGHTS

We destroy arguments and every lofty opinion raised against the knowledge of God, and take every thought captive to obey Christ.

2 Corinthians 10:5

It's fashionable to accept the popular saying; "what I do or think in private is nobody's business." It's true that we have the freedom to make our own choices. However, what we think about affects who we become and what we do. This will soon become public and everybody will know what we have thought about in our private time.

What do we think about when we are free to think as we please? If we will examine our thoughts, we will discover what we are and what we are going to become. The best way to control our thoughts is to offer our minds to God.

The Scripture tells us to *take thoughts captive* (2 Corinthians 10:5) and *whatever is true, whatever is honorable, whatever is just, whatever is pure, whatever is lovely, whatever is commendable, worthy of praise, think about these things.* (Philippians 4:8) These thoughts will kept us from falling into sin and dishonor.

PRAYER

Dear Heavenly Father, take control of my thoughts. Lead me in right paths. In Jesus' name I pray. Amen.

_____

_____

_____

_____

_____

_____

_____

_____

PREROGATIVE

And if it seem evil unto you to serve the LORD, choose you this day whom ye will serve; whether the gods which your fathers served that [were] on the other side of the flood, or the gods of the Amorites, in whose land ye dwell: but as for me and my house, we will serve the LORD.

Joshua 24:15

Joshua was one of the mightiest warriors within the Scriptures. His battles over foreign foes was continual and successful. The exploits and victories he won as a soldier are worth consideration as soldiers of today venture into their own battles.

One day Joshua came to an impasse. Either the people he was leading were going to serve the LORD or they were going to serve the former or current gods. There would be no alternative, and the choice had to be made. It was the people's prerogative, which way they chose. The results of their choice would be their own to bear. Joshua's prerogative was clear: *As for me and my house, we will serve the LORD.*

Everyone today has that same prerogative. The choice is ours and we, like the people Joshua governed, are responsible for the choices we make. If we are to be wise, we will choose as Joshua did. The awesome results from his choice are seen in the mighty victories he enjoyed.

PRAYER

Dear Heavenly Father, today I choose You. I realize that I have the prerogative to choose as I wish. As for me and my house, we will serve the Lord. In Jesus' name I pray. Amen.

_____

_____

_____

July 27
FAVOR

For his anger is but for a moment, and his favor is for a lifetime.

Psalm 30:5

There is a limit to our endurance. The strongest steel breaks if kept too long under unrelieved stress. Even Christ could endure the cross only because of the joy set before Him. God knows how much pressure each one of us can take. He gives relief just in time.

David, King of Israel, experienced times of great stress when it seemed that God was angry. He learned two great truths: one, the season of stress was limited and two, God's favor was forever. As sure as the morning came, his joy would return.

It may seem that the times of stress, when we don't see God in our circumstances, will last forever. The Scripture reassures us that it's God favor that lasts forever!

PRAYER

Dear Heavenly Father, thank You for Your favor. Give me Your strength to endure the stress. In Jesus' name I pray. Amen.

SOS

Three times I pleaded with the Lord about this, that it should leave me. But he said to me, My grace is sufficient for you, for my power is made perfect in weakness.

2 Corinthians 12: 8-9

A word of military wisdom says, "Flying the airplane is more important than radioing your plight to a person on the ground who is incapable of understanding or doing anything about it." There are times when nobody responds to our call for help. What should our response be when our attempts to send out a distress signal fails?

The experience of pilots who have survived that kind of an emergency is very simple, but not easy. First, avoid panic, and second, fly the plane. To be successful in that situation, pilots must trust their training. Panic uses negative energy and will prevent the mind from activating the maneuvers that will give the best chance at survival.

Paul, an apostle of Jesus, asked three times to be rescued, but the answer was similar to the military wisdom. The Scripture paraphrased says, "Relax and admit you're weak;" and "Put your trust in God— He's strong when you're weak."

PRAYER

Dear Heavenly Father, I prayed about this situation but You have not answered. You know that I am weak, so help me to trust in Your strength. In Jesus' name I pray. Amen.

July 29
FREE

And ye shall know the truth, and the truth shall make you free.

John 8:32

The principle and value of freedom is one of the predominant reason for military power in the United States of America. Many soldiers have given their lives so that others whom they do not even know may be free. "Let Freedom Ring" has been a motto since the beginning of this country and shall be its motto as long as this country survives.

The idea of being free is also important within the kingdom of God. Jesus Himself emphasized the way to true freedom. *The truth shall make you free* was His declaration thereby elevated the importance of the truth. Parenthetically, Jesus told those who listened that it was by continuing in His word that a person would truly be free. The implication is that any other route would be binding.

Many disregard Jesus' charge to continue in His Word. Rather than read, study, and obey the Scriptures, they endure the chains and bondage that life offers instead. The wise person knows the route to freedom, and then pays the price to stay there.

PRAYER

Dear Heavenly Father, thank You for Your words that lead to a life of being free. Please give me the desire to stay in Your word all the days of my life that I may truly be made free. In Jesus' name I pray. Amen.

_____

_____

_____

_____

_____

July 30

FALSE

Through thy precepts I get understanding: therefore I hate every false way.

Psalm 119:104

Abraham Lincoln said, "I am not bound to win, but I am bound to be true. I am not bound to succeed, but I am bound to live by the light that I have. I must stand with anybody that stands right, stand with him while he is right, and part with him when he goes wrong." The warrior knows these words to be true, and those who follow this resolve will find themselves turned away from that which is false.

But how do we know when something is true? The answer is in the precepts of God. The answer is found in the Bible. The Bible is the measurement and standard to which all ideas must be quantified. By receiving what the Lord indicates about a thought or way, we keep ourselves from false teachings. Without the standard of the Bible, everyone does what is right in their own eyes.

The Bible is exacting, demanding, and rigid about its standards, which are the standards and ways of God Almighty. His provision of the Bible is one of the greatest gifts given to man. If we use the Scriptures wisely, false methods will never enter our way of living.

PRAYER

Dear Heavenly Father, please give me a desire for Your word so that I will keep myself from every false way. In Jesus' name I pray. Amen.

HERO

And a cloud overshadowed them, and a voice come out of the cloud, 'This is my beloved Son, listen to him.

Mark 9:7

I suggest we all need to read the Mayflower Compact, a covenant by a band of settlers who helped establish one of the first communities in the new world. The Puritans first act at Plymouth Rock was to kneel, pray and dedicate the new colony to God.

God has blessed this nation! We should remember and be thankful for our rich history of God's miraculous intervention in the life of this nation. There are many examples of this blessing in our beginning history. General George Washington and his fledgling army of independence faced the British Commander, William Howe, and 30,000 veteran troops. They were outmanned and outflanked.

Their only hope was to escape across the East River. The wind was blowing and escape seemed impossible, so General Washington called a prayer meeting. The wind calmed, and a fog hid their retreat from the British. God intervened!

A more recent example of bravery and heroism occurred in what we call 911. We witnessed a modern generation of brave men and women who stepped forward. When those burning towers began to fall in New York City and thousands were fleeing, another group ran into those buildings. These modern heroes sought to rescue their fellow man even at the sacrifice of their own lives.

We owe a great debt to those past and present who act, in the face of danger, to defend and protect our freedom. Why do some shoulder this responsibility while others seem content to be a victim?

PRAYER

Dear Heavenly Father, there is only one who never disappoints, who is a genuine hero, and His name is Jesus. I ask for courage to use my gifts to help those in trouble. In Jesus' name I pray. Amen.

LEADERSHIP

And he said to them, 'Follow me, and I will make you fishers of men.

Matthew 4:19

The person who would be an effective leader must first be a devout follower. Jesus chose twelve men to place in charge of establishing the Christian church. In the beginning they lacked the qualities needed for the task, but in a short three and one-half years, these fishermen, tax collectors and other ordinary men were highly effective in achieving just that mission.

General Douglas MacArthur gave us a great definition of leadership. He said, "A true leader has the confidence to stand alone, the courage to make tough decisions, and the compassion to listen to the needs of others." No leader will be successful without the three qualities General MacArthur includes in his definition: confidence, courage, and compassion.

We can read about leadership, but having it modeled by someone we can walk with and learn from is the most effective way develop our skills. No one modeled leadership more effectively than Jesus. He invited the twelve to follow Him and the result was they became great leaders. He still calls men and women to follow Him today.

PRAYER

Dear Heavenly Father, I'm not seeking the role of leadership but I do desire to follow Jesus. My prayer is that You make me what You want me to be. In Jesus' name I pray. Amen.

_____

_____

_____

_____

FLASH

*And it came to pass, as they still went on, and talked, that,
behold, [there appeared] a chariot of fire, and horses of fire,
and parted them both asunder; and Elijah went up by a
whirlwind into heaven.*

2 Kings 2:11

People come, and people go. Challenges come, and challenges go, but
what about when they come and go like a flash in the pan? What
happens when a person or offering comes quickly today, but is gone
just as quickly tomorrow? How do we react to this sudden in-and-
out person or event?

The Bible tells the story of Elijah as he left the earth. In the story,
God comes down in a chariot and horses of fire and carries Elijah
away. As quickly as Elisha, Elijah's protégé and replacement, saw the
chariot come, he also saw it go. This is very symbolic of the nature
of the Heavenly Father, for He brings some in and takes some out.
Talent and abilities have no bearing upon His divine purposes.

Watch out for the flash-in-the-pan people and gimmicks that come
along. They sometimes have great promises, great wealth programs
or great weight-loss plans with them. If we are just a little patient,
most of those flashes fly away just as quickly as the chariot of God
that claimed Elijah.

PRAYER

*Dear Heavenly Father, I acknowledge that You know the
difference between that which is just a flash and that which
remains. Please help me today and throughout my life to
know the difference and to side with that which You have
ordained. In Jesus' name I pray. Amen.*

FISH

And he saith unto them, Follow me, and I will make you fishers of men.

Matthew 4:19

Those who need a break from it all know the relaxation that can come with fishing. Unless there are tasks, such as boats to ready, food to prep, bait to buy, or licenses to obtain, fishing can be a time away from it all. Those who involve themselves in busy activities like soldiers know how important just a little refreshment can be.

Many of the disciples were fishermen, and for some of them, it was their way of life. Fishing was how they made their living. One of the significant characteristics of Jesus was that He would enter directly into a person's world. He didn't try to alter their living, but He would use their living to relate to the kingdom of God. For the fishermen, they were to be *fishers of men*.

For us to understand how Jesus relates to our world, we must know our strengths. These strengths are often gifts from the Heavenly Father. He knows how to use them to have everyone be fishers of men. Fish with gifts given, and many will come to know the Lord Jesus through that casting of those lines.

PRAYER

Dear Heavenly Father, take today the blessings and gifts that You have given to me, and use them for fishing for men in Your kingdom. In Jesus' name I pray. Amen.

_____
_____
_____
_____
_____
_____

FIND

*He that findeth his life shall lose it: and he that loseth his life for
my sake shall find it.*

Mark 10:39

There is a certain joy that is associated with finding something that
is lost. Things such as lost keys, lost money, or lost people invoke
a certain amount of anxiousness and worry when they cannot be
found. Then, suddenly, that moment comes when we locate that
which was lost, and a sense of relief overwhelms us.

Jesus knows the association that most feel when something is lost. In
fact, the purpose of His mission was to seek and to save that which
was lost. According to Jesus, there is a method that is out of the
norm for finding ourselves. Jesus says that we do that by losing ourselves. In other words, we must forget about ourselves and be about
the things of Christ and His Gospel. This does not mean that we
have to give up what we do for a living, sell all, and go out and preach.
Rather, we should live our lives in such a manner that others see the
kingdom of God in them.

If we lose our lives, our own ambitions, and our own desires,
while replacing them with the importance of the Gospel, we
shall indeed find our own lives and know a joy in life like we
have never known before.

PRAYER

*Dear Heavenly Father, I know that it is right that I lose
myself and be about Your kingdom's work. Help me to
recognize where I lack in this area, and help me to live for
Your sake. In Jesus' name I pray. Amen.*

_____

_____

_____

FILL

And he said unto me, Son of man, cause thy belly to eat, and fill thy bowels with this roll that I give thee. Then did I eat [it]; and it was in my mouth as honey for sweetness.

Ezekiel 3:3

Filling one's stomach is one of the greatest parts of the day. To eat the morsels provided, especially when they are cooked to perfection, is a delight that people everywhere enjoy. Those who experience mess hall on the days when the food is the desired dish of the week know exactly the delight of which is written.

God Almighty understands the importance of eating. However, His standard for nourishment is not just within the physical body. God knows that the spirit of man needs, desires and longs for the nourishment that will only be provided by reading His Word. Ezekiel had to devour the Word for it to be sweetness within his mouth.

To be wise, we will keep a steady filling of the Word of God. The energy that the Word provides will help us make it through any situation, circumstance, or development. When we fill ourselves with God's ways and knowledge, every foe that rises against us shall fall. Any battles within our souls are brought to peace whenever the anguish is filled with God's whispers.

PRAYER

Dear Heavenly Father, thank You for Your word. I desire to fill myself with Your teachings, Your ways, and Your desires for my life. Help me to continually fill myself with You. In Jesus' name I pray. Amen.

FIGURATIVE

The thing that hath been, it [is that] which shall be; and that which is done [is] that which shall be done: and [there is] no new [thing] under the sun.

Ecclesiastes 1:9

Literal or figurative? Real or imagined? Fake or authentic? Many times when something of value is placed before some people, they want to know whether the object or saying is true, valid, honest or just an invaluable, worthless offering. The weight of a matter may depend upon it—the worth of an object certainly does.

When it comes to God Almighty, He knows the valid from the invalid. He knows when someone is using figurative language versus literal. He knows the difference between that which is real and that which is fake. Those who depend upon reliable, literal, factual information know the importance of having concrete facts rather than postulations.

The next time the words like, "There must have been like fifty thousand of us there" are stated, when it was actually two hundred, the wise person will realize that this statement is definitely figurative language. Sorting through that which is real and unreal is directly connected to the Heavenly Father, Who knows it all.

PRAYER

Dear Heavenly Father, please help me to distinguish between that which is real, and that which is figurative. I know Your perspective is right, and there is no disputing when I align there. In Jesus' name I pray. Amen.

_____

_____

_____

_____

August 7
FICTION

Prove all things; hold fast that which is good.

1 Thessalonians 5:21

Fairytales and stories are made up by people every day. From tales with morals to those stories that take us to fantasy land, entertaining stories have been written and told as part of the human experience for as long as man has been around. Legends, folklore, and traditional knowledge are as much a part of any culture as the eating of particular foods or the wearing of certain styles of clothing. Fiction is a major part of human existence.

However, what if the fiction is believed to be real? A soldier needs to know whether information is fictional or fact. Decisions are based upon knowledge, and that knowledge must be factual or wrong directives will be given. There must be a procedure for sorting through the story and obtaining the truth. Without it, lives may be lost.

Testing and validation of a story is right and worthy. Those who do so will be heroes—those who don't will be thought of as fools. When difficulties arise and facts mix with fiction, if we are wise enough to sort through, test all, and hold to that which is good, the decisions we make will be pleasing.

PRAYER

Dear Heavenly Father, please help me to know as You know. I realize that You can sort through all the fiction and relay to me the facts so that my decisions will be pleasing to You. In Jesus' name I pray. Amen.

FEELINGS

Then came his disciples, and said unto him, Knowest thou that the Pharisees were offended, after they heard this saying?

Matthew 15:12

Emotions such as anger, guilt, shame, joy, peace, and soberness are part of the basic makeup of mankind. These are just a few of the emotions that flow like waves in the human psyche. Those who have been through bootcamp know the abundance of emotions that flow and are dealt with on a constant basis. Feelings are real and sometimes feelings hurt.

There is, however, a marked place within man that goes beyond our feelings. Jesus "hurt" many people's feelings. The Pharisees were often offended by Him. Disciples were offended by Him, and the crowds were offended by Him. However, there was a mission that was far greater than one person's feelings. Jesus knew how to reach beyond the surface to accomplish the eternal.

The Word of God often offends feelings. If we are diligent to read His Word, there will be times where feelings come into conflict with God Himself. The key is to remember to go beyond feelings and reach for the Eternal purposes that God has in mind. Though feelings may be offended, the reward afterward will be well worth the anguish of heart now.

PRAYER

Dear Heavenly Father, I know that my feelings sometimes get in the way of Your dealing with me. Please help me to look beyond how I feel and see what You are doing eternally in me. In Jesus' name I pray. Amen.

_____

_____

_____

August 9
FAZE

For the Lord GOD will help me; therefore shall I not be confounded: therefore have I set my face like a flint, and I know that I shall not be ashamed.

Isaiah 50:7

Conflict often alters paths. Some engage and battle through it, and others avoid it altogether. Regardless of a person's lot in life, conflict shall arise. The question becomes, "Will it faze or not?" The idea is, "Will it disrupt, disturb or alter the path?"

For some, conflict and battle move them quickly. As soon as opposition arrives, off they go either avoiding or running away. Others will battle to the bitter end, and nothing will persuade them from meeting their objective. The difference is in the setting of the face and, as the Scripture says, "like a flint."

What shall it be: fazed or unfazed, moved or unmoved? Will we run or will we meet the mission? Will fleeing become our mantra or will the anthem be, fight until the goal is met? Only we know and only we will decide.

PRAYER

Dear Heavenly Father, I know there is a tendency to take the path of least resistance and avoid hardship. Help me today to be without faze and set my face like flint toward that which You would have me do. In Jesus' name I pray. Amen.

_____

_____

_____

_____

_____

_____

FANCY

And ye have respect to him that weareth the gay clothing, and say unto him, Sit thou here in a good place; and say to the poor, Stand thou there, or sit here under my footstool: Are ye not then partial in yourselves, and are become judges of evil thoughts?

James 2:3-4

Mercedes, Rolls Royce, Lexus, Ferrari, Lamborghini or limos, usually make people turn their heads when one of them drives by. Who owns this? Who owns that? They must be loaded. When passengers happen to step out of those fancy rides, a certain amount of respect is automatically given to them.

However, what if it's a smoking clunker like a 1983 Mercury Marquis or a 1982 Dodge with disheveled paint, ragged interior and multiple dents? These vehicles become marks of ridicule and targets of shame. The treatment is not the same and the level of respect falls quickly.

The Heavenly Father is not moved by fancy or not so fancy objects. In fact, those outward things move Him very little at all. Partiality does not constitute His character—preferential treatment toward those who have much of this world's wealth does not align with Jesus at all. If we show no respect of persons, we will be like the One who came to save us all from our sins, regardless of our belongings.

PRAYER

Dear Heavenly Father, please help me not to show partiality toward any person, regardless of their perceived wealth. May my life reflect Yours as I mingle among all people in this world. In Jesus' name I pray. Amen.

_____

_____

_____

_____

August 11
FALL

Now unto him that is able to keep you from falling, and to present [you] faultless before the presence of his glory with exceeding joy...

Jude 1:24

What should we do on an obstacle course when we fall? What happens when the falling occurs over and over again? The answer is simple—we get up and try again. There are still more obstacles to cross, more obstructions to pass, and more hindrances that must be moved.

But what if we fall and cannot get back up again? Is there such a place? Can we fall so far away from the Heavenly Father that we will never rise again? Not according to Jude. There is a watchful eye over all those who put their trust in the Lord Jesus. No matter how badly one falls, no matter what the circumstances may be, no matter how far we feel that we are away from God above, He knows, He cares and is ready to save.

Indications are that He keeps us in such a way that He will present them *faultless before the presence of his glory* and will do so *with exceeding joy.* Now that's a prevention to falling to which everyone should subscribe.

PRAYER

Dear Heavenly Father, I know there will be times that I fall in this life. Please keep me from falling so far away from You that You will never lift me up again. In Jesus' name I pray. Amen.

_____

_____

_____

_____

August 12
FAKE

And with all deceivableness of unrighteousness in them that perish; because they received not the love of the truth, that they might be saved. And for this cause God shall send them strong delusion, that they should believe a lie:

2 Thessalonians 2:10-11

Counterfeit dollar bills run everywhere in the country. An abundant supply of fakes is being made every day. Since there is value in the real, substitutions are fabricated and copies are manufactured. Though the fakes fool some, they never fool the One who made the originals.

Some people reject the Gospel of Jesus Christ to the point that they believe a total lie. One wonders how some people believe such things. In fact, some of the beliefs are so far out there that it takes more faith to believe in them than it does to believe in a Creator. For example, some believe that life began from the siliceous ooze. From this ooze, a worm-like creature formed and crawled out of the ooze to scrape itself onto dry land. From that scrape came an appendage that after millions of years became an arm. After several years more, another scraped occurred, and the worm-like creature grew another arm. Then a few more scrapes turned into a highly developed eye, so the creature could get around now and see where it was going. Need the writer go on?

No one enjoys a fake. Since the Heavenly Father is as real as it gets, why would anyone want to substitute something counterfeit for that which is the authentic?

PRAYER

Dear Heavenly Father, thank You for being real to me. Help me to identify that which is fake as I live in this world before Your eyes. In Jesus' name I pray. Amen.

August 13
CHARISMATIC

Now there are diversities of gifts, but the same Spirit.

1 Corinthians 12:4

Experts in marksmanship, professional technologists, and extremely skilled craftsmen are prevalent throughout the military. Some people are just more gifted than others in certain areas. Those who have charismatic abilities rise to the occasion when called upon. Those who surround individuals of this nature are advantaged by allowing these special individuals to do what they do best.

The Lord gives certain people unique gifts. Some have natural ability in music, while others cannot sing at all. Some are skilled with weapons, where others would be better off with kitchen duty. Some skills are well beyond the level of normal, such as a prodigy. Others seem to be very skilled at communications, technology or sports. The charismatic factor is employed in many areas.

The key is to realize the source of all charisma. Gifts come from the Lord. Once we discover our gifts, we should use them in humility and gratitude to the One who did the giving.

PRAYER

Dear Heavenly Father, thank You for the gifts You have given me. I open my life to You to use in any way that You deem fitting. I ask You to continue to add charisma to my life in everything I do. In Jesus' name I pray. Amen.

CHAOS

He, that being often reproved hardeneth [his] neck, shall suddenly be destroyed, and that without remedy.

Proverbs 29:1

Screaming! Yelling! Calling of names! People here! People there! The early education of a soldier can seem like madness. The basic training bootcamp is like a wildfire out of control. Those within its bounds run, walk, pace and march with an intensity that is unparalleled by any other environment. The chaos is regimented, with the desired result of being rigid, ruled and aligned.

The difference between a soldier before basic training and afterwards has to do with compliance. There is no room for one's own path, which differs from command or disunity from the rest of the troops, lest there be potential for future destruction, demise and rebellion. Thus, it is with a proud person. If soldiers reject correction over and over again, their destruction is imminent. There will be no putting back that which has been pridefully disdained.

Wise soldiers hear reproof and comply. The sooner they comply, the safer they will be. Quick agreement allows safety and lack of regret to enter their lives again.

PRAYER

Dear Heavenly Father, I submit my life to You, and I need Your reproof. Please help me to avoid consequences that have no remedy on the other side of their judgment. In Jesus' name I pray. Amen.

_____

_____

_____

_____

August 15
CELIBACY

Pure religion and undefiled before God and the Father is this, To visit the fatherless and widows in their affliction, [and] to keep himself unspotted from the world.

James 1:27

The attractions for military personnel for physical entertainment, especially overseas, can be inviting and intriguing. One of the characteristics rarely found is the trait of celibacy. Without regard to the future implications, many soldiers have sacrificed their health and souls for just a few moments of pleasure.

God Almighty designed man and created our desires. He also gave a proper place for these feelings. Whenever soldiers reach outside the bounds of His Divine safety net, they expose themselves to disease, heartbreak, and emptiness of the soul. This is the reason James writes to *keep himself unspotted from the world* as being related to pure religion and undefiled before God.

Celibacy may seem prudish and old-fashioned by most who consider it. However, for those who are wise enough to examine what the Creator says about it, there is nothing but reward for obedience to His ways and not their own.

PRAYER

Dear Heavenly Father, I want to choose to follow You in a pure religion and undefiled manner. Please help me to keep my commitment whenever temptation arises to alter that choice. In Jesus' name I pray. Amen.

CATCH

And the LORD said unto Moses, Go, get thee down; for thy people, which thou broughtest out of the land of Egypt, have corrupted [themselves]:...And Moses besought the LORD his God, and said, LORD, why doth thy wrath wax hot against thy people, which thou hast brought forth out of the land of Egypt with great power, and with a mighty hand?

Exodus 32:7,11

There are times when it seems that the enemy designs plans to play a cat-and-mouse game with battles. He is here—then he is there. He slithers from this hole and runs to the next one. There are those who are equipped in intelligence work to eliminate such foes and eradicate them with military precision. In other words, the cat-and-mouse game is reduced to a quick game of catch.

Sometimes, however, the Lord will work this way in the lives of Christians. The Lord spoke with Moses in such a manner. First God says, "thy people," to which Moses responds, "thy people." In other words, each one was putting the people off on the other. This is like a game of catch. One throws a ball and the other catches. Then, that one throws the ball and the other catches. Back and forth they throw and are relating to one another as they do.

Wise Christians know that the Lord will "throw" things their way. When He does, the key is to "throw them back." Those who learn this early will know that the Lord desires relationship. If it takes a game of catch to relate, He's throwing the ball their way.

PRAYER

Dear Heavenly Father, thank You for playing catch with me. Help me to recognize when You are throwing something my way that You only desire to have me throw back. In Jesus' name I pray. Amen.

August 17

CATAPULT

For unto every one that hath shall be given, and he shall have abundance: but from him that hath not shall be taken away even that which he hath.

Matthew 25:29

A catapult was an ingenious weapon used primarily in the medieval times. With such a mighty weapon, huge masses of material could be hurled through the air at opponents, and much damage could be caused. Today, military weapons far exceed those archaic ones, but nonetheless their usage is similar, as they are meant for greater progress toward victory.

Christians have certain responsibilities that they must apply. Bible study, prayer, witnessing and fellowship are vitally important to Christian growth. With them, we are catapulted far beyond what we encounter when these important weapons are left to the side. The greatest advantage comes by knowing Jesus through His Word, the Bible, and those who look into the Word, follow and study it, and obey the Word are catapulted far beyond those who neglect it.

PRAYER

Dear Heavenly Father, I choose to be catapulted by You into ways and paths that I cannot see. I know that through Your Word I will be put in places that I have never even dreamed of before. In Jesus' name I pray. Amen.

CAGEY

Now the serpent was more subtil than any beast of the field which the LORD God had made. And he said unto the woman, Yea, hath God said, Ye shall not eat of every tree of the garden?

Genesis 3:1

In the wealth of operations and standards that the military supplies, there is a certain amount of intelligent decisions that must be made with craft. Cagey designs within a plan to secure a city or dominate opposition shields the obvious and manifests itself best in the element of surprise. Often subtlety will be the determining factor for victory.

Christians must watch for their enemy who is cagey with his efforts. Satan doesn't usually walk up to someone's door, knock, and say, "I'm here to wreck your life today." No, rather he uses subtlety, craftiness and being cagey to pull us slowly into a life we never dreamed we would have. Destruction is just beyond the trickery and the enemy knows how to attack.

Pray, seek the Lord, and read His Word. With these three defense factors, every onslaught will fail, every attempt to seduce us will fall, and every effort to be cagey will be finished.

PRAYER

Dear Heavenly Father, I know that the enemy against my soul is cagey. Help me to stay in fellowship with You to be able to fight off every effort he makes. In Jesus' name I pray. Amen.

_____

_____

_____

_____

_____

August 19
COOPERATE

Two are better than one, because they have a good reward for their toil.

Ecclesiastes 4:9

I remember a lesson about cooperation I learned at a traffic light. The light was red, but as I sat there waiting, it dawned on me that I was in the wrong lane. At the next light, I needed to turn left but I was in the outside lane. I looked to my left to see if I could get ahead of the car next to me, when the light turned green. The driver saw that I was sizing him up and thought I was challenging him, so he revved his engine. My competitive nature kicked in, so when the light changed, we were off like two drag racers bent on finishing first. I was trying to get ahead so that I could get into the left lane and make my turn. I thought he wanted to show me he had the fastest car.

To my surprise, after he showed me his car was the fastest, he wanted to move over to the right lane. Both of us needed to make a turn at the next light. He wanted to turn right and I was turning left. Neither one of us was interesting in racing! Because of our mutual misunderstanding, we were competing when we needed to cooperate.

Teamwork requires cooperation to achieve a mutually beneficial goal. An old preacher once said, "I'm in competition with no man. Your success is no threat to me." There is room for us all to succeed. A team can accomplish more than any single individual.

PRAYER

Dear Heavenly Father, I have a competitive nature that works against cooperation. I want to be a part of Your team. Help me compete less and cooperate more. In Jesus' name I pray. Amen.

August 20

CALL

Behold, I stand at the door and knock. If anyone hears my voice and opens the door, I will come in to him and eat with him, and he with me.

Revelation 3:20

... I came not to call the righteous, but sinners.

Mark 2:17b

There is nothing more disturbing than a telephone call or a ringing doorbell in the middle of the night. It seems those occasions always bring bad news. Conversely, there's nothing more exciting than a long-anticipated call from a family member or old friend. It seems like time stands still when we're waiting for that special person to call.

I suppose all of us prefer to receive calls that bring good news. Some of my favorite calls are from family, announcing the arrival of a new grandchild, my son calling to say hello, my daughter wishing me a happy birthday or a grandchild just wanting to talk. My least favorite calls include someone's dying—you need to come or your house payment is overdue or you've won a four-day vacation—all you have to do is ...

The most important call I've received came, not from family or bill collectors, but from God. When I was fourteen years old, I heard a message in church that told me God came to seek and save me. Through reading the Bible, I learned that I was a sinner and that God's gift was eternal life. I opened my heart and like He promised, Jesus came into my heart. I've never been sorry.

PRAYER

Dear Heavenly Father Your word says, For all have sinned and fall short of the glory of God, (Romans 3:23) For the wages of sin is death, but the free gift of God is eternal life in Christ Jesus our Lord. (Romans 6:23) I am a sinner, forgive me. I accept Your gift of eternal life in Christ. In Jesus' name I pray. Amen.

August 21
COMMAND

My son, do not forget my teaching, but let your heart keep my commandments, for length of days and years of life and peace they will add to you... So you will find favor and good success in the sight of God and man.

Proverbs 3:1-2,4

How do we respond to a command? What is our gut reaction? Do this little checkup the next time a police car or a state trooper appears. Do we slow down? Then check our speed? I admit, my first reaction is to back off the accelerator, then check my speed. I'm not sure if respect for authority or fear of getting a ticket is my primary motivation.

Respect for authority is necessary in our training to be good soldiers. Fear also can be a positive factor in disciplining our relationship to those in command. We don't always know the reason for the command and may want to test the boundaries, like a child with its parents. The pain of touching something hot reinforces the command, "Don't touch that!"

We won't live long enough to learn by experience all the lessons of life, so there is wisdom in learning to obey those whose experience exceeds our own. The Scripture promises that we'll not only gain wisdom but add years of life, along with favor and success.

PRAYER

Dear Heavenly Father, Your commandments are for my benefit. Forgive me when I am rebellious and seek my own way. In Jesus' name I pray. Amen.

_____

_____

_____

_____

CHECKPOINT

And all who believed were together and had
all things in common.

Acts 2:44

The experts tell us that the definition of old age is changing. A sixty-five year old is now considered to be the new forty. Sixty-five used to be the retirement age, but now retirement no longer means what it did twenty years ago. Instead of looking forward to retiring from work, more people are looking to a change of pace. People are understanding that life itself is what matters, and it matters much more than just collecting a paycheck.

There's no denying the effects of time on our bodies. Hair turns grey or falls out. Skin wrinkles and senses like hearing and sight can begin to dull—as can our short-term memory. Mitch Anthony suggests five ways to keep us alive and relevant no matter our age. 1. Connect - Stay connected to people who value us. 2. Challenge - Don't stop being stimulated and challenged. 3. Curiosity - Be a lifelong learner. 4. Creativity - Listen, explore and observe. 5. Charity - Be concerned, generous and unselfish.

The first century church was characterized by a passion for learning and generosity toward those in need. The evidence is overwhelming that our quality of life is improved by an attitude of generosity. It doesn't take money to live charitably, it just takes concern, generosity and unselfishness.

PRAYER

Dear Heavenly Father, I want to know You better and share
unselfishly with those in need. In Jesus' name I pray. Amen.

August 23

EAR

Know this, my beloved brothers; let every person be quick to hear, slow to speak, slow to anger, for the anger of man does not produce the righteousness of God.

James 1:19-20

Developing good listening skills requires that you listen to what "is" said and what "is not" said. The term, "listening with the third ear," denotes paying attention to body language, emotions, and facial expressions. The ear is vital to being a good listener, but not the only component of the process. Someone once said, "What's happening isn't always what's going on!"

One of the Bible's most practical books was written by James, and he taught, *Be quick to hear (listen); slow to speak and slow to anger.* Someone observed, we have two ears and one mouth, which suggests that it is wise to listen twice as much as we talk. The superior lesson is that excellent listening is essential to intelligible communication.

James' application is very practical: good listening leads to constructive conversation and avoids destructive anger, but the most important lesson is to put into practice what we learn. Hearing without action leads to stagnation. A lake can have a beautiful spring flowing into its reservoir, but unless it has an outlet, it becomes stale. For example, the Jordan River flows into the Sea of Galilee, which in turn empties into the Dead Sea. The Dead Sea has no outlets and, as a result, nothing lives in its salty waters. Good listening prepares us to act wisely.

PRAYER

Dear Heavenly Father, I am impulsive, tending to speak before I thoroughly grasp the situation. Help me to be quick to listen and slow to speak. I pray that when action is necessary, I'll rely on You. In Jesus' name I pray. Amen.

August 24

DELAY

The Lord is not slow to fulfill his promise as some count slowness, but is patient toward you...

2 Peter 3:9

"Hurry up - and wait!" This refrain reflects the frustration of soldiers and civilians who chafe at delays. Waiting is an acquired skill that we admire in others but seldom desire for ourselves. Our favorite restaurant has to do with the quality not only of the food, but also the promptness of the service. Waiters that earn our loyalty are those who don't make us wait for service.

In Afghanistan, the battle of Tora Bora teaches that delay can be costly. Arriving on the scene, Special Forces troops sought to assault the caves through the mountains to the south, but were denied that action by headquarters. A similar request to mine the passes south to Pakistan was also denied. Forced to conduct a frontal attack, the Special Forces were delayed when their Afghan allies negotiated a ceasefire with the enemy. This delay most likely allowed bin Laden to shift to a new position.

Life will bring delays—the question is, how will we respond? The waiter in our favorite restaurant and the troops on the front line must juggle expectations that are frustrated by lack of progress. The waiter who keeps their patrons' glasses filled while the entree is being prepared will defuse much of the frustration. The troop that channels the energy of frustration into a positive action, such as cleaning the equipment, will redeem the time.

God promises to hear and answer the prayer of all who call upon Him. Sometimes the answer is not yes or no, but wait. We have a choice to spend our time waiting either in frustration or in developing patience.

PRAYER

Dear Heavenly Father, I am frustrated with delay! I am impatient with people, but I greatly appreciate those who are patient with me. I need to turn my frustration into patience. Please help me. In Jesus' name I pray. Amen.

August 25

BLIND

... whose minds the god of this age has blinded, who do not believe, lest the light of the gospel of the glory of Christ, who is the image of God, should shine on them.

2 Corinthians 4:4

Jesus identified a blindness that is worst than the inability to see with our eyes. In the Gospel of John, chapter nine, there is an account of a man blind from birth. The disciples attributed the man's blindness to some sin he had committed. Jesus rejected this reasoning, and healed the man's eyes.

The miracle of healing the blind man's eyes exposed a greater blindness. A group of religious leaders, who could see with their eyes, refused to see that Jesus was the Messiah. Jesus came to heal blind eyes and blind hearts, but those who refuse to admit their need for healing remain blind.

There is a god of this world that would blind us to this truth. Tragically, many live without admitting that they are blind, even though they enjoy the bounty of a gracious Creator. Those who have been healed can proclaim in the words of John Newton, "I once was blind but now I see."

PRAYER

Dear Heavenly Father, I have been blind. Heal my eyes and my heart. In Jesus' name I pray. Amen.

Remembering Vietnam

ANXIETY

Be careful for nothing; but in every thing by prayer and supplication with thanksgiving let Your requests be made known unto God.

Philippians 4:6

Has there ever been a time when anxiety comes in because there is a big test ahead, a huge task at hand, or an unknown outcome is on the horizon? Worry is common to everyone, yet some people seem to fret much more than others. Huge bills, health concerns, and job wonders are fairly commonplace. The concern over these events can cause sleepless nights and disturb and create restless activities for those who are overcome by them.

Paul, the apostle, has a direct solution when worries come. His words are basically, *Pray with thanksgiving and let your requests be made known.* So often rather than pray, people try to work the worry out for themselves. They wrestle and struggle. They plan, and they plot. They think and they act, but they do not take the time just to pray.

The Lord Jesus above knows all our concerns. He knows all the questions and He knows all the answers. The wise person goes to the source of those answers and then rests in the ability of the One who knows it all.

PRAYER

Dear Heavenly Father, I bring to You all my worries and concerns today, and lay them at Your feet. Please remind me to find the pathway to You every time a worry arises. In Jesus' name I pray. Amen.

_____

_____

_____

August 27
ATTITUDE

But unto Cain and to his offering he had not respect.
And Cain was very wroth, and his countenance fell.
And the LORD said unto Cain, Why art thou wroth?
and why is thy countenance fallen?

Genesis 4: 5,6

From the very beginning, attitude has directed man's steps. Because Cain was aloof and did not put forth the best offering, his offering was not accepted. Although the Lord offered him a chance to redeem his actions, he decided to challenge and kill his brother instead. The pending results from his bad attitude caused the first murder—Cain paid the price for it the rest of his life.

There are some situations that cannot be altered or changed. They are the way they are. When we encounter one of these situations, we have the opportunity to decide how we will approach them. We may choose to have a bad attitude, so the reflection of our countenance will show for it. We can also choose to have a good attitude and that countenance will also be observed. The reward for proper attitude is not readily seen, but over time, does not go unnoticed.

Jesus is the best example of keeping the proper attitude. Even when He was reviled, He reviled not again. When He hung on the cross, His words were, Father forgive them, for they know not what they do. Now that's an attitude worth adopting and one that is pleasing to the Heavenly Father.

PRAYER

Dear Heavenly Father, help me to have a proper attitude that pleases You today no matter what the circumstances or situations may be. In Jesus' name I pray. Amen.

ASSIGNMENT

But he knows the way that I take; when he has tried me, I shall come out as gold.

Job 23:10

The obstacle course in our lives may seem designed to defeat us or to send us packing. Actually, its purpose is to equip us for victory.

Some obstacles test our physical endurance, while others measure our mental and emotional strength. The dreaded exams in school aren't to torture us, but to show where learning needs to improve.

As men and women of God, we can be assured our assignments will challenge us, but also provide opportunity for us to grow. Moses protested that his assignment was too much for him and God's reply was: I'll go with you. (Exodus 3:12)

PRAYER

Dear Heavenly Father, I am prone to see how difficult the situation is. Please open my eyes to Your power and presence. In Jesus' name I pray. Amen.

AFFLICT

Before I was afflicted I went astray, but now I keep your word...
It is good for me that I was afflicted, that I might learn your
statutes.

Psalm 119:67, 71

Self-protection is very basic to our survival. Nobody wants to suffer unnecessarily—most of us want as much comfort as possible. Life usually doesn't provide us with total comfort, does it? Thankfully we don't get all comfort or all affliction.

Could it be we actually benefit from affliction? Some hold a view that if we are moral and do more good than evil, we will be protected from suffering and pain. But life teaches that all of us will endure hardship. There is training in these experiences that is helpful.

The question isn't, "Will I be afflicted?" but, "How will I respond?" The truth is that the world has benefited from the service of those men and women who have suffered great hardships in performance of their duty. The author of Psalm 119 said, *I went astray before I was afflicted and it is good that I was afflicted.* Why? I learned God's statutes (laws). The benefit of affliction could be that I learn when I'm going in the wrong direction and I'm not self-sufficient!

PRAYER

Dear Heavenly Father, I don't want to waste the lesson of this pain. Turn me around, I need You. In Jesus' name I pray. Amen.

ALL

I have sworn by myself, the word is gone out of my mouth [in] righteousness, and shall not return, That unto me every knee shall bow, every tongue shall swear.

Isaiah 45:23

When a command is given, most who are under authority obey it. Soldiers know the consequences of disobedience and the punishment or the threat thereof motivates all to follow command. However, there are those defectors who push the limits, and some of them go AWOL. Those who act in this manner receive their just reward.

But when it comes to God's directives, are there any who are exempt? Are there any who will not bow? Are there any who will not confess? No, no, and a thousand times no. When God Almighty speaks, not a word He shares will fall to the ground. In other words, every word He speaks must, will, and indeed shall come to pass. Those who desire to disobey shall not be able to reject the bowing of the knee and the confession of the mouth that Jesus Christ is indeed Lord. Disobedience will fail, and insubordination will have no place, for everyone everywhere will follow this command.

The question of submission is whether it will be in this life or the life to come. All will bow and all will confess. It's just a matter of time before they obey.

PRAYER

Dear Heavenly Father, I bow my knee and confess with my mouth that You are Lord. Help me to share with others in a way that they will know that all people will follow these commands. In Jesus' name I pray. Amen.

_____

_____

ANARCHY

For rebellion [is as] the sin of witchcraft, and stubbornness [is as] iniquity and idolatry. Because thou hast rejected the word of the LORD, he hath also rejected thee from [being] king.

1 Samuel 15:23

A society without rules results in anarchy. Military operations without principles become lawless and rebellion reigns when boundaries are not set. There must be law to keep order or else no one will survive.

The Bible has much to say about anarchy, which is another word for rebellion. Those who rebel against God Almighty are anarchists to the highest degree. In fact, they are likened to witchcraft, iniquity and idolatry. Basically, anyone who "dethrones" God and His principles surmises that they know better than God. In other words, they are their own God.

The wise person obeys the Word of God. Those who comply will find themselves in greater positions than they ever thought possible within the resources of their anarchist minds.

PRAYER

Dear Heavenly Father, I realize that You have Divine order, Divine rule, and Divine principles. Please help me to recognize Your authority and be willing to obey those to whom that authority has been handed down. In Jesus' name I pray. Amen.

September 1

FLEXIBLE

*O LORD, I know that the way of man [is] not in himself: [it is]
not in man that walketh to direct his steps.*

Jeremiah 10:23

One of the greatest traits a person can have is to be flexible. Pastor
Chuck Smith says, "Blessed are the flexible, for they shall not
break"—this is so true. Events change, circumstances are altered,
and expectations sometimes come up short. If we are flexible, we can
alter plans, move in a different direction, and purpose to continue
until a new pattern or path is realized.

There are very few guarantees in life, so as we learn early that things
do not always go the way we plan, we will be ready for alterations.
Being in a mode of flexibility allows us to plan, but also to react
should the plan not go accordingly. Wisdom says that we should be
ready to move as planned, but also be ready to change on the fly
should it become necessary.

PRAYER

*Dear Heavenly Father, I know that You have all knowledge,
and You care for me very deeply. I know that You have the
knowledge of how things will be for me in the future. I give
You my life to be flexible and ready to respond to any changes
that may come my way, and I give all my plans to You. In
Jesus' name I pray. Amen.*

FEET

Thy word [is] a lamp unto my feet, and a light unto my path.

Psalm 119:105

Soldiers know the importance of keeping their feet in good condition. Blisters, cuts, and marring of the feet can impede progress, slow succession, and induce excruciating pain. Provision for the feet must be of utmost priority, if mobilization is going to be at its maximum.

Spiritually, it is important to know where a person's feet are being led and what they are being led by. The Psalmist employs the Word of God as the lamp for his feet. In other words, the Word of God directs any place that we go. If the word shines in this area, the path is clear. If it shines in that area, access is permitted. However, should the Word of God show danger, trouble, or alienation from the Heavenly Father, that path must be avoided.

If we know the importance of a guide for our feet, we will seek the Bible's direction daily. To forgo the illumination of the Word of God is to walk down a very dark path with no light.

PRAYER

Dear Heavenly Father, thank You for the light of Your Word. Please help me to keep my feet on the path that You have set for me. In Jesus' name I pray. Amen.

September 3

CHART

And I saw the dead, small and great, stand before God; and the books were opened: and another book was opened, which is [the book] of life: and the dead were judged out of those things which were written in the books, according to their works.

Revelation 20:12

When soldiers are sent on missions, charts and maps are used to plan, give direction, and denote goals where opposition is to be defeated. Many times those charts become sheets of progression and motivate commanders as they make choices for the next move. Charts also demonstrate in a microcosmic way the true progress or path in which the soldiers have moved. They also become historical documents for future judgment about other missions.

We have something like a chart in our lives. Books are kept in heaven and every move of our lives is recorded. One book is the book of life where all those who trust in Jesus as their Savior have their names written. Other books have every act, thought and movement each of us makes in our lives. The interesting part about the books is that people are judged out of those things that are written in them.

One wonders, for those without the saving grace of Jesus Christ, what will be on the charts of those who failed to trust in the greatest Authority of all.

PRAYER

Dear Heavenly Father, I know that my life is being charted before You. I ask You to forgive me when I go off-course, and please help me to live my life before Your eyes in a manner that is pleasing to You. Thank You for Jesus, and it's in His name I pray. Amen.

CHARADE

And [that] they may recover themselves out of the snare of the devil, who are taken captive by him at his will.

2 Timothy 2:26

Symbols and gestures are used by military personnel where verbal speech is inadequate or unsafe. Underwater, flying through the air, and in intense military covert operations soldiers use charade-like movements with their hands, head, feet and body to communicate with fellow soldiers. These gestures are foreknown in most cases, and the communication is clear.

Sometimes people travel through life as though they are living in a charade. From one movement to the next, they go this way, then they go that. The never-ending cycle is generally a trap of the devil to keep us from following the direction of the Almighty God. We can be trapped within our movements, and our power to be released from such movements can be overwhelming.

Jesus came to set the captives free, and those who recognize the source and ways of the enemy of their souls can come to Jesus, Who doesn't have to communicate with charades, but shares His information with all who will receive it.

PRAYER

Dear Heavenly Father, I tire of the charades, and I know that You have much better for me. I come to You fully and completely to be removed from the snare of the devil who would have me trapped all my life. In Jesus' name I pray. Amen.

_____

_____

_____

_____

CHAINS

*Because that he had been often bound with fetters and chains,
and the chains had been plucked asunder by him, and the fetters
broken in pieces: neither could any [man] tame him.*

Mark 5:4

Huge chains bind military ships to port docks around the world.
Massive steel forged link by link bound together creates a strength
that keeps the massive vessels in place while soldiers go on furlough
or resupply. The mere weight of the chains is enough to crush a man,
and the power within them would fail all efforts to escape should
they be wrapped around him.

The man Jesus encountered in Gadera was wrapped in multiple
chains. Not only were there chains physically, but also the chains
that bound him spiritually and within his soul. No man could tame
this man, and no amount of chains could bind the forces within him.
There was the need for someone more powerful than the foe who
bound him to concur and release this man. Jesus was the only person
who could free him.

There are many people in this world who are bound by chains that
are not visible to the human eye. The chains are within and are such
as these: fear, anxiety, loneliness, depression, depravity, sadness, guilt,
and shame. There is only one who can truly free these chains—Jesus.

PRAYER

*Dear Heavenly Father, I know that no one can remove
chains like You. I submit all my chains to Your care, and I
ask You to help me to lead others to You who are likewise
bound. In Jesus' name I pray. Amen.*

September 6
CATCALL

*And beheld among the simple ones, I discerned among the youths,
a young man void of understanding,*

Proverbs 1:7

There are various tempting attractions around the world. Some are meant for good and some are meant for evil. Soldiers who work so diligently for their country will often visit these places for recreation and playful activity. The key to this entertainment is to understand the seduction of it all. Those military men and women who have been caught in the catcall of the sparkling lights have often paid for it later on.

Christians must understand that the enemy of the soul is dangling traps all over the world. His catcall and invitation is to partake in the very things that later will bring regret, cause shame, and malign character. Those who heed his traps will pay dearly, be a poor example, and suffer greatly for the momentary pleasure.

Beware of the enemy's catcall. He desires to steal, kill and destroy, and should he get even a small claw within one's soul, he means to devour the entire life.

PRAYER

Dear Heavenly Father, help me to identify the enemy's catcall. I know he desires to devour me, and I choose to follow You all the days of my life. In Jesus' name I pray. Amen.

_____

_____

_____

_____

_____

_____

September 7

COLD

The lazy man will not plow because of winter; He will beg during harvest and have nothing.

Proverbs 20: 4

Procrastination effectively serves to avoid taking an undesirable action. Sharing an oral report in school prompted me to put it off, hoping that the class would be over before my report was to be given. The truth was that I wasn't lazy, but afraid. Standing in front of a class and talking caused me to sweat, blush, and tremble. Rather than seek help to overcome this stage fright, I sought to avoid the problem.

One teacher refused to let me run from my fear. She very firmly, but kindly, said, "You can do it and you are going to do it." It was her firmness and encouragement that guided me through my lack of self-confidence and timidity. As a result my life was enriched, and my vocation became the very thing I had so sought to avoid. I have spent the last forty years speaking to people and encouraging them to conquer their fears.

What if I had allowed my fear and poor self-confidence to control my life? One thing is for sure, I would have missed meeting many wonderful people. I would not have experienced the joy of overcoming fear and timidity. Could it be that some people who are labeled lazy are just afraid?

PRAYER

Dear Heavenly Father, You helped me to overcome my fear of speaking. Thank You for the opportunities to encourage others to face their fears. In Jesus' name I pray. Amen.

_____

_____

_____

_____

CLIMB

Truly, truly; I say to you, he who does not enter the sheepfold by the door but climbs in by another way; that man is thief and a robber.

John 10:1

An old man taught me a valuable lesson in using a shovel. We were preparing a foundation for pouring a concrete floor. Sand had been dumped and needed to be spread and leveled. Several volunteers had shovels and were energetically scattering the sand. It soon became apparent that many of us were using lots of energy, but accomplishing very little. The older man, however, made each shovel of sand count. He didn't move it twice.

We can always learn from someone with more experience, even in the area of moving dirt. We can learn that energy needs to be directed by wisdom or it can be wasted. Every task can be accomplished more effectively and many times with less effort, if we are willing to learn from others.

Jesus taught lessons about life that apply His experience. God stands ready to help anyone who will come to Him and ask for His help. We cannot accomplish the good life by ourselves. We must admit that we are not good, as the Scriptures says, *There is not one righteous, no not one*, for only then can we receive the gift of eternal life.

PRAYER

Dear Heavenly Father, forgive me for trying to climb the ladder of success by my strength, and forgive me for substituting good deeds for faith in Your Son, Jesus Christ. In Jesus' name I pray. Amen.

_____

_____

_____

ACCIDENTAL

*But as one was felling a beam, the axe head fell into the water:
and he cried, and said, Alas, master! for it was borrowed.*

2 Kings 6:5

Elisha, the prophet, gave permission to build a place down by the Jordan River. While the men around him worked, one of the men had a borrowed ax head fall into the water. Elisha put a stick into the water, and the ax head floated. Now this story seems remarkable, if not impossible in the natural realm, but within the story is a fundamental principle of living if one looks hard enough.

Accidents happen. No human being alive, whether civilians or soldiers, can live without accidents occurring in their lives. Sometimes the accidents happen because of negligence or disregard. Other times they materialize out of nowhere, and no one is personally at fault. In other words, sometimes things just happen differently than we expect.

Those who follow Jesus know that one thing is assured and that is their existence is no accident. When we realize that we are made for the pleasure of God Almighty, and that God stands ready to rescue any time the ax head of their lives fall into disturbing waters, we will know the purposes of God are intentional and not accidental at all.

PRAYER

Dear Heavenly Father, thank You for my existence. I realize that my life has purpose and is not accidental at all. Please be by my side to rescue me as accidents occur in my life. In Jesus' name I pray. Amen.

_____

_____

_____

_____

ABSOLUTE

Every good gift and every perfect gift is from above, and cometh down from the Father of lights, with whom is no variableness, neither shadow of turning.

James 1:17

Some decisions require pinpoint accuracy. Failure to align with the absolute right choice can be fatal. Warriors know this, and one mistake can mean their lives. There are times when thought and performance must align absolutely, and there is no room for a mistake.

God Himself has areas that are absolute. He knows with perfection when no variable may be allowed and where not even a shadow of turning is permitted. If we choose to inspect His absolutes, one of these areas is in giving good and perfect gifts to men and women.

There are attributes and gifts within people who have no other explanation than that God Almighty has showered down upon them. Prodigies and specialists who easily conform to the disciplines in certain areas are well-known and often envied. Those who acknowledge the source of their gifts are wise, as all glory must be given to Him. Those who believe in their own ability to provide such a gifting are absolutely wrong.

PRAYER

Dear Heavenly Father, I know You are the source of my gifts. Thank You for Your steadfast absoluteness in this area of my life. In Jesus' name I pray. Amen.

_____

_____

_____

_____

_____

September 11
ABRUPT

But as they sailed he fell asleep: and there came down a storm of wind on the lake; and they were filled [with water], and were in jeopardy.

Luke 8:23

Things sometimes change in a moment. One minute everything is okay, and then suddenly, everything is not okay. Peace can be altered abruptly, and that which was supposed is now vanished.

The disciples knew about abrupt changes. At one moment they were traveling across the lake peacefully, and the next moment they were in jeopardy. They feared for their lives, and when they searched for Jesus, they found him asleep. It appeared that Jesus did not care, and the disciples let him know of such. It appeared that Jesus was unaware, and the disciples informed. It appeared that Jesus could do nothing about their situation, and the disciples incorrectly assumed the worst.

Be assured, when abrupt changes come, Jesus cares, Jesus is aware, and Jesus is quite capable. The wise person will keep these promises close in mind and heart, so that fear subsides when the waves of life change abruptly.

PRAYER

Dear Heavenly Father, thank You for the assurance that You care, know and are capable no matter what comes my way. In Jesus' name I pray. Amen.

September 12
ALONE

And after he had dismissed the crowds, he went up on the mountain by himself to pray. When evening was come, he was there alone...

Matthew 14:23

Technology makes it very difficult for anyone to experience wholesome solitude. Cell phones, email, Facebook and television have become such a part of our lives that reflection and quiet meditation are nearly impossible.

I experienced a three-day weekend where phones, television and watches were not allowed. In that imposed quietness, I found a new sensitivity to life's real priorities. In this solitude, I renewed my commitment to faith, family and integrity.

Sometimes solitude is imposed by others for a period of time and other times, we just long for a time alone. Whether involuntary or by choice, we need time to be still, reflect, listen and renew our soul.

PRAYER

Dear Heavenly Father, I feel alone, but You are always with me. Use this quiet time to renew my passion for things that really matter. In Jesus' name I pray. Amen.

AMERICAN

Let every soul be subject unto the higher powers. For there is no power but of God: the powers that be are ordained of God.

Romans 13:1

Lee Greenwood sings, "I'm proud to be an American, where at least I know I'm free." Those around this great country know the significance of being a citizen of the United States of America. It is indeed the greatest country in the world. Those who protect it know the significance of the ideals for which this country stands.

The Bible is clear about the idea of "higher powers." They are ordained by God. In other words, the position of authority has been handed down by the Almighty. Those who realize this understand that at any moment that authority can be retracted by Him. God is in control and, by His mercy and grace, America stands where it is today.

Regard and worship given to the God of all creation must be preeminent within all Christian hearts. Knowing that we are ambassadors for the kingdom of God must hold the highest kinship. As an agent for the Heavenly Father, we are commissioned to keep that which has been committed to us. Doing so gives highest praise to the One who runs it all.

PRAYER

Dear Heavenly Father, thank You for the blessing of being an American. Please help me at all times to keep in mind that You have given the power we enjoy. In Jesus' name I pray. Amen.

_____

_____

_____

_____

_____

September 14

ALOOF

[Yet] a little sleep, a little slumber, a little folding of the hands to sleep: So shall thy poverty come as one that travelleth, and thy want as an armed man.

Proverbs 6:10, 11

Being aloof incorporates the idea of being distant either emotionally or physically. It's being detached, not into it, or without care. Some people approach their missions in such manner. They have no personal engagement or opinion, and rather than engage, they simply drift.

This manner of living wouldn't be so harmful if there were not pending results. If there were no repercussions, sleeping through a matter would not be so important. However, results come and repercussions matter. Those who are wise understand that attitude reflects our obedience or rebellion. Others are watching, and those with good attitudes are rewarded—those with non-caring, aloof attitudes are not.

God Almighty gives advance notice to some unpleasant events in life. He also notifies His followers that those who follow His ways advance, so engage, put aside aloofness, and follow the One who knows.

PRAYER

Dear Heavenly Father, thank You for the opportunity to serve You with a good attitude no matter what is put before me. Help me to stay on task and never be aloof in anything. In Jesus' name I pray. Amen.

_____

_____

_____

_____

_____

_____

JUDGE

Judge not, that you be not judged. For with the judgment you pronounce you will be judged, and with the measure you use it will be measured to you.

Matthew 7: 1-2

Many people have rejected the belief that there is absolute truth. They take a little piece from one religion and a little piece from another, add a little from Christianity and presto—they create their own religion … like constructing a Lego model. The popular thinking that many are embracing is, "There are many roads (choices) and they all lead to God."

In defense of this idea, many people use Jesus' words, *Judge not, that you be not judged.* He did say, "Judge not," but that's not all He said and it's not all He meant by what He said! Instead of prohibiting judging, Jesus actually taught that we will be judged. The measurement we use to judge others will be the same measurement used to judge us.

Jesus taught that we should first judge ourselves and then we can clearly see the faults in others. His words say it best: *… first take the log out of your own eye, and then you will see clearly to take the speck out of your brother's eye.* (Matthew 7: 5b) The lesson of Scripture is that all of us should take care of our own faults and then we can see clearly how to help others.

PRAYER

Dear Heavenly Father, Your Word is the mirror that shows me my faults. Take the log out of my eye, and fill me with grace toward those who need Your forgiveness. In Jesus' name I pray. Amen.

_____

_____

_____

EVACUATE

...from the end of the earth I call to you when my heart is faint. Lead me to the rock that is higher than I, for you have been my refuge, a strong tower against the enemy.

Psalm 61:2-3

Florida residents are familiar with evacuation routes that direct traffic away from the threat of major hurricanes. During a recent extremely active hurricane season, major highways became virtual parking lots as anxious residents fled the approaching storm. Some evacuees left in such haste, they failed to adequately prepare for the unexpected delays. Some were caught in the bumper-to-bumper traffic and ran out of gas on the interstate.

Most of us attempt to prepare for emergencies in life. We purchase insurance to cover health, property and even income emergencies in the event of a major catastrophe. Coastal residents are repeatedly reminded to rehearse their evacuation plan. Recent history has taught us that despite our planning, disaster takes a tremendous toll on people and property each year.

We prepare for natural storms to the best of our ability. What about the storms that can't be covered by insurance or planning? Many people live as though trouble will never threaten them or their family. Every year we read the tragic story of someone who decides to ride out the storm and becomes a victim to its fury.

Life brings unexpected storms into people's life. It may be the death of a spouse or friend, a major illness, job loss or desertion by a spouse. God offers us a place of shelter in our storms and a sanctuary in the good times. It's good to remember that we don't have to be in a storm to need God.

PRAYER

Dear Heavenly Father, whether I'm in a storm or not, You are my refuge. Thank You for providing security and peace. In Jesus' name I pray. Amen.

September 17
RETREAT

The times of ignorance God overlooked, but now he commands all people everywhere to repent, because he has fixed a day on which he will judge the world in righteousness by a man whom he has appointed; and of this he has given assurance to all by raising him from the dead.

Acts 17:30-31

Soldiers are intent on taking the battle to the enemy, always on the move. "Charge!" is the mantra of their advance and the command to retreat is difficult to process. However, in war, retreating may be the best strategy for protecting the troops and exposing the overreaching advance of the enemy. The frontline can advance beyond the reach of their supplies.

Success can lead to pride, which can foster decisions that set a trap for our defeat. Acting as though we are self-sufficient and invincible provides the enemy opportunity to cut us off from our supply lines. History teaches that armies need to maintain contact with their artillery, air and food supplies. Individuals who fail to learn this lesson will find themselves exposed and vulnerable.

The retreat that keeps mankind in touch with their spiritual sources is called repentance. It begins with a realistic appraisal of our vulnerability. None of us are self sufficient and nobody is sinless. The Bible reveals that we've *all sinned and come short of the glory of God.* (Roman 3:23) Understanding that sin is not just a religious myth, but a condition that leads to eternal death, opens the heart to the gift of forgiveness and life. *For the wages of sin is death, but the free gift of God is eternal life in Christ Jesus our Lord.* (Romans 6:23)

PRAYER

Dear Heavenly Father, I pray that You will keep me close to You. Pride causes me to act as though I don't need You, but I confess my sin and put my trust in Jesus Christ. In Jesus' name I pray. Amen.

September 18

PRESUMPTION

Now when the Pharisee which had bidden him saw [it], he spake within himself, saying, This man, if he were a prophet, would have known who and what manner of woman [this is] that toucheth him: for she is a sinner

Luke 7:39

Many people who live today believe that they know better than God. When events occur that do not make sense, presumption of facts and predetermination of what is taking place is normal. However, when it comes to Jesus, presumption is often misplaced.

The Pharisee, who was a religious leader of Jesus' day, had invited Jesus over to his home to eat with him. While Jesus visited, a woman who was known in the city as a sinner came in to wash His feet with an alabaster box filled with ointment. This act met with the disapproval of the Pharisee. His presumption was not only that Jesus must not be a prophet, but that this woman was not worth Jesus saving. His presumption was wrong and Jesus corrected it.

Many situations and circumstances and even people appear one way, when in reality, they are completely different. The wise person considers all things and all people with the aid of the Heavenly Father and His thoughts in mind. Through prayer, a difficult and trying time or person may be the very one God uses for His great purposes.

PRAYER

Dear Heavenly Father, please remind me to keep You involved in every situation, every circumstance, and with every person that comes my way. In Jesus' name I pray. Amen.

_____

_____

_____

PREDISPOSED

Beloved, now are we the sons of God, and it doth not yet appear what we shall be: but we know that, when he shall appear, we shall be like him; for we shall see him as he is.

1 John 3:2

What's on the other side of that hill? Where exactly is the enemy hiding? What kind of weapons does he have and how many of them are there? If these questions were known in advance, the battle and its outcome would be much different. The idea of predisposition is to know in advance. The question becomes, "What does the Christian know in advance?"

Christians know that we are the sons and daughters of God. Although we don't know the full future, this much can be known—when Jesus appears, *we shall be like him.* Whatever shall that be like? To think as Jesus, talk and listen like Him, and to help as Jesus will be the greatest attributes that anyone could ever obtain. There is no greater height of existence. There is no precipice of belonging that exceeds and there is no grander mountain to be climbed.

The reason for all this splendor will be the visual of Jesus as he is. Someday everyone will be face to face with Jesus. For those who know Him, there is more in store than any words could ever describe.

PRAYER

Dear Heavenly Father, I know You have great plans for me, and I long to see Your face one day. Help me today to live in such a manner that I reflect Your love to everyone I engage. In Jesus' name I pray. Amen.

_____

_____

_____

September 20

PUNISHMENT

*For he hath made him [to be] sin for us, who knew no sin; that
we might be made the righteousness of God in him.*

1 Corinthians 5:21

When someone commits a crime, there is usually a punishment that
fits the crime. Statutory laws fill the pages of law books with limits and maximum penalties that should be administered by a judge
when someone is convicted of a crime. Sometimes a judge is more
lenient and at other times, the maximum sentence is employed.

But what if another person were to pay the punishment for the
crime of someone else? Would the sentence be fulfilled? Would the
price have been paid for the wrongdoing? Would it be fair and just to
allow the lawbreaker to go free while another paid the price? These
questions are answered by none other than Jesus Christ himself.

Jesus was made to be sin for us, even though He never sinned. In
other words, he took our place of punishment. He paid the price. He
paid the penalty. Why? Because to live with God someday, people
needed to *be made the righteousness of God in him.* Without this righteousness, every person would be banished from God's throne.

PRAYER

*Dear Heavenly Father, thank You for bearing my
punishment through Jesus Christ. I look forward to being
before Your throne in a righteous state because of what Jesus
did. In Jesus' name I pray. Amen.*

_____

_____

_____

_____

PENALTY

Who gave himself a ransom for all, to be testified in due time.

1 Timothy 2:6

Whenever there is wrongdoing that incurs a conviction, there is usually a penalty to be paid. From the "time out" chair to incarceration, limitations and punishments are placed upon individuals who violate the "law." In other words, a penalty or price must be paid.

Jesus' purpose in coming to the earth was driven by a penalty that had to be paid. Mankind sinned, violated the law of God, and broke the perfect will of God. For this reason, a penalty was due and that penalty was death: *For the wages of sin is death.* Jesus came to pay that penalty, that ransom for all. Everyone is guilty and all people owed the price. However, Jesus came and paid the price by giving His life.

All people have had to pay a price for some behavior, act, or wrongdoing at some time or another in their lives. However, for the nature of sin that is within every man and woman, every boy and girl, only one could pay the ransom due. That one paid the penalty in full, and that one is Jesus.

PRAYER

Dear Heavenly Father, thank You for the price that Jesus paid for my sin. Once again I come to You with a grateful heart. Help me to appreciate the penalty He paid. In Jesus' name I pray. Amen.

September 22

PATIENT

Wherefore seeing we also are compassed about with so great a cloud of witnesses, let us lay aside every weight, and the sin which doth so easily beset [us], and let us run with patience the race that is set before us,

Hebrews 12:1

Hurry up! Get there quickly! Are we there yet? All of these phrases have to do with waiting for something to occur. Usually those with little patience want the event or characteristic to happen now. Most people hate waiting and to stand in line, sit at a red light, endure trials, or last through hardships is the last thing they want to do.

Life is filled with times that require patience. Whether it is making it through a difficult obstacle course or finishing a scholastic class, patience is a required virtue. No amount of trying to make it go quickly will ever expedite the process.

There is a race going on and this race is a marathon. Those who heed the Word of God know that trials during the race come to form patience that will help us cross His finish line as a victor.

PRAYER

Dear Heavenly Father, patience does not come naturally to me, so I come before Your throne yielded to You working patience within me. In Jesus' name I pray. Amen.

_____

_____

_____

_____

_____

September 23
REWARD

But when thou doest alms, let not thy left hand know what thy right hand doeth: That thine alms may be in secret: and thy Father which seeth in secret himself shall reward thee openly.

Matthew 6:3,4

In Jesus' day there were people who would give to the poor by using a trumpeter blowing his horn to give notice to poorer people to come around. This was a supposed alert them that monies would be given to the underprivileged. However, it became a notice of personal publicity for the individual who was giving.

Some of the greatest deeds every done by people have been done in secret. However, the tendency within the world is to be noted by others for accomplishments, giving, and achievement. Pins, bars, trophies and notices are symbols of great merit, award and honorarium. Those who seek such notoriety are often consumed by self-aggrandizement, and perpetual pursuit of such repels rather than draws.

Jesus, who is most noted among mankind, says that when alms are given, they are to be given in such a way that they do not bring fanfare. In other words, some of the greatest accomplishments will be done when no one else sees but the Heavenly Father, and publicity with Him is unmatched.

PRAYER

Dear Heavenly Father, help me to know the tendency to desire notoriety within me. May my duties seen and unseen be before Your eyes. In Jesus' name I pray. Amen.

_____

_____

_____

_____

September 24
PURITY

Blessed are the pure in heart, for they shall see God.

Matthew 5:8

Purity has to do with integrity. For a us to have a pure, unadulterated heart, we must be washed in the water of the Word of God regularly. The idea is to have a heart that is toward God.

As King David in the Old Testament, the man or woman who would be pure in heart must be *after God's own heart*. In other words, the pure in heart desires to have the same heart as God Almighty.

Those who are in battle understand integrity. It is imperative that fellow soldiers tell each other the truth, especially when it comes to combat missions. The misinformation or impure intelligence might compromise the mission. Those who adhere to the principle of purity will find themselves in the place of seeing God. There is no mission of greater importance than that.

PRAYER

Dear Heavenly Father, please help me know the importance of purity. In Jesus' name I pray. Amen.

PRACTICE

But refuse profane and old wives' fables, and exercise thyself
[rather] unto godliness.

1 Timothy 4:7

Practice sessions can be time-consuming, boring, and requiring of a lot of effort. Most teams know the long hours of endurance that must be put in before the big game. Swinging the bat, hitting the dumbbells, or running the course over and over again can seem to be on an endless path to nowhere. However, practice and the way one practices will be manifested when the game is played. Those who have prepared well will perform well—those who have not prepared will not be ready when the big play comes.

It is imperative for those who succeed to endure the practice time. Although it is day by day, hour by hour and minute by minute, practice and the discipline of it must be in place. Reality calls for it, and the preparation time will be well worth the effort.

So it is with godliness. If we practices godliness, when reality comes and opportunity for ungodliness arrives, we will not fail. If godly practice has been in place, no opposition will conquer. The failings come when someone forgets to practice the idea of godliness and, oh, how many have suffered the losses that last a lifetime from simply not practicing God's Word.

PRAYER

Dear Heavenly Father, remind me to practice godliness at all times, so when the opposition arises, I shall not fail. In Jesus' name. Amen.

September 26
PRIVILEGE

For in him we live, and move, and have our being; as certain also of your own poets have said, For we are also his offspring.

Acts 17:28

The breath within every man and woman has been given by Almighty God, and without breath no one shall live. Every breathing person has been given a commission of duty, responsibility, and adherence to the privilege of living and there are none who are exempt. There is no escaping the presence of the Creator above.

God is everywhere present, and there is no place whether dangerous or safe that is outside of His being. The comfort for those who recognize His presence is the privilege of access to Him at all times. His counsel, direction, comfort and leading are readily at hand. To call upon the One who oversees it all is a relational benefit to those who deem Him, "Heavenly Father."

Avoiding His outstretched hand is like rejecting the advice of one who knows in advance what is going to happen. Call upon Him.

PRAYER

Dear Heavenly Father, please remind me daily of the privilege of living and the access I have to You at all times. In Jesus' name I pray. Amen.

_____

_____

_____

_____

_____

_____

_____

_____

TARGET

I have fought a good fight, I have finished [my] course,
I have kept the faith:

2 Timothy 4:7

One of the most important parts of a battle is to know who the enemy is and what the targets are that one is to hit. If there is no enemy, and if there are no targets, military men and women might as well stay home for their missions would be mute. Commodore Oliver Hazard Perry (1813) said, "We have met the enemy, and they are ours!" Now that's a man who knew who the proper perspective on the enemy, and in knowing the enemy, he knew what the mission was to be.

Christians have a mission but we also have an enemy. There is an ensuing battle every day within the Christian's life. Ignoring the enemy and not focusing upon the target will only find the Christian weak, weary and defeated. Paul knew there was a fight on hand and he knew the battle was to keep the faith. No matter what the battle looked like, no matter what the circumstances were, Paul knew there was fighting, finishing and keeping involved.

Fight, finish, and keep the faith by knowing who the enemy is. With Jesus' help, make him ours, and victory every day will be the mantra lived by.

PRAYER

Dear Heavenly Father, help me to keep in mind who the enemy is and who is the target. I desire to be victorious over him every day with Your help. In Jesus' name I pray. Amen.

_____

_____

_____

_____

TALK

I will meditate also of all thy work, and talk of thy doings.

Psalm 77:12

There are many subjects to talk about in the world. Talking is one of the greatest forms of communication known to man. Cell phone companies thrive on it and commercial sales depend upon it. Talking is part of relaying a mission, giving commands, and communicating plans even for covert operations.

The psalmist gives a preclusion to talking, "I will meditate also of all thy work." In other words, this psalmist will mull over and over again the works of God. Thoughts of the planets, the stars, the universe, and creation will permeate his mind. Thoughts of the work of God in men and His purposes for them will be in the forefront of the psalmist's mind. All the works of God will be meditated upon before, during and after he speaks.

If we are wise, we will withhold speech until we can considers a matter completely. Those who have meditated in all the work of the Heavenly Father will be more easily heard than those who speak without thinking.

PRAYER

Dear Heavenly Father, I come before You today meditating upon Your great works. Help me to keep Your work in the forefront of my mind. In Jesus' name I pray. Amen.

September 29
SIGNS

... When it is evening, You say, "It will be fair weather, for the sky is red." And in the morning, "It will be stormy today, for the sky is red and threatening." You know how to interpret the appearance of the sky, but you cannot interpret the signs of the times.

Matthew 16:2b-3

Our history is still being written. Many writers are pessimistic about this generation. They write about the decline in SAT scores, the breakdown of the family unit; the increase of violence, the decline of public trust in authority figures and increasing climate changes. Clearly it's easier to catalog societal problems than it is to offer solutions.

Just visit the archives of a major city newspaper, and read the headlines of a century ago. Pick up a history book of the great empires of the past and note the similarities to our present day problems. We shouldn't belittle the seriousness of today's problems, but keep them in perspective. The fact that these problems exist is cause for concern but not despair.

We need to see beyond the obvious. We need someone who not only sees the problem but wants to make a difference. Jesus Christ came into a world that knew the letter of the law but was ignorant of how to live it. He taught that we should admit our own sins before we attempted to point out the faults of others. The solution Jesus offered the sinner and the saint was peace with God. He demonstrated that there are none so bad that God won't forgive them. Sadly, there are thousands who are so good that they don't think they need to be forgiven.

PRAYER

Dear Heavenly Father, I find it easier to see the faults of others than my own. I know more about God than I've applied to my everyday walk. I want that to change. I want to make a difference in my life and in my generation. In Jesus' name I pray. Amen.

September 30

TOMORROW

Do not boast about tomorrow; for you do not know what a day may bring.

Proverbs 27:1

What do you call a person who puts off until tomorrow what needs to be done today? They might be a procrastinator, that is, someone who needs encouragement to attempt the job or they might lack enough information to finish the task. One thing is certain, we are assuming that tomorrow will actually provide the opportunity to take any action.

If we presume that we will have another day, that makes us a procrastinator and a bit arrogant. We presume that plans are ours to make. What about the person who fails to do what they know to do? This is called omission and is equivalent to disobedience. What if we boast of things which we are unable to do? This is all three qualities—presumption, omission and boasting—they are barriers to wise planning for the future. Soldiers who deliberately put off obeying a command or complete a mission are guilty of disobedience.

The Bible gives us a formula for achieving excellence in our personal life and our service to our country. First, we should remember the many blessings God has bestowed upon us. He has given us so much, so we miss the mark when we fail to do what the Lord is calling us to do. Instead of presuming, boasting or missing the mark, we should commit ourselves to the Lord and do His will. Second, we need to be sensitive to the world around us and their needs. We need to respond to the needs of others in the way He has blessed us.

PRAYER

Dear Heavenly Father, I have today, so let me live it mindful of Your many blessings to me. Help me to share information and encouragement to those who are struggling. In Jesus' name I pray. Amen.

FUNDAMENTAL

And now abideth faith, hope, charity, these three;
but the greatest of these [is] charity.

1 Corinthians 13:13

Basic training is filled with the fundamentals for military training. From learning how to march to understanding obedience when commanded, learning the foundational elements is essential, if a soldier is going to be effective in the field and in the world.

The Bible lists three fundamentals: Faith, hope, and love. Upon these three attributes lay all that a person is compositely made of within the soul. Where there is faith, there is hope, and where there is hope, there is love.

When functioning as Christian soldiers in the middle of a war-torn battlefield called the world, it is imperative that we have faith, hope and love. Without them, we are subject to be destroyed at any time.

PRAYER

Dear Heavenly Father, I desire the divine traits of faith, hope
and love. Help me to find them abundant in the fundamental
foundation of my life. In Jesus' name I pray. Amen.

October 2

FULLY

And being fully persuaded that, what he had promised, he was able also to perform.

Romans 4:21

Those who engage in battles know that there is high risk in anything but full commitment. Resolve to accomplish a mission is imperative, and there is no place for compromise. Without a fully committed plan and action, harm and failure may occur.

Paul, the apostle, believed that God Almighty was fully committed to His promises. There are literally thousands of promises in the Bible. Christians who seeks them out will find that God is faithful to His word. Not only does the Lord make promises, but He keeps them and performs them.

Doubt will creep into our lives, if we allow it, but when doubt comes, remember the promises of God and His full commitment to perform that which He said He would do.

PRAYER

Dear Heavenly Father, thank You for Your promises, and thank You for being fully committed to keep them. May I live my life in a manner that is fully committed to You. In Jesus' name I pray. Amen.

October 3
FRAUD

Be not deceived; God is not mocked: for whatsoever a man soweth, that shall he also reap.

Galatians 6:7

One of the greatest acts of fraud is not when a person embezzles millions of dollars from a company nor is it when there is an act of counterfeiting or writing worthless bank checks. No, one of the greatest acts of fraud is when soldiers act evasively toward their training. Not only does this act endanger others, but it may also be detrimental to oneself.

There is a Divine principle called "sowing and reaping." Whatever people sow into their lives will bring up a crop later. For example, when an orange seed is sown, it brings forth oranges. When a lemon seed is sown, it brings up lemons, and on and on. So it is with individuals who sow good or bad seed into their lives. If bad seed is sown, bad is reaped, but if good is sown, good is reaped.

The key to this principle is to continually sow good seed. Anything other than this action will be a fraud, as it brings forth a harvest that is promising in the beginning, but the end results are horrific. Be careful as to what kind of seed is being sown, and fraud will flee as abundant fruit arises.

PRAYER

Dear Heavenly Father, please help me to sow good seed today. May my life be a garden of fruit for You to pick and not a life of fraud that has no meaning. In Jesus' name I pray. Amen.

_____

_____

_____

_____

_____

October 4
FRAGILE

Likewise, ye husbands, dwell with [them] according to knowledge, giving honour unto the wife, as unto the weaker vessel, and as being heirs together of the grace of life; that your prayers be not hindered.

1 Peter 3:7

Hummers, bazookas, heavy transport trucks, and construction machinery are considered hearty, tough, and rugged equipment, and they can be handled in a tough manner. However, there are other military items such as: landmines, hair-trigger rifles, and flight controls that needed to be treated gingerly and with respect toward their fragile state. One mistake in dealing with fragile items can mean loss of life.

The Bible gives direction in all areas of life. One in particular is when a husband relates to his wife. Peter calls her the "weaker vessel," and this description has significance far beyond less strength. The idea is that she is like a fine piece of fragile china. Her value is great, and she must be handled with care. Husbands who understand this principle and practice the same are usually those who continue in their marriages. Those who do not usually find themselves in grief or alone.

PRAYER

Dear Heavenly Father, please help me to distinguish between that which is fragile and that which is not. May my behavior toward each be pleasing before Your eyes. In Jesus' name I pray. Amen.

October 5

FLY

*Then we which are alive [and] remain shall be caught up together
with them in the clouds, to meet the Lord in the air: and so shall
we ever be with the Lord.*

1 Thessalonians 4:17

Those who fly the fighter jets know the thrill of pushing past the
sound barrier in speed. (Some know the thrill of mach two!) Who
knows what the future may hold for planes that might reach mach
three, four, five or more. There is something exciting about flying at
those kinds of speeds.

However, even the Bible refers to a time when Christians will "fly."
When the Lord Jesus left the earth almost two thousand years ago,
angels asked why the disciples were standing and gazing up at him.
The answer they gave was that He would come again in like manner
as they had seen Him leave. Paul, the apostle, further wrote that the
Lord would descend from heaven. Those who are alive and remain
shall be caught up (or fly) to meet him in the air. What an exciting
flight that will be!

The key to this flight is to be ready in advance to fly. Pilots know
the importance of a fight plan. Those who have a relationship established with Jesus Christ before He returns will have logged all the
flight plans they shall ever need. Up, up, and away!

PRAYER

*Dear Heavenly Father, thank You for the promise of Your
return. I ask to have my entire flight plan in order, so that
when You return, I will fly away to You. In Jesus' name I
pray. Amen.*

_____

_____

_____

_____

FLUCTUATE

A double minded man [is] unstable in all his ways.

James 1:8

There is nothing more discouraging or harmful than indecision when it comes to engaging the enemy. Hesitation and vacillation may cost lives. Those who encounter such engagements know how important it is not to fluctuate between two choices.

Examples of those who fluctuate are like this: a leader chooses this and then chooses just the opposite—perhaps choosing left, but turns right or selecting up, but then goes down. The choice may also be the difference between choosing liberal, but remaining conservative. In other words, vacillation and indecision are predominant and is manifested when a person fluctuates back and forth, back and forth.

One of the keys mentioned throughout the Bible is to be a person who chooses and sticks with the choice. In some places it refers to "setting one's face like flint." When the choice is between a godly choice and an ungodly one, decisiveness is imperative, and holding fast to that decision makes one wise.

PRAYER

Dear Heavenly Father, help me to make the right decisions today. May I not fluctuate back and forth on anything that has to do with You. In Jesus' name I pray. Amen.

FLOP

So there went up thither of the people about three thousand men: and they fled before the men of Ai.

Joshua 7:4

Some battles end in loss and sometimes a person is not on the winning side. From one engagement to the next, people and groups go in with victory in mind, but do not have the result of their thoughts. Some losses are relative to skill or training, while others have to do with numbers. Whatever the cause, the flop that is incurred is neither enjoyable nor relished by the participants who lose.

The Bible speaks of the victory that Joshua and the people of Israel enjoyed over Jericho. Their march into the promised land was progressing, but the small little village of Ai stood within their path. Because of its size, there was no assumed need to pray, no need for a large army, and the victory was assumed to be assured and quick. However, the mission became a flop as the men of Ai put Israel to flight.

Sometimes the "flops" within a person's life are because of disregard to the things of the Heavenly Father. He may know of sin, presumption, or preparations that the person who engages may never have in mind. Wise soldiers always pursue the battles in advance at the feet of the Creator before they ever go out on the field.

PRAYER

Dear Heavenly Father, help me in the battles ahead and remind me to come to You before I ever go out into the engagements ahead. In Jesus' name I pray. Amen.

_____
_____
_____
_____

FLOAT

Thrice was I beaten with rods, once was I stoned, thrice I suffered shipwreck, a night and a day I have been in the deep;

2 Corinthians 11:25

Waiting is not usually a fun event in life. Having to endure a process, outlast training, sit through a class or hold on for an advancement is difficult for most people. Soldiers know how difficult it is to wait. Waiting for chow, waiting for promotion, waiting for directives, waiting for reserves, and other factors that require that soldiers bide their time. Having to sit afloat is a taxing demand.

Paul, the apostle, knew what it was to wait. In fact, he actually did float for a night and day in the sea. What did he think of there? What were his worries? What were his words? What were his contemplations and concerns of the future? One is sure that many thoughts raced through his head as he just floated. There is one thing for certain—he thought about the Lord Jesus. However, thinking of the hardships mentioned in the Scripture reading for today, his plight only verified that he was a "minister of Christ."

When life brings about troubling circumstances that require soldiers to float, they must keep the perspective of the Lord who reigns above. They must realize that ministering for Him is above every waiting circumstance that shall ever flood the way.

PRAYER

Dear Heavenly Father, I desire to patiently wait for and minister to You. May my life be a reflection of the benefit of waiting on the Almighty God. In Jesus' name I pray. Amen.

_____

_____

_____

_____

FLIPPANT

*And Nadab and Abihu, the sons of Aaron, took either of
them his censer, and put fire therein, and put incense thereon,
and offered strange fire before the LORD, which he commanded
them not. And there went out fire from the LORD, and
devoured them, and they died before the LORD.*

Leviticus 10:1-2

If an order is taken with a flippant attitude, a soldier is likely to be
reprimanded immediately. To be nonchalant and aloof only makes
those who give directives angry, and to be treated with such insolence usually is met with great discipline. A soldier with a flippant
demeanor is usually begging for a yelling.

Nadab and Abihu treated the holy work of the Lord with a flippant
attitude and it cost them their lives. They were "fired," so to speak.
When the Lord gives instruction in holy things, they are to be followed. There is to be no strange fire offered in their place. A person is
greatly advantaged by listening to and heeding the commandments
of God. Not doing so hurts the cause of Christ and oneself, too.

Lessons can be learned from Nadab and Abihu, but they are ones
no one wants to experience personally. However, soldiers are well-
benefited if they learn how not to be flippant from someone else.

PRAYER

*Dear Heavenly Father, please forgive me for being flippant,
especially about spiritual things. Help me to always consider
Your works holy and treat them as they should be. In Jesus'
name I pray. Amen.*

_____

_____

_____

_____

FLESH

For the flesh lusteth against the Spirit, and the Spirit against the flesh: and these are contrary the one to the other: so that ye cannot do the things that ye would.

Galatians 5:17

There is a war going on—this war is not just between factions or countries. Soldiers are aware and they know the opponent is dangerous. In fact, many have their lives on the line dealing with the enemy. Alertness, carefulness, strategic planning, and constant observation are necessary. Victory will be obtained if soldiers just plan and follow directives.

Within the soul, there is also a battle being waged. The soul is the seat of emotions, the resting place of intellectual thought, and the throne of judgment for the will. This soul will be influenced by fleshly desires, related to desires of the body, or they will be influenced by the Spirit of God that dwells within the Christian. The battle rages—sometimes the flesh wins and sometimes the spirit wins. The difference in the number of victories for each side is directly dependent upon the closeness of the relationship that the Christian has with God Himself.

The key to winning the battle against the flesh is to grow in the Spirit. One grows by spending time in the Word of God, praying, being in fellowship with other believers, and being busy about the kingdom of God venue. With these strategic plans engaged, victory in the battle of flesh versus spirit is surely gained, but to forsake these plans is to fall to the enemy's destruction.

PRAYER

Dear Heavenly Father, please help me to stay engaged in Your strategies for defeating the flesh. Forgive me for my failings, and help me to continue to grow in the spirit that I might win the battles ahead. In Jesus' name I pray. Amen.

FLAW

There is none righteous, no, not one.

Romans 3:10

When a product, such as a gun or scope, shoots off-target, no matter how skillful the shooter is, that product is said to have a flaw. There was something that went astray in the manufacturing of the product that doesn't allow anyone to use the equipment properly.

People have flaws—they make mistakes. Those flaws are much more evident in some than in others. One of the most difficult parts of living with others is existing among their flaws. These errors cause conflict, fighting and sometimes even war.

The key to living around the flaws of others is to understand that every person has these flaws—even the reader. *There is none righteous,* and the word "none" there means none—no one escapes or is without fault. Some even surmise that the flaws that we see in others are most notable, because those same flaws are evident within our own lives. Before we condemn another for their flaws, it might be best to examine within to clear the same flaw from ourselves.

PRAYER

Dear Heavenly Father, I know that the illumination of Your Word once again will reveal the flaws in me. Help me to know them that I might not be so harsh when I see the flaws in others. In Jesus' name I pray. Amen.

_____

_____

_____

_____

_____

October 12

FLARE

But of these who seemed to be somewhat, (whatsoever they were, it maketh no matter to me: God accepteth no man's person:) for they who seemed [to be somewhat] in conference added nothing to me:

Galatians 2:6

There are certain people who seem to have a certain flare about themselves. Some today call it the "x" factor and those who have it are usually singled out in a group as excellent or above average. There are certain abilities that have been divinely given and there are no other explanations for their prolific talents.

Paul, the apostle, recognized people have a tendency to elevate others who have special talents, positions or authorities. To put someone on a pedestal is as common as breathing for most people. However, most cannot maintain that position for very long. Eventually the extremely good ball player, the talented pianist, or gift-given golfer becomes feeble and cannot perform as they once did. In other words, this type of flare is temporary.

As Christians, we are challenged to seek the fruit that remains. Temporary acknowledgment for flare-like traits are like the fireworks during the Fourth of July display. They shine brightly for a short time and then fizzle out. Stars, however, keep on shining well after the flare of the fireworks is gone.

PRAYER

Dear Heavenly Father, please help me to not think of myself more highly than I ought and to remember that all gifts come from You. May my life be as the shining stars in this world for You. In Jesus' name I pray. Amen.

_____

_____

_____

October 13

FLACK

And when king David came to Bahurim, behold, thence came out a man of the family of the house of Saul, whose name [was] Shimei, the son of Gera: he came forth, and cursed still as he came.

2 Samuel 16:5

An insubordinate soldier is dealt with quickly and with ready judgment. Those who have experienced this form of rebellion and disobedience know the impact that one person can make upon an entire group. There is no room for flack within the military, as there is no room for flack in the kingdom of God.

The Bible tells the story of one man who gave "flack" to his king. Shimei, a relative of the previous king, Saul, railed upon David as he left his kingdom behind to Absalom, David's insubordinate son. David was in a crisis in his life and yet, Shimei cursed him as he fled his country. Although David at this point in the Scriptures did not allow one of his men to lop off Shimei's head, he later told his son, Solomon, to take care of him. Shimei gave flack and Solomon returned the retaliation.

Obedience to God and His established authorities is peremptory for the soldier. Rebellion is contagious. Those who depend upon the unity of a team must not involve themselves in such behavior. Submission is the key to moving out all forms of flack. Those who are wise will remove it before it begins to flourish.

PRAYER

Dear Heavenly Father, thank You for the authorities that You have placed above me. Help me to be obedient and not give flack to their instructions that ultimately tie to You. In Jesus' name I pray. Amen.

October 14

FIX

*In that day will I raise up the tabernacle of David that is fallen,
and close up the breaches thereof; and I will raise up his ruins,
and I will build it as in the days of old:*

Amos 9:11

Walls of the city are broken down, and buildings have large holes from missiles within them. People are scattered, and the effects of war and battles show on their faces. Peace has been reestablished, and now the rebuilding begins. Who will repair this place? Who will rebuild these lives? Who will fix this mess?

The Bible is clear about restoration when it comes to the Heavenly Father. He is in the "fixing" business. Often lives when examined look like war zones within the soul. Those with many hurts from the past have much rebuilding to do. When Jesus came to the earth, He came to fix it and those who dwell upon it—*to seek and to save that which was lost.*

Sometimes life comes in like a battle, and damage is done. When those times arrive, we do best when we submit our war-torn lives to the one who is the Master rebuilder. It is He who can fix any broken life, no matter how badly damaged it is.

PRAYER

Dear Heavenly Father, I submit to You my wartorn life and ask You to fix any damage that may have been done. In Jesus' name I pray. Amen.

FIRE

*I indeed baptize you with water unto repentance: but he that
cometh after me is mightier than I, whose shoes I am not worthy
to bear: he shall baptize you with the Holy Ghost, and [with] fire:*

Matthew 3:11

There is something awesome about fire. The flames, the heat, the
consuming and the power of fire are an attraction to those who look
upon it. But fire can also be destructive, damaging, and destroying
of things that are important within a person's life. Those who have
experienced house fires know what this means.

The Scriptures are clear about the consuming fire of God Almighty.
There are places within a person's heart, and ways within a person's
life that need to be consumed, removed and destroyed. Bad attitudes,
awful language, and maligned practices will be "fired" for the person
who follows after Jesus Christ.

The Holy Spirit of God brings the fire of conviction within our souls
as He cleanses from within to without our lives. A little fire here and
a little fire there from the Spirit of the Living God will purify. Those
who desire it shall know the effects of a fired-up and redeemed life.

PRAYER

*Dear Heavenly Father, I make myself available for Your
Holy Ghost and fire. Burn away all that is within me that is
not like You. In Jesus' name I pray. Amen.*

_____

_____

_____

_____

_____

_____

_____

October 16

FILTHINESS

Wherefore lay apart all filthiness and superfluity of naughtiness, and receive with meekness the engrafted word, which is able to save your souls.

James 1:21

There are some places in the world where the garbage and filth are so thick that it feels like a person is ingesting it just to be in its presence. Trash, garbage, and refuse from animals and humans alike make such a place unbearable—never mind livable—yet, there are those who live there. Soldiers who have trod these places know exactly what they are like and the smells of them still resonate within their minds.

The apostle, James, writes that *one should lay apart all filthiness and superfluity of naughtiness.* The idea is that our minds could be like those filthy places within the world. Filth and naughtiness are natural for some—adherence to the Word of God never even crosses their mind.

Perhaps some filth has been allowed. Perhaps naughtiness has taken hold and now we are beginning to smell of them. Transformation begins when we take a spiritual bath by receiving the engrafted Word, which will clean the filth, wipe away the naughtiness, and come to save our souls.

PRAYER

Dear Heavenly Father, I need to be cleansed by Your Word. Please wipe away any filth or naughtiness that is within my life, and help me to receive Your engrafted Word today. In Jesus' name I pray. Amen.

_____

_____

_____

_____

October 17

FERTILE

Herein is my Father glorified, that ye bear much fruit; so shall ye be my disciples.

John 15:8

If our hearts could be measured for their hardness, what would that measurement read like? Would it be soft and ready to receive God's Word or would it be hard and resistant to the Scriptures? Is there a natural tendency to be inclined toward the things of God or is there a natural tendency to stray or stay away from holy things?

Whether we have fertile or fallow ground is realized through our actions and activities. Our speech, interests, places we go, and activities in which we choose to involve ourselves give clarity to that which we really believe. Many who claim to have fertile hearts mainly ascribe to them, but in no way manifest it in their lives.

To be fertile and bear much fruit for the Lord Jesus, we must have our hard ground broken. The repetitive action of an outside source will break up the most difficult of dirt. Those from whom the Lord desires the most will experience breakup after breakup after breakup to receive fruit. Only the wise receives the plowing.

PRAYER

Dear Heavenly Father, break up the fallow ground in my heart today. I want to be fertile and bear much fruit for You in Your kingdom. In Jesus' name I pray. Amen.

FORGIVE

But Joseph said to them, Do not fear, for am I in the place of God? As for you, you meant evil against me, but God meant it for good, to bring it about that many people should be kept alive, as they are today.

Genesis 50:19-20

Think about a time when someone had intentionally hurt or wronged us. Later, they acknowledged their trespass and asked to be forgiven. We had a choice to forgive or seek revenge. What helped us make our decision?

The Old Testament records the life of Joseph, son of Jacob, who had eleven brothers. Family rivalry had divided Joseph's brothers against him. In short, they conspired to sell him into slavery. Years later, the brothers meet Joseph, and he held their fate in his control. He was faced with a choice—to forgive or retaliate. Joseph's choice is found in the Scripture for today; ... *you meant evil ... but God meant it for good ...* (Genesis 50:20a)

Joseph's faith in God had prevented bitterness from taking over his life. While acknowledging the true nature of his brothers' wrong, Joseph saw the good that had come to him. He refused to act as God towards his brothers. Joseph could forgive his brothers, because of God's grace to him.

PRAYER

Dear Heavenly Father, You have turned that which was meant to harm me into a blessing. Thank You for Your grace. In Jesus' name I pray. Amen.

_____

_____

_____

_____

RISEN

If ye then be risen with Christ, seek those things which are above, where Christ sitteth on the right hand of God.

Colossians 3:1

If an enemy is before us, we would be wise to look in that direction. If the enemy is behind, we might want to turn around. If the enemy cannot be seen, huge difficulty arises, and the danger level increases. The reason for knowing where the enemy is would be for protection, perception, and strategy. Our focus often determines response and appropriate engagement.

Paul writes to the church of Colossae to *seek those things which are above*. There are battles that are unseen, and battles that are won and lost within the soul of a person. Those who have their focus in the right place win, while those who neglect do not.

We Christians are in a battle and the enemy desires to kill, steal and destroy. By keeping our attention upon Christ, Who sits on the right hand of God, the enemy's attacks fail. Those who are wise forget not the advantage that is found in Christ Jesus.

PRAYER

Dear Heavenly Father, thank You for Jesus, Who sits at Your right hand. Please help me today to keep my attention upon Him as I perform my tasks. In Jesus' name I pray. Amen

ASSENT

Whoso [is] simple, let him turn in hither: [as for] him that wanteth understanding, she saith to him, "Come, eat of my bread, and drink of the wine [which] I have mingled."

Proverbs 9:4-5

If we give our assent to something, we are agreeing with that item. Whether it is an idea, a venture, a way of living, or an act, we align ourselves in commitment. Direction for wise Christians is to be sure that we are assenting to the right things. If we assent to the right things, we have it made, but if we assent to the wrong things, we have it unmade.

Battles ensue every day, and pressures from without can make anyone weak. Moral choices are tested the most in times of frailty and insecurity. Giving assent to behaviors that cause future distresses and penalties are most prominent at this time. The vulnerable and simple shine greatest in the darkest of times.

Jesus knows our tendency to "give in" in trying times, so He has orchestrated a plan in the Bible for preventing and avoiding future consequences that bring regret. The wise person assents to the Almighty God's plan—there is no greater assent than this.

PRAYER

Dear Heavenly Father, please help me to give my assent to You. I know You have my best interest in mind, and I want to walk in Your ways at all times. In Jesus' name I pray. Amen.

October 21

ADVANCEMENT

For promotion [cometh] neither from the east, nor from the west, nor from the south. But God [is] the judge: he putteth down one, and setteth up another.

Psalm 75:6-7

Why does it seem that one person gets promoted over another who is doing the exact same job? Why does there seem to be favor in one direction and not in another? What is it about those who are elected who do not seem worthy, credible or qualified? How is it that this seems so unfair, biased or one-sided? The answer lies in the source of advancement.

God Almighty puts it within His supreme sovereignty to advance one and not another. The Bible is very clear on where true promotion comes. Though sometimes it does seem unfair, the wise person will realize that the Lord knows the authorities that should be in place. He has the advantage of foreknowledge and His decisions are based upon His own purposes for individuals and countries. Though promotion of one seems correct, only the Divine knows for sure. Those who follow Jesus must align with His perfection or become terribly bitter at His superior knowledge.

PRAYER

Dear Heavenly Father, thank You for Your Divine perspective. When promotions are given that are contrary to my way of thinking, please help me to align with Yours. In Jesus' name I pray. Amen.

_____

_____

_____

_____

_____

_____

October 22
ANALYST

For the ways of man [are] before the eyes of the LORD, and he pondereth all his goings.

Proverbs 5:21

Analysts step back and survey. They review and contemplate. Analysts look for better ways, better paths and better solutions to problems. Their function is necessary. They often only surmise, but many do not get involved in practical repair. However, the best analysts engage in the alteration and have greater success.

The Heavenly Father is an analyst. He is consistently and constantly pondering our goings. His careful eye is involved and His ways of correction are obvious to those who stay in tune with Him. The fulfilling of His work is the mission, and when conditions are unfavorable, He engages.

There is advantage to those who recognize the Almighty. When He analyzes, those who are wise submit to His findings.

PRAYER

Dear Heavenly Father, analyze my life today. Correct that which needs corrected and show me Your ways at all times. In Jesus' name I pray. Amen.

October 23

ALTOGETHER

Every one of them is gone back: they are altogether become filthy;
[there is] none that doeth good, no, not one.

Psalm 53:3

Has there ever been a thought about one person being much more wicked than another? Is there someone who is deemed the lowest of the low? Is there one particular person who has rank, authority or privilege, who seems to not deserve even the time of day? One supposes everyone has someone in mind when they think about such things. However, the Bible is clear on one point: *Every one of them is gone back: they are altogether become filthy.*

This thinking just doesn't seem possible when people are measured against one another. Surely this person is better than that one, right? Surely this person is more moral and that one is more wrong, correct? Well, it all depends on the standard of measurement, which is a Holy God and not other men or women.

Who measures up to the holiness of God? Who is totally pure in thoughts and actions? Who cares like God does and who is perfect like the Divine? None. None, and once again, none. There are none who are that righteous, that holy, that perfect, and thus "altogether" people are in this thing.

PRAYER

Dear Heavenly Father, thank You for the standard of perfection and holiness that You exhibit. Forgive me for my failings and help me to see others and myself in a manner that measures according to You. In Jesus' name I pray. Amen.

_____

_____

_____

_____

_____

October 24

EVIL

If possible, so far as it depends on you, live peaceably with all.
Beloved, never avenge yourselves, but leave it to the wrath of God,
for it is written, Vengeance is mine, I will repay, says the Lord.

Romans 12:18-19

Getting even is the natural way to handle conflict in human relationships. Evil is a reality that exists in the world, and evil men will cause us suffering and pain. But Scripture gives us a better way to respond to evil instead of getting even.

To apply this response, we must do two things: one is negative, the other positive. The negative factor is to refuse to respond to an evil action with evil. How can I do that? Remember the example of Jesus—when He was reviled, He refused to answer. He said, *Blessed are you when they revile and persecute you and say all kinds of evil against you falsely for My sake.* (Matthew 5:11) The blessing isn't because I enjoy persecution, but because I choose to follow Jesus.

Now, the positive response: Vengeance belongs to the Lord. Our society doesn't agree on what is good, but as a Christian, I know that God will ensure that right and good will prevail. How can I live peaceably with those who are intent on making war? I just do the possible, as much as depends on me, and I leave the impossible to God. *If possible, so far as it depends on you, live peaceably with all.*

PRAYER

Dear Heavenly Father, I'm not the judge or punisher of evil. I want to overcome evil with good. In Jesus' name I pray. Amen.

_____

_____

_____

_____

October 25

ENEMY

And the Lord restored the fortunes of Job, when he had prayed for his friends. And the Lord gave Job twice as much as he had before.

Job 42:10

There are critics of the book of Job who say: "Hold on, only fairy tales end with 'and so they lived happily ever after.'" The ending of the book of Job is just too good to be true. After all, Job has lost his family, possessions, health and his friends. How could he possibly recover?

During the time of Job's suffering, those who called themselves friends had turned into accusers and tormentors. The key to Job's recovery is connected to his prayer for these accusing friends. The Scripture says, *And the Lord restored the fortunes of Job, when he had prayed for his friends.* Personally, I would have difficulty calling them my friends and definitely struggled to pray for them.

Why is Job's recovery linked with his willingness to pray for these men? After being confronted with his own inadequacies, Job utters, *I spoke things that I did not understand, I had heard of you by the hearing of the ear, but now my eye sees you; therefore I despise myself, and repent in dust and ashes.* (Job 42:5-6) Job needed grace for himself, and this perspective allowed him to pray for his enemies.

PRAYER

Dear Heavenly Father, thank You for the grace You've poured into my life. I will give grace to those who have offended me. In Jesus' name I pray. Amen.

October 26

EMPTY

And Elisha said to her, "What shall I do for You? Tell me; what have You in the house?" And she said, "Your servant has nothing in the house except a jar of oil."

2 Kings 4:2

What will we do when we are backed into a corner with no way out? It is possible that in our panic, we overlook a resource that holds the key to our success. The Scriptures tell the story of a widow who faces the creditors with no apparent assets to pay her deceased husband's debts. The law of that time demanded that her sons be taken as slaves to satisfy the debt.

Attempting to avoid her sons becoming slaves or going to prison, she asked the prophet for help. He asked the widow to identify her assets, so she replies, "I have nothing except a jar of oil." That which she had overlooked became the instrument of her recovery. The jar of oil alone wasn't enough, but when blessed by God, her debts were paid and her sons freed.

The lesson we can learn is: panic will cause us to overlook a valuable resource. Little is much if God is in it. We are not alone when life overwhelms us. Cry out—God hears our prayers.

PRAYER

Dear Heavenly Father, I see my problem. You see the solution. Open my eyes to see Your blessings. In Jesus' name I pray. Amen.

_____

_____

_____

_____

_____

_____

October 27

WAIT

Wait for the Lord; be strong, and let Your heart take courage;
wait for the Lord!

Psalm 27:14

The command to "be strong" and "take courage" resonates with people who love action and adventure. Soldiers want to be where the action is taking place. Three-mile hikes, obstacle courses and wilderness survival are made tolerable by the expectation of the real battle.

David, the second king of the young nation of Israel, learned that military readiness and might wasn't always enough. He was clearly God's choice to be the next king, but he waited until the timing was right. Psalm 46:10 records the lesson he learned: *Be still, and know that I am God.* In David's case, waiting and being still are linked to God's purpose for himself and the nation.

We want to be people of action. We feel better if we're doing something to address the situation. Waiting is often viewed as idling away valuable time or indecision. Instead of being frustrated by the delay or season of waiting, we can utilize the time to strengthen our faith in God. David took advantage of the delay in being the king to shore up family ties and to recruit additional colleagues.

PRAYER

Dear Heavenly Father, I am impatient with delays in my life. Teach me the lessons I need to learn while I wait. I need to rely more on You. In Jesus' name I pray. Amen.

October 28
WORK

Whoever is slack in his work is a brother to him who destroys.

Proverbs 18:9

All of us have a name that identifies who we are in the eyes of those who know us best. It may not be the name given to us at birth or even the nickname some of our friends call us. This name reflects the character we demonstrate and reveals much about our personality. What does our work say about who we are? What does our commanding officer say to our sergeant about our performance?

The quality of our work says a lot about our character. Earning a coveted promotion will depend upon how well we take care of the small things. If we fail in small tasks, like cleaning, we will never succeed in any aspirations to lead. In baseball, the successful team is the one that makes the routine plays.

We may encounter an attitude of indifference, sleepwalking, or let's have a party. Good soldiers are exhorted to guard against these attitudes, to be sober, alert and armed with faith in God. It's our watch, so don't quit. Resist the impulse to blame someone else or to be a slacker. God, our country, and our family are counting on us.

PRAYER

Dear Heavenly Father, I serve my country as an act of worship. I want my work to be done with an attitude of excellence. In Jesus' name I pray. Amen.

October 29
RICH OR POOR?

Let the lowly brother boast in his exaltation, and the rich in his humiliation, because like a flower of the grass he will pass away.

James 1:9-10

Would we rather be rich or poor? The overwhelming majority of people would answer: "Are you crazy? I'd rather be rich!" A survey of people who are rich by the measurement of money and property found that most felt that they needed just a little more. Obviously, we have trouble knowing when we're rich enough.

Anyone desiring to be rich needs to hear the warning in Scripture concerning wealth. Listen to these words in 1 Timothy 6:10 *For the love of money is a root of all kinds of evils* ... Does this mean that money and riches are evil? No, but it tells us that the love of money can lead to thinking we don't need God. Another danger is that we are deceived to believe money can provide happiness. The teaching of Scripture is that wealth is like flowers—temporary. We are to use them, but not put our trust in riches.

The lesson for the poor is that they are to be encouraged that their poverty is temporary. They belong to the kingdom of God, so their present lowly circumstances are not all they'll ever know. However, they should avoid thinking that riches will make them happy.

Consider these words of Solomon, one of the world's richest men, *He who loves money will not be satisfied with money, nor he who loves wealth with his income; this also is vanity.* (Ecclesiastes 5:10) Jesus taught that a man is a fool who lays up treasure for himself on earth and is not rich toward God. (Luke 12:21)

PRAYER

Dear Heavenly Father, I confess that I aspire to have money and the things it can provide. But I never want earthly possessions to become my god. I want my treasure to be my faith in You. In Jesus' name I pray. Amen.

October 30

PRESENT

Take therefore no thought for the morrow:
for the morrow shall take thought for the things of itself.
Sufficient unto the day [is] the evil thereof.

Matthew 6:24

Some people worry so much about what is going to happen tomorrow that they forget to live today. Although there may be troubles on the horizon or preparations for future events, there are enough activities that may be enjoyed today if we make them priority.

There is no one who knows more about how to live than Jesus. When He gives a directive on living—if we are wise, we will take heed. In the Sermon on the Mount, Jesus taught in a manner that was relative to everyone's situation. He knows the tendency to allow tomorrow's worries to overwhelm the events of today. His words were, *Sufficient unto the day is the evil thereof.* In other words, there is enough evil going on today that one doesn't need to add tomorrow's evil to it.

Live today for today and allow the worries of tomorrow to be for tomorrow. Those who listen to these words will not let any day just pass them by and be wasted away.

PRAYER

Dear Heavenly Father, please help me not to waste one day upon this earth. I put my future in Your hands and ask You to bless me as I live before You today. In Jesus' name I pray. Amen.

_____

_____

_____

_____

_____

October 31

PENITENT

I tell You, Nay: but, except ye repent, ye shall all likewise perish.

Luke 13:3, 5

Whenever Jesus says something twice within a couple verses, it would be wise to pay particular attention. In this instance, Jesus is referring to people who encountered horrific circumstances. The first group was slaughtered and their blood was mingled with Gentile sacrifices. The second group, which included eighteen people, had the tower in Siloam fall and slay them. Each of these incidents were well-known. However, Jesus relates them to everyone's condition. In other words, everyone must repent.

The Heavenly Father knows that people fail, and mistakes are made every day. The difference between the penitent person and the unrepentant is whether they acknowledge God's presence in their lives. God watches and God sees. He knows failure as it occurs, and He knows the ones who will heed His conviction and turn to Him. Those who are penitent are not perfect, but they know enough to go to the Heavenly Father when failure comes.

PRAYER

Dear Heavenly Father, please forgive me when I fail to keep Your word. May my life be one that is in a constant state of turning from sin and toward Your Heavenly throne. In Jesus' name I pray. Amen.

November 1

CASUAL

And say to Archippus, Take heed to the ministry which thou hast received in the Lord, that thou fulfil it.

Colossians 4:17

"Ten-hut" and "At ease" are two very familiar phrases to military personnel. Whenever those words are spoken, action follows. Those who are used to hearing these phrases know the importance of obeying them. There is a formal and casual position that relates to both commands, but the wise soldier knows which position to be in accordingly.

There are times as Christians where casual behavior is normal, but there are also times when we must pay particular attention to our service. There is a ministry for all Christians and those who understand the authority under which they serve know the importance of compliance. Obedience in serving the Lord aligns with the greatest service any of us will ever do in our lives. There is no room for a casual effort, but a full-on work mode must be pursued.

Whenever the Lord assigns, He also equips. Those who hear His marching orders snap to attention just as if they heard, "Ten-Hut!"

PRAYER

Dear Heavenly Father, I know that You have an assignment for me in this world. Please help me not to treat it in a casual manner, but to understand the importance of that which You would have me to do. In Jesus' name I pray. Amen.

CAPTIVATE

So Manoah took a kid with a meat offering, and offered [it] upon a rock unto the LORD: and [the angel] did wondrously; and Manoah and his wife looked on.

Judges 13:19

There are sites soldiers see that most other human beings are not allowed to view. Some of these sites repel, but many of them captivate. There is something mesmerizing about some of the tremendous usages of the equipment available to the military. Those who have the privilege of watching them perform have a great advantage.

Manoah and his wife were captivated once with an angel. Although God had promised them a son who would deliver Israel, Manoah especially had some doubts. Although Samson was on his way, doubt found a pathway. The angel helped to remove doubt, and by being captivated by the things of God, belief replaced unbelief and faith pushed away the uncertainty.

The next time doubt arises, be captivated by the things of God. Replace doubt with faith. Look through the Bible for stories where the Lord showed up just when someone needed Him the most.

PRAYER

Dear Heavenly Father, I desire to be captivated by You. May all my doubts and fears be removed by the overshadowing of the wonder of You. May my life be filled with all You have for me. In Jesus' name I pray. Amen.

_____

_____

_____

_____

_____

November 3

HAPPY

He who heeds the word wisely will find good,
and whoever trusts in the Lord, happy [blessed] is he.

Proverbs 16:20

"Our habits do affect our happiness …, Habitual thoughts and behaviors create … pathways in the wiring in our brains, the way water
flowing downhill creates a groove in the earth." is a quote from the
book, *Happy for No Reason; The Secrets of True Happiness.* Research
tells us that unhappy people tend to have more negative pathways in
their brains. If a person repeatedly thinks, feel and acts in a different
way, the brain actually rewires itself!

The apostle, Paul, encourages this rewiring with these words, Finally
brothers, whatever is true, whatever is honorable, whatever is just,
*whatever is pure, whatever is lovely, whatever is commendable, if there
is any excellence, if there is anything worthy of praise think about these
things.* (Philippians 4:8)

The performance of our duty as a soldier in the military will bring
contact with a variety of people and situations—not all of them will
be positive. Remembering that we have a choice in how we think,
feel and act will make us happier persons and assets to our unit.
Circumstances will not produce happiness. They merely reveal what
is on the inside of us. A truly happy person will be the one who
trusts in the Lord.

PRAYER

*Dear Heavenly Father, I find that when I'm around negative
people, my thoughts become more negative. Help me to think
on good things and to train my mind to meditate on Your
Word. In Jesus' name I pray. Amen.*

_____

_____

_____

November 4

HELP

Our soul waits for the Lord; he is our help and our shield.

Psalm 33:20

Driving around any city, we're likely to see someone standing at the intersection holding a sign saying, "Will work for food or need help." Notice that most of these beggars don't look directly at us. Unless we're disposed to give assistance, we don't make eye contact. Why? It is easier to pass them up without stopping if we don't actually look at the person. Also, the beggar will not approach every person, because from experience, they can tell the ones most likely to give.

The question that's important to remember: "Is what these beggars are asking for what they really need?" Experience has shown that many actually use any help received to purchase alcohol or drugs. In giving what they ask for, we actually perpetuate their condition.

The book of Acts records such a situation where a man is begging at the gate of the Temple. Peter and John are on their way to pray when they are approached by this man. Their response is instructive for us. First, Peter and John saw the man and they made eye contact. Then Peter said, Look on us. Why? Because the beggar was still calling out to others, while he had two prospects. Next, Peter said, What I have I give to you.

Let's remember what Peter and John had to give. Both had left fishing and family to follow Jesus and spent three years learning from him. Both swore to follow all the way, even to death. Both failed when the test came. What they now had to give was the confidence that someone prayed for them to be restored. Peter and John knew the pain failure caused those who loved them. Both now possessed a willingness to repent and return.

PRAYER

Dear Heavenly Father, many times I have asked for things I didn't need. Thank You for giving me the things I needed most, forgiveness and restoration. In Jesus' name I pray. Amen.

PRELIMINARY

But continue thou in the things which thou hast learned and hast been assured of, knowing of whom thou hast learned [them];

2 Timothy 3:14

A popular speaker once said, "I believe everybody ought to go out and get them some learnin', and then when they have learned, they ought to go out and get themselves some more learnin' so that they don't look down on those who haven't learned yet." There is much wisdom in that advice, because many who receive extra education tend to think themselves superior to those who have not received that extra education.

However, there is knowledge that we have that we should use in present and future events. There are things that we have learned. It is only wisdom to continue to use education that has come from others. Carrying that wisdom forward will only expedite future educational opportunities.

There have been preliminary opportunities given. Rather than throw them away like a wadded up piece of paper, we should use those thoughts, those ideas, and those experiences now and refer to them in the future. Doing so marks us with preliminary advantage.

PRAYER

Dear Heavenly Father, please help me to realize the benefits of the preliminary education and experiences You have brought me through. I know they are from You, and I thank You for them. In Jesus' name I pray. Amen.

November 6

PRODIGY

And unto one he gave five talents, to another two, and to another one; to every man according to his several ability; and straightway took his journey.

Matthew 25:15

How does that three-year-old play the piano like a person who has played for thirty years? How is it that a twelve-year-old boy has two college degrees and graduated from high school when he was six? Why does that sixteen-year-old throw the baseball one hundred miles per hour and gets to sign a ten-year contract worth one hundred million dollars? Of course, these are unusual examples of people called "prodigies."

Prodigies are certain individuals who have extraordinary talent in one or more areas. They are noted for their great abilities—some of them become quite rich and famous. However, Jesus tells a story that precludes that all servants are given talents. Some have more, and others have less. The amount of the talent is not what is emphasized, but rather the way we use the talents we are given.

Some are given a few talents or even just one talent, which they use in a disciplined manner. Others are given many talents and they squander them with wasteful living. Everyone gets to make a choice as to what they do with the talents given. As one person said it, "Discipline is what makes talent ability." Those who are wise will spend their talents knowing the master will return to make an accounting of their use.

PRAYER

Dear Heavenly Father, help me to realize my God-given talents today. May I use them in a manner that is pleasing when You come to account for them. In Jesus' name I pray. Amen.

November 7
TAKE

*And as they did eat, Jesus took bread, and blessed, and brake [it],
and gave to them, and said, Take, eat: this is my body.*

Mark 14:22

Most of the time, the Christian is charged to "give." Jesus said, *Give
and it shall be given unto you* ... There is also a special place where the
Christian should "take."

Jesus knew that His departure was at hand. He knew the suffering
that was ahead for Him and His followers. He also knew the need
for a resource by which they would be reminded that He was with
them in those times. When suffering was imminent, they were to
take and eat the bread as a reminder of His broken body.

There is a perfect time when "taking" is not being greedy, not being
presumptuous nor stingy. Taking the body of the Lord Jesus is one of
the greatest practices that will ever be offered to man. Take.

PRAYER

*Dear Heavenly Father, I take of Your broken body today
as a reminder that no matter what I face, You were broken
and suffered for me. I take this in Jesus' name. In Jesus'
name I pray. Amen.*

_____
_____
_____
_____
_____
_____
_____

November 8

THIRST

As a deer pants for flowing streams, so pants my soul for you, O God. My soul thirsts for God, for the living God. When shall I come and appear before God?

Psalm 142:1-2

Thirst is one of the basis drives of human beings. A cool drink when we are tired and hot is refreshing. Appetite is also a good thing—it tells the body when we need fuel necessary for life. However, when our appetite goes beyond meeting essential requirements for preserving life and we become excessive in satisfying these drives, we get into trouble.

The soul that thirsts for God will be healthy. All our senses can alert us to important needs in our bodies, but they also can lead us into gratification and self-indulgence. It is natural that we will become thirsty and hungry, but as we satisfy these appetites, let us remember our soul's need for God.

PRAYER

Dear Heavenly Father, I need You more than the necessary food for my body. In Jesus' name I pray. Amen.

FORWARD

Brethren, I count not myself to have apprehended: but [this] one thing [I do], forgetting those things which are behind, and reaching forth unto those things which are before,

Philippians 3:13

"Forward, march!" How many times has a soldier heard those infamous words? Marching regiments are given from the very beginning of basic training to the final days before release. The soldier understands the discipline and control, the unifying and allegiance that is gained just by the act of marching.

In the Christian faith, there are marching orders as well. The idea is to forget the things of the past and continue forward. Some of those forgotten things will be good, and some will be bad. Some memories are fond, while others we would rather never visit again. Whichever the case, the idea is to leave them behind and continue forward.

Troubles occur, and good times roll. However, if we are to make progress in the kingdom of God, we must not allow accolades or failures to impede our journey. Keep marching until the final day, when the Heavenly Father releases us from earthly duty.

PRAYER

Dear Heavenly Father, I realize that both bad and good has occurred within my life. I desire to leave the past behind no matter which category it falls within and to continue marching forward for You. In Jesus' name I pray. Amen.

_____

_____

_____

_____

_____

_____

FURIOUS

Therefore the anger of the LORD was hot against Israel, and he sold them into the hand of Chushanrishathaim king of Mesopotamia: and the children of Israel served Chushanrishathaim eight years.

Judges 3:8

When a drill sergeant gets angry, everyone in the barracks knows. Many fly low, so as not to be discovered. Others just try to avoid having that anger taken out upon them. Anger that turns to wrath and aggravation that turns to furious behavior may leave lasting marks upon recipients for the rest of their lives.

However, consider the anger of the Lord. Over 90 times in the Bible does it speak of "the anger of the Lord." The Lord God Almighty does get angry and His fury is like no other. Entire cities and nations have been eliminated by His power. The world, remember, was once flooded entirely, so that only Noah's family of eight survived.

Thank the Lord for Jesus, who bore the brunt of the anger of the Lord for those who have strayed away from Him. Our Creator knows the power of His fury. He gave in advance the solution that appeases the one who could eliminate everyone with one small word.

PRAYER

Dear Heavenly Father, thank You for Jesus, and thank You for giving me an escape from Your fury. May every day of my life bring glory and thanks to You for the good that You have provided for me. In Jesus' name I pray. Amen.

_____

_____

_____

FRUSTRATE

*I do not frustrate the grace of God: for if righteousness [come]
by the law, then Christ is dead in vain.*

Galatians 2:21

There is nothing more uninviting than a drill sergeant who is frustrated. The intimidation factor is at a nearly intolerable level, without having frustration as a motivation. Those troops who have known the wrath of a frustrated drill sergeant understand the importance of doing things exactly as he says. Otherwise, there is a sure price to pay.

Paul, the apostle, wrote of a frustration in the Bible. His writing was related to the "grace of God." The idea of frustrate here means "to do away with, set aside, disregard or to thwart the efficacy of anything, to nullify, make void, reject, refuse or to slight." In other words, the grace of God is so significant and complete on its own that it needs no other additive for righteousness. There is nothing else that someone must do to earn the unmerited favor of God. God's grace cannot be worked for in any manner. The work has been completed by Jesus Christ.

The easiest way to avoid frustrating the grace of God is to just believe and enjoy it. Some say, "Just roll around and bask in it." The price of God's favor is paid in full.

PRAYER

Dear Heavenly Father, thank You for Your grace. Though it's hard to believe sometimes, thank You for paying the full price for my salvation. In Jesus' name I pray. Amen.

_____

_____

_____

_____

FRUGAL

*And he called him, and said unto him, "How is it that
I hear this of thee? Give an account of thy stewardship;
for thou mayest be no longer steward."*

Luke 16:2

Military ventures cost millions and billions of dollars to fulfill. Those who appropriate funds for battles and training know the heavy costs for protecting a nation. Being a frugal entity is imperative should those in control of the purse strings desire to continue protecting as they have in the past.

Christians are considered stewards to all that the Lord has placed within our keeping. Whether it is much or little makes no difference—the idea is to be frugal and not wasteful with whatever the portion is. Those who foolishly believe that all things are theirs have not considered what will happen to those things once they are gone. Stewards within the kingdom of God are to be frugal with finances, time and energies. The question becomes, "Will any who read this take the time to examine themselves in the area of being frugal?" Time will measure out that which has to be properly stewarded over and will reveal that which has been made a waste.

PRAYER

Dear Heavenly Father, I desire to be a frugal steward with all that You have provided for me. Help me to examine my life today to realize areas that I need to be a better steward within. In Jesus' name I pray. Amen.

_____

_____

_____

_____

_____

FRINGE

And Peter followed him afar off, even into the palace of the high priest: and he sat with the servants, and warmed himself at the fire.

Mark 14:54

Troops sent to the heat of the battle know engagement up close and personal. The onslaught of the enemy is frightful and awing. Those who have taken enemy fire know the dangerous situation they are within. They are not on the fringes—they are involved.

Peter did what is natural to most people when the times get tough. He stayed on the peripheral. He stayed on the fringe. When it comes to Christianity, sometimes there are battles to be fought and missions to be completed. Only those who engage fully know the heat of the trials or the onslaught of the enemy. Those who stay on the fringe, as though Christianity is just another religion, will never know the agony of the battles. However, they also will never know the victories that come from engagement.

The key is to be in the battle, fight the good fight, and occupy until the Lord Jesus comes again. This battle is not on the fringe, but on the battlefield. Those who choose to pursue will have trophies to lay at Jesus' feet.

PRAYER

Dear Heavenly Father, I know there is a tendency within me to stay on the fringe. Help me to be in the battle, engage the enemy, and win the victories with the help of Your Holy Spirit's power within. In Jesus' name I pray. Amen.

_____
_____
_____
_____

FORESHADOW

For the law having a shadow of good things to come, [and] not the very image of the things, can never with those sacrifices which they offered year by year continually make the comers thereunto perfect.

Hebrews 10:1

Testimony, witness, stories of old, accounts in battle, strategic memories, and previous battles are all used to determine current engagement plans. Experience from other people and previously tried exploits help to determine what to do and not to do in the battle ahead. These conglomerate preliminaries are blessed foreshadowings of battles ahead.

The law of God, the sacrifices, the feasts and the holy days were also a foreshadowing. Each of these fine examples were signs that pointed to Jesus Christ, Who is our ultimate victor over sin. Every cloth, every piece of metal, every skin and arrangement made a declaration of some sort about the Messiah.

These were, however, not the real thing like a battle ahead—they were only a foreshadowing of them. As it would be foolish to try to hug a shadow, one must keep in mind that these only point to Jesus and are to be managed and used as only a map to Him.

PRAYER

Dear Heavenly Father, thank You for the foreshadowing parts of the Scriptures that point to Jesus. I acknowledge their significance, and pray that I will always see them as pointing to Him. In Jesus' name I pray. Amen.

FOREIGN

There shall no strange god be in thee; neither shalt thou worship any strange god.

Psalm 81:9

There is nothing like being on foreign soil no matter even if it is run by one's own government. Being away from home is emotional and the return to home has nothing with which to compare. There is indeed, "no place like home."

The Bible declares that this world is not the Christian's home. This earth is foreign land and those who know Jesus Christ as their Savior are promised that there is a place whose builder and maker is God. The key is to be sure not to worship any foreign god or strange god. There are those out there whose entire mission is to thwart the plan of God Almighty for making something great out of His children.

As with a foreign country, a person should be delighted to be upon his or her own turf. Those who delight in Jesus will find no foreign alternative that even comes close to compare.

PRAYER

Dear Heavenly Father, thank You for Jesus and thank You for the relationship that is like home with Him. May everything I do be aligned with Your ways and let no foreign idea, way or god interfere with Your plan for me. In Jesus' name I pray. Amen.

FOOLISH

*And every one that heareth these sayings of mine, and doeth them
not, shall be likened unto a foolish man, which built his house
upon the sand:*

Matthew 7:26

Soldiers who listen to orders and directives and then choose to obey
a different direction will soon know the consequences of insolence.
When they are told to do something, they are expected to do so.
Behind the orders, there may be greater purpose of which soldiers
aren't aware. To take it upon themselves to do something entirely
different might as well be AWOL of the mind. Foolish soldiers may
take it upon themselves to direct and command their own army in
the midst of such authority.

Jesus gives directives and commands in his famous Sermon on the
Mount. He finalized this teaching with the example of the wise man
and the foolish man. The difference between the two is the foundation upon which they built. One had great regard for his house
standing, while the other didn't take the time. The foundation for
the one who follows Jesus is hearing and doing the sayings of Jesus.
There is no greater foundation than this.

Today there will be opportunity to obey the Supreme Creator of the
Universe. Those who are wise will obey Him and watch their lives
stand in the storms. Those who are foolish will not and will watch
their lives be blown away.

PRAYER

*Dear Heavenly Father, I choose to be wise today and follow
Your teachings. Please remind me when I seem to be building
upon a foundation of sand. In Jesus' name I pray. Amen.*

_____

_____

_____

November 17
FOLLOW

And he said to [them] all, If any [man] will come after me, let him deny himself, and take up his cross daily, and follow me.

Luke 9:23

The point man has one of the most important and yet dangerous jobs of any mission. He who is up front is subject to be the first person attacked—therein lies the danger. Soldiers who take point must be able to deny their own thoughts of self-preservation and think about the preservation of the whole group. Although they will be a hero, there is a great cost. Those who follow must rely heavily upon whatever happens with the leader.

Jesus said there is a way that we should follow Him. The presumption is that everyone would be inclined to think about following Him, but not all will. There is a cost, and those who follow after Jesus know that denial of self is number one on the list. For most, this is the stumbling-stone that keeps us away.

Wisdom calls out for all to realize the leader is Jesus who takes the point in our lives. He came. He lived. He died and rose again, as one who has taken the point in advance. Those who follow Him, follow a leader who never fails. The point ahead may be completely relied upon in Him.

PRAYER

Dear Heavenly Father, thank You for taking the point in my life. I ask You to help me follow You all the days ahead and to rely fully upon Your perfect leading. In Jesus' name I pray. Amen.

November 18

FLIGHT

Then we which are alive [and] remain shall be caught up together with them in the clouds, to meet the Lord in the air: and so shall we ever be with the Lord.

1 Thessalonians 4:17

The marvel of flying has revolutionized the way wars are fought. Having military aircraft available to engage the enemy or his territory puts distinct advantage in the way of the attacker. Much devotion, time, effort and money is put toward the air divisions within the armed forces because of it.

There is, however, a flight that shall take place that the Bible speaks of in which no aircraft will be needed. There will be no need for a pilot, resources or air control towers. No flight plan will be accessed, and neither will any license need to be obtained. The flight promised will be when the Lord Jesus returns in the sky, just as was promised by the angels as Jesus left this earth.

At that moment, that flashing moment, all who rely upon, trust in and cling to Jesus Christ will meet the Lord in the air, and so shall they ever be with the Lord. It will be the flight of flights, and those who love Jesus' appearing will be ready when it comes. The key is to constantly be ready for takeoff, for when the trumpet of God sounds, it will denote that the flight of flights begins.

PRAYER

Dear Heavenly Father, I know that You have promised to return in the same manner in which You left. Help me to be ready to take off in flight at the moment of Your trumpet sound. In Jesus' name I pray. Amen.

_____

_____

_____

_____

FIB

Thou shalt not bear false witness against thy neighbour.

Exodus 20:16

How many military people want to plan missions based upon lies? How about just a little lie like a fib or a "white lie"? How many people who are in combat want to risk their lives based upon someone else, who has not presented fact, truth, and good intelligence? Not many, if any, would be the proper response.

So, how is it that people believe that lies or untruths are somehow okay? How is it that there are varying degrees of permission to lie? For example, if someone asks about our age, weight, marital status, or wealth, how are we to respond? What if there is a blatant disregard for orders or directives and a person could blame another for the failing and get away with it? What if we are asked directly whether we cheated on an exam or taxes or other important documents? One supposes the examples could go on and on.

Although most people are guilty of telling a lie at one time or another, the standard does not change. God Almighty said, Thou shalt not bear false witness against thy neighbor. For many who struggle with keeping just this one command, there is a great appreciation for Jesus and His redemption through the cross for their sin.

PRAYER

Dear Heavenly Father, thank You for Your Word. Thank You for Your commandments. Help me today to keep this one about lying, and help me give no excuses for not telling the truth. Thank You for Jesus. In His name I pray. Amen.

_____

_____

_____

_____

_____

PRAYER

Pray without ceasing.

1 Thessalonians 5:17

The configuration of man is created in such a way that he can continue in activities without talking with God. Even though God is everywhere present and very conscious of every move, thought and word of man, sometimes people do not take the time to pray. Though the Bible exhorts over and over again in illustration, exhortation, and example that prayer is a key component for relating to the Heavenly Father, still many do not take advantage of it.

Jesus prayed. In fact, many times we see examples of Him praying all night long. Prayer was an important part of Jesus knowing the will of the Father. Many of the decisions Jesus made publicly were determined during the quiet hours alone with the Father. If Jesus prayed, everyone should pray.

The idea of praying without ceasing is to be in a manner of prayer throughout the day. Talk with God. Listen to God. He is involved. He knows the situation and His interest is greater than any other who might listen to our pleas.

PRAYER

Dear Heavenly Father, remind me to pray, and help me to listen to You as I do. In Jesus' name I pray. Amen.

_____

_____

_____

_____

_____

_____

_____

PERSUASION

For I am persuaded, that neither death, nor life, nor angels,
nor principalities, nor powers, nor things present,
nor things to come, Nor height, nor depth, nor any other creature,
shall be able to separate us from the love of God,
which is in Christ Jesus our Lord.

Romans 8:38-39

Peer pressure is huge in a person's life. The invitation to participate in activities that counter the inner voice inundates everyone who lives in this world. The indication that an invite is detrimental comes from within our souls. Deeply implanted ideas that are Godlike within people sometimes are cast aside for the adventure, the risk, or the excitement of a moment. Unfortunately, those moments come with a price, and some of them are for a lifetime.

The determinate is according to persuasion. If we are persuaded in the things of God, there will be no failing when the tempter comes. If, however, there is no real persuasion, falling will be easy, and the resistance after the first offering will be much less, as we are invited again and again. Resistance breaks down with each acquiescence.

The key is to be persuaded before the temptation. If "no" is already deeply implanted, and that "no" is based upon a relationship with Jesus Christ, then to violate that "no" would be to slam the door upon the closeness of Jesus in our lives. This mistake would be tragic, and the fallout will be much greater than the price we determined. There is no substitute for being from the love of God, which is in Christ Jesus our Lord, who helps overcome any offering others may make.

PRAYER

Dear Heavenly Father, please help me to be persuaded in my relationship with You, so that when temptations come, I will not fall away. In Jesus' name I pray. Amen.

PECULIAR

But ye [are] a chosen generation, a royal priesthood, an holy nation, a peculiar people; that ye should shew forth the praises of him who hath called you out of darkness into his marvelous light:

1 Peter 2:9

A lady I once knew used to speak of some individuals as "strange birds." In other words, their behavior was weird, uncanny and eldritch. When one speaks of being peculiar, it doesn't always mean a behavior that is antisocial, odd, and bizarre. No, rather it can mean, "specially selected or chosen." Being peculiar in this group is a place of honor, notoriety, and respect. There is no higher position than the one given by a Holy God.

Being peculiar has with it a sense of transparency. For us to be peculiar in God's kingdom, we must live a life that is on display. Others are watching and observing the way those of us who are peculiar react to circumstances, situations, and people. Others often desire to see the peculiar fall, make a mistake, or fail at something. We make them feel uncomfortable, but if there should be an error, that feeling can dissipate.

Great honor is bestowed upon those who recognize the benefits of being a peculiar people. Those who keep their peculiarity in an honorable way will reap huge eternal rewards.

PRAYER

Dear Heavenly Father, help me to recognize the honor of being one of the specially selected people in Your kingdom. May I bring honor to that privilege. In Jesus' name I pray. Amen.

FULL

And they did all eat, and were filled: and they took up of the fragments that remained twelve baskets full.

Mark 14:20

When a fine meal is prepared like at Thanksgiving, getting full is extremely easy. Soldiers know when the mess hall has the best meal served—eating until one can eat no more is a luxury. There is nothing like having a full stomach to satisfy hunger.

Jesus knew that people needed sustenance to survive and many people were following Him who did not have food. Jesus supplied food in such a manner that there were leftovers! The people were stuffed and Jesus was their hero. He satisfied their physical needs, but they were most likely soon hungry again.

The full soul, the complete soul, is the one in which satisfaction and fullness goes well beyond physical food. There is the satisfying of the soul, and only Jesus can fulfill that vacancy. No other food, filling, morsel or otherwise can satisfy the longing of a person within. Today if there is a vacuum inside, an emptiness, or a loneliness that is longing to be satisfied, come to Jesus. He has sufficient supply to satisfy the most lonely of souls.

PRAYER

Dear Heavenly Father, I choose to be satisfied with You today. Fill me to capacity that I may be ready to serve You in any manner You choose. In Jesus' name I pray. Amen.

November 24

THANKFUL

And let the peace of Christ rule in Your hearts, to which indeed You were called in one body. And be thankful.

Colossians 3:15

Some people are bitter, not because they do not have anything, but because they do not have everything. We learn to be greedy and ungrateful. Commercials remind us of what we do not have and create a perceived need for them. Most of us are well-fed, have shelter and money to spend. Because we have grown too accustomed to them, we take them for granted.

The American holiday of Thanksgiving is a special time of the year. It is a time we look back on the blessings God has given us, and a time when we look forward to the blessings we will enjoy. What is the basis for true thanksgiving? The Pilgrims, from whom we draw our inspiration for this holiday, recognized that their provision (food and life) came from God. They acknowledged the greatest gift was Jesus Christ!

Most unhappy people are unthankful. They are unthankful not because they're unhappy, but unhappy because they are unthankful. Do we spend significant amounts of time thinking about what we don't have or do we direct our thoughts to our many blessings? Thankfulness has the power to transform us.

PRAYER

Dear Heavenly Father, even on my worst day, I am blessed. Thank You for the daily provision of food, shelter and family. I am thankful for Your gift of peace, a freedom from guilt and condemnation. In Jesus' name I pray. Amen.

_____

_____

_____

November 25

THANKSGIVING

I will praise the name of God with a song; I will magnify him with thanksgiving.

Psalm 69:30

Thanksgiving Day in the United States started as a way of giving thanks for food collected from a good harvest or problems that were fixed. It originated in 1621 and was a religious festival. However, it is now largely a secular holiday that falls on the fourth Thursday of November.

There are claims that the first Thanksgiving Day was held in the city of El Paso, Texas in 1598. Another early event was held in 1619 in the Virginia Colony. Many people trace the origins of the modern Thanksgiving Day to the harvest celebration that the Pilgrims held in Plymouth, Massachusetts in 1621. However, their first true Thanksgiving was in 1623 when they gave thanks for rain that ended a drought. These early Thanksgivings took the form of a special church service rather than a feast as is common now.

Military service takes men and women to a variety of countries and cultures. Some of the assignments are stimulating and fulfilling. In most, there is an element of danger and in all, there are personal sacrifices. Regardless of the convenience of the accommodations provided, soldiers miss the familiarity of home. Separation from family, friends and home remind them of blessings often taken for granted.

PRAYER

Dear Heavenly Father, I am blessed to live in a nation that has freedom to worship You. Thank You for the privilege of serving in the military to protect that freedom for my fellowman. And I thank You for my family. In Jesus' name I pray. Amen.

UNIFORM

And being found in human form, he humbled himself by becoming obedient to the point of death, even death on a cross.

Philippians 2:8

There will be occasions when duty requires wearing camouflage. Camouflaged soldiers seek to avoid detection by the enemy and secure an advantage for their mission. Their uniform identifies their authority and makes them an easy target for the enemy. Camouflage allows them to conceal their location and equipment to gain an advantage.

The Bible tells us that Jesus put on human nature to identify with those He came to rescue. He wasn't avoiding detection but identifying with humanity. Mankind had failed to obey the law of God, so the Father sent His Son in the form of man to fulfill the demands of the law. Jesus put on our uniform and through faith in His death, burial and resurrection, we are free to access divine resources.

Fatigue, weariness, sorrow, loneliness, and separation are normal to every person no matter what our mission in life. It's not uncommon for us to camouflage our feelings of weakness out of fear that we'll be rejected. Jesus entered our world of weakness to give us His strength.

PRAYER

Dear Heavenly Father, when I am afraid I will trust in You. In Jesus' name I pray. Amen.

November 27

TANTAMOUNT

And now abideth faith, hope, charity, these three; but the greatest of these [is] charity.

1 Corinthians 13:13

Missions have different classifications. Some are high priority, like covert operations. Others are low on the totem pole, like policing the trash around the barracks. One supposes the rankings are determined by those making them. However, discipline and danger factor into most tasks. The propensity for each determines whether the mission is tantamount or not.

Jesus knew the greatest thing and Paul later relayed it—love. Without love, there would be no Savior. Without love, there would be no mankind to save and without love, creation would have been extinguished long, long ago. Nonetheless, there is a Heavenly Father above who loves beyond measure, and the greatest characteristic of Him is that, God is love.

Those who know God, love—those who do not know God, do not know the greatest love that ever shall be. Above all else in life, love is indeed the greatest drive.

PRAYER

Dear Heavenly Father, thank You for loving me. I ask You, today, to help me love as You love. May love be my greatest characteristic, like unto You. In Jesus' name I pray. Amen.

November 28

CHANGE

In a moment, in the twinkling of an eye, at the last trump: for the trumpet shall sound, and the dead shall be raised incorruptible, and we shall be changed.

1 Corinthians 15:52

When recruits reach basic training camp for the first time, one thing is very evident—things are about to change. From the time they reach those who are designated to train them until the time basic training graduation occurs, physical, mental, emotional and spiritual changes are priorities. Those who were once in authority over these recruits are replaced, and new authorities have reign.

The Bible speaks of change. For those who seek a relationship with the Heavenly Father, this change begins with the Word of God, continues with the Word of God, and ends with the Word of God. The new authority within Christian lives is the Word of God and what He has to say about life and living. This priority brings Christians into an expectation that there will be a day when Jesus returns. The corruptible body in which we now live will be changed in a moment in time.

Those who do not desire change should not consider Christianity, for those who walk on the Christian pathway know that continual change is imperative, and the expected final change is desired.

PRAYER

Dear Heavenly Father, I desire change in my life not only in my living now, but also when You return to the Earth again. Help me to continually look for You in every area of my life that needs to be altered. In Jesus' name I pray. Amen.

_____

_____

_____

November 29

CHARACTER

A [good] name [is] rather to be chosen than great riches, [and]
loving favour rather than silver and gold.

Proverbs 22:1

Honor and integrity are two of the greatest traits within a soldier's character. The highest respect is given to those who exhibit these traits, and the lowest respect is given to those who disregard them. The advancement, assignments, and responsibilities of soldiers are directly related to how they carry out day-to-day operations. Those with a good name are trusted, relied upon and promoted accordingly.

The Bible emphasizes the importance of a good name. It places the value of a good name above great riches. Christians who understand this principle are used greatly by the Lord to carry out His operations. Those who do not have good character bring reproach upon the name of Christ. They can do more damage to the cause of Christ than if they never became a Christian in the first place.

Give place to good character. Regard integrity and honor as traits highly esteemed. Live in such a way that others know who is being represented. May a poor character never be attributed to the one who considers these words.

PRAYER

Dear Heavenly Father, I desire to be a person of good character. Help me to recognize any place that I come short, and may my witness of You and Your kingdom shine at all times. In Jesus' name I pray. Amen.

November 30
SUCCESS

This Book of the law shall not depart from your mouth, but you shall meditate on it day and night, so that you may be careful to do according to all that is written in it. For then you will make your way prosperous, and then you will have good success.

Joshua 1:8

The fear of failing can be a powerful motivation in times of crisis. One of history's greatest moments, World War II, was shaped by Sir Winston Churchill. It has been written of him that he *"gave the British back their roar."* Here's a quote from one of his many speeches as he rallied both the British and world to stop the onslaught of the Nazis:

Never give in, never give in, never, never, never, never – in nothing, great or small, large or petty – never give in except to convictions of honor and good sense! Never yield to force; never yield to the apparently overwhelming might of the enemy. We stood alone a year ago, and to many countries it seemed that our account was closed, we were finished...Very different is the mood today.

Churchill's courage and persistence persuaded a reluctant President Roosevelt to commit the resources of the United States to the war.

The success of the allied forces changed the course of history. However, the cost was great in terms of human lives and effort required to preserve the world from one of history's most evil empires. Success doesn't mean the mission will be easy or the resistance weak. Joshua, who led Israel into the promised land, was successful because he obeyed God's commandments. Our personal success will present tests of our determination to remain true to God's Word.

PRAYER

Dear Heavenly Father, when I'm weak, it's easy to realize I need You, but when I'm successful I am tempted to take the credit myself. Keep me dependent on You in failure and success. In Jesus' name I pray. Amen.

343

December 1

GRACE

The Lord repay you for what you have done, and a full reward be given you by the Lord, the God of Israel, under whose wings you have come to take refuge!

Ruth 2:12

Robert Rogers, an old country preacher, gave a sermon many years ago, entitled, *Grace Is Not a Blue-eyed Blonde!* The attention-getting title quickly dimmed in the brilliant light of God's grace to sinners. I want my grandson, who reads this devotional book, to know the life-changing truth of grace. I grew up attending church, but rarely hearing about the grace of God. The emphasis of the teaching was on separation from sin and personal purity, which I sorely needed. But, I mistakenly thought this was achieved by works not by faith. Later, I came to know the truth, *For by grace you have been saved through faith. And this in not your own doing; it is the gift of God.* (Ephesians 2:8)

The story of Ruth and Naomi in the Bible beautifully illustrates the message of grace. Ruth is a foreigner and Naomi is her mother-in-law—both are widowed and homeless. A widow in that culture had no social or legal recourse. They were totally dependent on the kindness of the community. Boaz became their benefactor and the one who bestowed grace in the form of food and ultimately, a home.

Family and friends can provide a safe place for us to grow and prepare for our life's mission. However, the day will come when we must make our own choices and build our own life. Our family desires to spare us as many hardships as possible. The truth is, however, we will make choices that bring us and those who love us pain. They have prayed that we would never turn away from God, but all of us have done so many times.

So, when that time comes in our lives, receive the message that family and friends have to share: *If we say we have no sin; we deceive ourselves, and the truth is not in us. If we confess our sins, he is faithful and just to forgive us our sins and to cleanse us from all unrighteousness.* (1 John 1:8-9) They have received grace and extend that grace to us.

PRAYER

Dear Heavenly Father, I cannot be good by keeping the rules. I confess my sin and place my faith in the gift of Your grace. In Jesus' name I pray. Amen.

GUARD

... which is why I suffer as I do. But I am not ashamed, for I know whom I have believed, and I am convinced that he is able to guard until that day what has been entrusted to me.

2 Timothy 1:12

The person assigned guard duty is entrusted to protect or oversee another. The value of the property or person being guarded demands absolute attention to the task. There was a time when guards who failed to protect the person or property would pay for that failure with their lives. We see an example in the armor bearer of the king or commander of the army. If the king or commander died in battle, the armor bearer would take his own life.

The ceremonial guards of Buckingham Palace are an excellent picture of precision and commitment to the mission of protecting the royal family. They stand at absolute attention and will not be distracted from their mission. Their discipline and ability to tune out all distractions sets the standard for all who serve both in the military and civilian life.

Paul, the apostle, who wrote most of the New Testament, reverses the role. Instead of mankind protecting a valuable treasure, he sees God guarding and protecting the treasure in us. The faithful guard will endure momentary hardship but will gain true riches. God sees the believer as valuable and worthy of His protection. (1 Timothy 6:17-19) God will guard what we entrust to Him.

PRAYER

Dear Heavenly Father, I am humbled by Your mercy and I commit all that I have to Your care. In Jesus' name I pray. Amen.

_____

_____

_____

December 3

GREAT

First of all, then, I urge that supplications, prayers, intercessions, and thanksgivings be made for all people, for kings and all who are in high positions, that we may lead a peaceful and quiet life, godly and dignified in every way.

1 Timothy 2:1-2

The United States of America is 233 years old. In the history of nations that means we're still young compared to other nations such as Egypt, Japan or China. The Declaration of Independence, which our founders drafted, stated: "We hold these truths to be self-evident, that all men are created equal, that they are endowed by their Creator with certain inalienable rights, that among these are life, liberty, and the pursuit of happiness."

Certainly our recognition of man's right to freedom from tyranny and political oppression was instrumental in the success of our form of government. However, we dare not ignore the primary assumption of the authors of this bold declaration, which was the existence and blessing of Almighty God. Our freedom comes with great responsibility. We are not free to live selfish and excessive lives. Our independence should not make us infidels.

How can we keep America great? Paul, the apostle, admonished Timothy and us to pray for our country and her leaders. We have a responsibility to live as godly citizens and share our many blessings with those who are in need.

PRAYER

Dear Heavenly Father, I pray for the United States of America and her leaders. I don't always agree with the president and Congress, but I ask You to protect them and their families. Give them wisdom and strength to perform their duties. In Jesus' name I pray. Amen.

FURTHER

And whosoever shall compel thee to go a mile, go with him twain.

Matthew 5:41

Obedience to command is essential and extremely necessary when the occasion arrives for life-threatening engagements. Submission to authorities may not be natural or comfortable, but without it, chaos reigns and anarchy prevails. Many find those who will readily obey commands, but finding those who go further than the instruction is rare. Those who go beyond, further than the expected or required, are those who excel above the pack.

Certain behavior is expected and required for Christians. When onlookers see something different, something beyond, something further than the normal response, they see a witness of Jesus Christ prevailing in a Christian's life. Anyone can simply fulfill a charge—it is those who go further than the expected who give the greater witness.

All eyes are upon the Christian. Every occasion that lends itself to go further than the rest of the pack simply gives opportunity for others to see Jesus reigning in our lives.

PRAYER

Dear Heavenly Father, please help me to recognize those places where I might be a witness for You. I desire to go further than that which is expected or required of me. In Jesus' name I pray. Amen.

FRESH

Therefore if any man [be] in Christ, [he is] a new creature: old things are passed away; behold, all things are become new.

2 Corinthians 5:17

There is nothing like having fresh socks, clothes, and shoes to put upon our bodies. There is no taste like the taste of fresh fruit, fish, and appetizers during a dinner engagement. Anyone who has experienced left-over, day-old, and aged foods, knows how important it is for foods to be fresh. Those who have worn smelly, nasty, and ragged clothing know how important new clothes are. There is just a significance to something being fresh and new.

In Christianity, when a person gives their heart and life to Jesus Christ, the entire life becomes new. Every sin, every mistake, and every wrongdoing is forgiven, and like a whiteboard that has been erased, the person's life begins new and fresh. Everything has become new, and the feeling associated with such a relief is out of this world.

Some people need a fresh start, a new direction, and a fresh change of course. The simplest and best way to find a life that is totally fresh and new is to give one's life to Jesus Christ. Sometimes, this must be repeated, as some forget the freshness of relationship that Christ Jesus brings. Today is a good day for a fresh start. Why not start right now?

PRAYER

Dear Heavenly Father, I desire a fresh start with everything. Cleanse me anew and afresh. May my life be lived as a testimony to the wonderful way that You provide for all things to be made new. In Jesus' name I pray. Amen.

FORFEIT

Who, being in the form of God, thought it not robbery to be equal with God: But made himself of no reputation, and took upon him the form of a servant, and was made in the likeness of men:

Philippians 2:6-7

Retreating and forfeit are not necessarily most desired, but both are often important. Giving up position to later return to conquer it is as much a part of a battle plan as a full frontal assault. Those who study war and combat know there are times where the most strategic part of the engagement is momentary forfeit.

Jesus knew the idea of forfeiting. He is God. He has it all and made it all. All power, all knowledge, and the ability to be everywhere at one time were His and yet, He humbled Himself to become a man. Some wonder why He would give up so much for such a paltry return. The answer lies in the fact that Jesus treasured man and His relationship with man. Without His forfeiting, mankind would be lost, and those who can comprehend this move, bow in humility before Him.

PRAYER

Dear Heavenly Father, I realize how much You gave up for me. May I live my life before You in acknowledgment of all You forfeited for me. In Jesus' name I pray. Amen.

_____

_____

_____

_____

_____

_____

_____

_____

FOREMOST

Nevertheless I have [somewhat] against thee,
because thou hast left thy first love.

Revelation 2:4

Whatever is the most important part of a mission is the foremost in the mind. Whether it is a particular function, machine, operation or maneuver, the soldier knows the order in which a procedure should take place. Altering from this order is damaging at the least and life-threatening at the most.

The kingdom of God has an order that incorporates a thought that is foremost. John in the book of Revelation sheds light on this most important function. Christians are to continue with their first love. The love of Jesus must be foremost and those who have left it have everything out of order. The foremost element is revealed by the way one acts in their Christianity today and doesn't rely upon the sensitivity of the past. If there seems to be a dryness, a coldness or a distance in the relationship with Christ, then someone has moved away from their first love, and that someone is not Jesus.

The beautiful part of being a Christian and reading the Bible is that there are reminders that are spread throughout the Word of God to bring a person back into love with Him. If the first love is not the foremost, read His love letter, the Bible, and restore that love once again.

PRAYER

Dear Heavenly Father, thank You for the reminders in Your Word to stay in love with You. Help me to remember to keep my love with You foremost in everything I do. In Jesus' name. Amen.

December 8

LOST

For the Son of Man came to seek and to save the lost.

Luke 19:10

It is difficult to describe the feeling of being lost. On one occasion I had made a wrong turn on an unfamiliar road and thought I was traveling west when actually I was driving north. Being a little stubborn, I refused to stop and ask for directions. Some twenty miles later, I admitted my error and turned around.

Another incident occurred at Turner Field in Atlanta, where I was watching a baseball game with my grandson. We left our seats to visit the concession stand and on our way, saw some other family members. I stopped to talk, but my grandson kept going and disappeared into the crowd. In panic, we began looking for him. After a few scary minutes (it seemed like hours), he found us!

When we're lost, our senses can deceive us. We fail to recognize familiar landmarks. Admitting I was going in the wrong direction was embarrassing, but essential, if I was to go in the right direction. Realizing my grandson was missing activated the search for his recovery.

In Luke, chapter 15, there are accounts of a lost sheep, a lost coin, and a lost son. In each of these lessons, a search continued until the sheep was found, the coin was recovered and the son was restored. Jesus proclaimed that this was His purpose in coming to the world. The mission of the church is to find and restore the lost.

PRAYER

Dear Heavenly Father, I have difficulty in asking for directions. My pride keeps me from admitting that I am lost. Thank You for searching for and finding me. In Jesus' name I pray. Amen.

LED

For as many as are led by the Spirit of God,
these are the sons of God.

Romans 8:14

Are we good soldiers? Is it true that good soldiers follow orders? There are many qualities that define those who would serve in the military. It would be safe to say that if we refuse to obey the orders of our commanding officer, we would not be considered good soldiers. Look at this question from another angle. What is our attitude toward those who give orders?

There's an old saying, "You can lead a horse to water, but you can't make him drink." A little boy was instructed by his mother to sit down. When he refused, she placed both hands on his shoulders and firmly placed him in the chair. Defiantly he said, "I may be sitting on the outside, but I'm still standing on the inside!" It's possible to comply to authority externally and at the same time, be defiant in our attitude.

Are we willing to lead or do we have to be driven by someone with superior authority or rank? God is capable of pulling rank or using power to coerce us to yield to His moral authority. He chooses not to force his will, but to beseech us to follow His path. Anyone who would be God's son must believe that He is and that He is a rewarder of those who diligently seek Him. (Hebrews 11:6b)

PRAYER

Dear Heavenly Father, You have revealed Your mercy through the life of Your Son, Jesus. I want to follow You out of awe and love, not out of fear of punishment. In Jesus' name I pray. Amen.

December 10

LIGHT

*This is the message we have heard from him and proclaim to you,
that God is light, and in him is no darkness at all.*

1 John 1:5

Every day we are told that the economy is bad, and businesses,
families and governments are struggling to survive. How will we respond? Some adjustments are needed and even necessary. Businesses
are looking for ways to cut expenses and still provide quality services.
Many have adopted the slogan, "We have to get leaner," meaning cut
expenses, even if it means eliminating someone's job.

The news often reports the negative effect this is having on some
people. A terminated employee reacts in rage and vents his anger
with violence against his former employer. More and more, we see
anger, irritability and rage driving people to unspeakable aggression.

We need to be reminded that regardless of our circumstance, God
is light! God is good! God is in charge! We don't have to carry the
world on our shoulders. We don't have to fix it. We just have to have
faith in God with it. He is the Light forever. The darkness of my
circumstance is temporary.

PRAYER

*Dear Heavenly Father, my business may be down and the
economy may be struggling, but You are good! You are still
God, and I will trust You. In Jesus' name I pray. Amen.*

_____

_____

_____

_____

_____

_____

COMPASS

*From Mount Hor they set out by the way to the Red Sea,
to go around the land of Edom. And the people became
impatient on the way.*

Numbers 21:4

The compass was the GPS for travelers in the 20th century. The greater the distance to be traveled, the greater the importance to know where true "north" is found. A few years ago, a Korean airliner was shot down by a Soviet jet because the pilot had strayed into Soviet airspace. The navigational error resulted in the death of over 200 people and a tense cold war escalation between the U.S. and the Soviet Union.

Moses depended upon a divine guidance system when he led Israel out of Egypt. God provided a pillar of fire by day and a cloud by night to show the way to the promised land. The children of Israel became impatient, much like our modern-day kids and they asked; "Are we there yet?" God didn't always choose the most direct route. Sometimes He wanted to teach them a lesson and sometimes avoid a battle, because they were not ready to fight.

How patient are we? Do we look for God's guidance before choosing a path or do we rely on our own instincts? Proverbs says: *There is a way that seems right to a man, but its end is the way to death.* The Bible reveals the truth and has proven to be the most reliable compass for our souls.

PRAYER

Dear Heavenly Father, I need Your compass for my soul. Forgive me for becoming impatient and relying on my own choices. Teach me that Your way is always best. In Jesus' name I pray. Amen.

CONDUCT

…but as He who called you is holy, you also be holy in all your conduct, because it is written, "Be holy, for I am holy."

1 Peter 1:15-16

Remember the report cards from elementary school? One section was citizenship and it recorded our progress in social skills. We probably paid more attention to our grades in reading, writing and arithmetic, but our teacher paid attention to our behavior.

Every organization with whom we associate has a code of conduct. It may be formal and written down or informal, but it is expected. Recent years has seen a discussion about public versus private behavior. Who has the right to require me to submit to their code of conduct? Privacy seems to have won in the public arena, where it's popular to give everyone the right to do what is right in their own eyes.

One thing we cannot escape however is the law of consequences. Newton's third law of motion says, "For every action there is an equal and opposite reaction." God's law says, *For whatever one sows, that will he also reap.* (Galatians 6:7b) Self-sufficient and self-reliant people may reject the authority of anyone to tell them what to do, but they cannot escape the law of consequences.

God's law calls us to be accountable for our behavior. He sets a standard for our conduct that if followed will produce good fruit in our private lives and in our society.

PRAYER

Dear Heavenly Father, I cannot be holy in my own strength. I've fallen far short of Your standard in the past and will, no doubt, in the future. Pour out Your grace in my life. In Jesus' name I pray. Amen.

December 13
HOME

*But our citizenship is in heaven, and from it we await
a Savior, the Lord Jesus Christ.*

Philippians 3:20

*But as it is, they desire a better country, that is, a heavenly one.
Therefore God is not ashamed to be called their God,
for he has prepared for them a city.*

Hebrews 11:16

Young people often are anxious to leave home, ready to explore and experience adventure. Travel appeals to our desire to be independent. It's not uncommon to feel trapped by the familiar and feel unfulfilled in attaining our full potential. A new job or a new location can provide new enthusiasm for a fresh start.

The older we become, the more attractive home seems to grow. Life has a way of bringing us to a new appreciation of childhood places and people. We may find ourselves thinking about the places where we grew up or where we attended school. Occasionally, we long to go home and remember those carefree days of our youth. Sometimes we're weary, tired and need to escape.

But could there be more to this longing for home? Truthfully, when we do return to the place of our childhood, it's not as we remembered. The house may look the same, but the people have changed, and try as we may, we can't recapture those early emotions. The Scripture talks about our true home being a relationship with God. It is not a place, neither is it earthy accomplishments. An old preacher once said, "Life is not a destination, it is a way of travel."

PRAYER

Dear Heavenly Father, I live in this world, but this is not my home. I desire to know You better and to live with You eternally. In Jesus' name I pray. Amen.

December 14

HONESTY

But we have renounced disgraceful, underhanded ways…

2 Corinthians 4:2a

Benjamin Franklin is reported to have said, *"Honesty is the best policy."* When we purchase a gallon of milk, we expect to receive a gallon, not a quart. When we fill our automobile with gas, we count on the pump to deliver the amount of fuel that we purchased. Aren't we glad there's a standard for what constitutes a gallon of milk and a gallon of gas? There would be mass confusion and probably a total revolt if every merchant had their own different standards.

There exists a Bureau of Weights and Measures so we can trust that a gallon of milk purchased in Tallahassee is the same as a gallon bought in New York. If we expect honesty from those we are buying gas or milk or automobiles, does that expectation also apply to us? Would we be honest people, if we demanded honesty from others but failed to operate by the same standards?

Our government wisely established a standard for weights and measurements, and God has given us a code of conduct for life. Psalm 15:2-4 *He who walks blamelessly and does what is right and speaks truth in his heart; who does not slander with his tongue and does no evil to his neighbor, nor takes up a reproach against his friend; in whose eyes a vile person is despised, but who honors those who fear the Lord; who swears to his own hurt and does not change.*

PRAYER

Dear Heavenly Father, Your standard is high because You are holy. I can only attain Your ways through faith in Jesus' righteousness. Help me! In Jesus' name I pray. Amen.

_____

_____

_____

PRE-APPROVED

The Lord is not slack concerning his promise, as some men count slackness; but is longsuffering toward us, not willing that any should perish, but that all should come to repentance.

2 Peter 3:9

Solicitations fill mailboxes every day throughout the United States. We are "Preapproved" for this. You are "Preapproved" for that, and so goes the story of trying to solicit buyers by giving them advance approval for loans or gifts. These promises are often empty and meant to incur business from people who really are not in need of the particular business being solicited.

Jesus, however, also makes promises, and He always keeps His promises. His desire is for everyone to know that they are pre-approved by the sacrifice of His body and blood for their sins. Unlike many of the shenanigans that are played by the "pre-approval" business world, Jesus has already paid the price of admission. The only measure that must be met now is belief that Jesus indeed already paid.

Jesus in not willing that any should perish—only those who reject His offer will find themselves rejected. The offer is so rich, so true, and so easy that all who come will find themselves already approved in His sight.

PRAYER

Dear Heavenly Father, thank You for the finished work that You did for me on the cross. By Your work and to Your glory alone I know I am pre-approved with You. In Jesus' name I pray. Amen.

December 16

TROUBLE

I have said these things to you, that in me you may have peace.
In the world you will have tribulation. But take heart,
I have overcome the world.

John 16:33

So much of our time and resources involve protecting people and property. National and personal security occupy the time and resources of the federal and local governments. Military and law enforcement agencies are diligent in protecting us as much as possible. Yet, despite their vigilance, all of us face very real danger every day. We live in a troubled world in which none of us can escape danger. Jesus taught, in the world you will have tribulation, but He also offered another option: in me you may have peace. Yes, we live in a trouble world, but we can live in this world and have the peace of Jesus!

The peace of God is predicated upon peace with God. We have peace with God through Jesus Christ by renouncing our sin and accepting His gift of eternal life by faith.

PRAYER

Dear Heavenly Father, I receive the peace You offer me through Jesus Christ. You have overcome all the trouble and danger I will ever face. Thank You. In Jesus' name I pray. Amen.

December 17
FANTASY

*And I knew such a man, (whether in the body, or out of the body,
I cannot tell: God knoweth;) How that he was caught up into
paradise, and heard unspeakable words, which it is not lawful for
a man to utter.*

2 Corinthians 12:3-4

In Disney World, there is a section called "Fantasy Land." In this
portion of the amusement park are rides that depict fantasy, like
"Cinderella's Golden Carrousel," "Dumbo's Flying Elephant" and the
most notable, "It's a Small World." There is something about fantasy
that is attractive to human beings—being among such fantasy helps
a person to escape from reality for a while.

Paul, the apostle, spoke of an experience that seems like fantasy, and
yet it is very real. His body was broken to the point that he actually
died and went to heaven. He called it "paradise", and he heard words
there that he felt it would be unlawful for a man to try to repeat
them.

This place, this real place, this non-fantasy place, is one that is promised to all who follow after Jesus Christ. Heaven is real, and no fantasy on Earth will ever match that which is reserved for those whom
the Heavenly Father calls His own.

PRAYER

*Dear Heavenly Father, thank You for the promise of heaven.
I know I cannot even begin to imagine how wonderful it
is. Help me today to live as though heaven is just another
breath away. In Jesus' name I pray. Amen.*

_____

_____

_____

FAST

And, behold, I come quickly; and my reward [is] with me, to give every man according as his work shall be.

Revelation 22:12

Almost two thousand years ago, the King of Kings stated that he was coming quickly. That seems to be a long, long time, and yet, it remains closer than it was back then.

The difficulty with the idea of being fast in today's society is that people are use to an instant way. Instant coffee, fast food, and ready-made items have redefined our outlook. Fast means now or at least a few moments from now. The impatience that is inbred manifests itself by anger every day.

Soldiers must be alert, but patient. They must be ready, but not too quick. Allegiance to those superior in position and knowledge is imperative. The authorities know when to move and how quickly to do so. The Heavenly Father has the timing down on all of life, according to His immutable plan and ways. Trust Him.

PRAYER

Dear Heavenly Father, I trust You with the timing of the issues of my life. Help me to be patient, as I feel an urgency for things to move faster than Your master plan. In Jesus' name I pray. Amen.

_____

_____

_____

_____

_____

_____

December 19

FIELD

Say not ye, There are yet four months, and [then] cometh harvest? behold, I say unto you, Lift up your eyes, and look on the fields; for they are white already to harvest.

John 4:35

Fields are used for multiple purposes. From engaging in battles to planting corn, people use fields to carry out actions, grow food and engage in warfare. If we stop for a moment and think about the significance of fields, we will find the purpose of the Master.

God Almighty is not unfamiliar with fields. He created them and many of the activities of His relationship with people were in the very fields of His creation. Sometimes there were battles to be won and sometimes, there was just a meeting place with God. Sometimes people would lose their lives, while at other times, they would find them. Nonetheless, God uses the resource of fields to do much of His mighty work.

Jesus looked upon mankind as a field of sorts. His observation was one of an eternal agrarian view in that He saw people like a field that was ready to be harvested. People surround Christians every day. Although they do, many of us either ignore them or are unwilling to work in the fields. The harvest is ripened and the fields are white. Who will go and work for the Lord of the Harvest today?

PRAYER

Dear Heavenly Father, please help me to see the fields as You see them. I know there is a great harvest that You desire to reap and I would like to be a part of it. In Jesus' name I pray. Amen.

FINGERS

When I consider thy heavens, the work of thy fingers, the moon and the stars, which thou hast ordained; …

Psalm 8:3

The universe is filled with stars and galaxies that overshadow everything that happens on the earth. The vastness of the heavenly expanse boggles most people's minds as they try to imagine such vastness. Whenever we considers the heavens, we are generally brought to smallness, tininess, and ineffectiveness in comparison.

Yet, the Heavenly Father flung out stars and galaxies with His fingers. The moon and the stars were no great feat for Him. The massiveness of His power moved celestial balls like a man would move grains of sand, and that which is not even possible with man was performed with very little effort.

The question becomes, "Who holds us in His hand, and is that hand powerful enough to keep us from falling?" The answer is found in the might of the hand that holds—remember, with just His fingers, He flung out the stars. With that kind of power at His disposal, we are certainly safe in His hand.

PRAYER

Dear Heavenly Father, I desire to be in the middle of Your mighty hand, so that Your powerful fingers will keep me safe no matter what comes against me. In Jesus' name I pray. Amen.

_____

_____

_____

_____

_____

FLABBY

Therefore be ye also ready: for in such an hour as ye think not the Son of man cometh.

Matthew 24:44

There is nothing more disheartening than for a person to be unfit for a task in the future. One of the reasons there is bootcamp is because people tend to be "flabby" in their bodies and in their minds. Through great discipline and intense training, each of those characteristics will be sharpened for the day of battle. Without this training, failure is assured.

For Christians, discipline is also a must. No one knows the time of Christ's return, but it could be at any moment. The idea is to be sharp in body, mind and spirit whenever He comes back. The ideal of occupying until He returns is the stimulus for being in shape. No fleshly desire, bodily appetite, or mental accomplishment can take precedence. There is no room for flabby Christianity.

It's about that time. Being fit for the days ahead is imperative for those who await Jesus' return. Although it was announced almost two thousand years ago, the signs of the times tell us to look up, your redemption draweth nigh.

PRAYER

Dear Heavenly Father, please help me to keep fit and not be flabby in my Christian walk. I know the tendency is to be slack, but I want to be ready when You return. In Jesus' name I pray. Amen.

December 22

PEACE

*Glory to God in the highest, and on earth peace among
those whom he is pleased!*

Luke 2:14

John Lennon once said of the Beatles, a musical group of the sixties and seventies of which he was a part, that they were more popular than Jesus. During that era, he might have been right, but they were not and are not better known. Julius Caesar, one of the most powerful of the caesars in the Roman Empire, was considered to be god in his lifetime. It was said of him that he came to a Rome made of bricks and left it a city of marble.

Who determines history? The caesars, the kings, or the presidents? Despite their popularity, the Beatles ceased to perform as a group. Julius Caesar was a powerful leader who transformed not just Rome, but the entire world with his roads and his armies. President Ronald Reagan was instrumental in bringing down the Berlin Wall and ending Communist domination of the former Soviet Union. All these leaders were mortal. They saw history happen, but didn't determine history.

Jesus was born in Bethlehem, and it was Caesar Augustus who facilitated this prophetic fulfillment. But it was God who directed it. Jesus proclaimed to the world, *I am the Bread of Life, and he who comes to Me shall never hunger, and he who believes in Me shall never thirst.* (John 6:35) The message of peace is for us—it is available for all . When we receive Jesus, we have peace. The passing years reveal that it is God who directs history, not presidents, kings, nor caesars.

PRAYER

Dear Heavenly Father, human personalities and leaders come and go, but Your word is forever. Thank You for the promise and reality of peace. In Jesus' name I pray. Amen.

RULES

*Rejoice, O young man, in your youth, and let your heart cheer
you in the days of your youth. Walk in the ways of your heart and
the sight of your eyes. But know that for all these things
God will bring you into judgment.*

Ecclesiastes 11:9

I grew up in a church that seemed to me, at that time, intent on
taking all the fun out of life. The teaching we received focused on
avoiding sinful activities, but little training in biblical standards. The
result was I knew what was wrong, but I didn't know much about
what or why I believed.

Youth are prone to test the boundaries and ask the reason for the
rules. We ask for more freedom than we are mature enough to handle. When I read, *Rejoice, O young man, in your youth, and let your
heart cheer you…Walk in the ways of your heart and the sight of your
eyes,* I heard freedom! It sounded like the Bible was on my side for
a change.

Now I have learned the truth of that Scripture. God is willing to
give us freedom, but He holds us accountable for how we use it. God
gives us the truth, but He gives us the freedom to choose our own
way. The truth is: *We're free to have it our way; but know this: for all
these things God will bring you into judgment.* As a grandfather, I've
learned that reaping wild oats isn't as exciting as sowing them.

PRAYER

*Dear Heavenly Father, You love me enough to give me
freedom, but You love too much not to tell me the truth. In
Jesus' name I pray. Amen.*

_____

_____

_____

December 24

PERFECT PEACE

And the peace of God, which passeth all understanding shall keep your hearts and minds through Christ Jesus.

Philippians 4:7

Peace is often sought but rarely found. Wars, skirmishes, battles and fights occur every day between human beings. How will peace ever be resonant within the world with all the commotion going on? If there could ever be peace, would it last? Only those who know the importance of peace with God and the peace of God will know.

Peace with God is established by a person realizing the salvation that is offered through Jesus Christ. When people come before Jesus and recognizes their need for salvation, immediately they have peace with God. However, this does not always ensure everyone will have the "peace of God". There is a difference. The one who has the peace of God enjoys peace, no matter what the outside situations or circumstances may be. Those with the "peace of God" know that God is in control, and nothing they go through is greater than the Heavenly Father.

Peace is made perfect in His strength. When people understand the power that is over all, there will indeed be peace on Earth and goodwill toward men.

PRAYER

Dear Heavenly Father, I desire peace with God and the peace of God. May my soul rest today in knowing that You have it all in control. In Jesus' name I pray. Amen.

CHRISTMAS

Behold, the virgin shall conceive and bear a son, and they shall call his name Immanuel (which means, God with us).

Luke 1:23

In one of the historic churches in Rome, there is a beautiful painting called, "Aurora." It's a must see for tourists, but because it's painted on the ceiling, people get tired staring upwards. Someone came up with an idea to install a mirror just above floor level. Now people can look down at the mirror and see the painting from the ceiling.

The message of Christmas brings a similar encounter to those searching for good news. Ever since creation man has gazed toward the heavens in search of God. It is true that the created world bears the imprint of the Creator, but the glory of God cannot be understood by the majesty of the heavens.

Nature has many interesting lessons, but man has never understood God through the study of the universe. One of the Russian cosmonauts observed, "I didn't see God in space." But when we look at Jesus—when we see Him healing the sick, when we see His compassion on the hungry and fainting, when we see His concern for little children or His dealing with those who were demon-possessed, when we see His anger against hypocrisy, and His passion for sinners—we see God and understand what He is like.

Man has never been successful in finding God. Christmas is the good news that God came to where we are.

PRAYER

Dear Heavenly Father, thank You for sending Jesus Christ to be with us. In Jesus' name I pray. Amen.

FINAL

Finally, my brethren, be strong in the Lord,
and in the power of his might.

Ephesians 6:10

The end. The Finish. The last step. The final voyage. Anyone who has been around long enough knows the significance of the previous words. There is something about the finality of things: The final day before graduation. The final text before certification. The final, the final, the final ...

There will be a final day for everyone who lives upon the earth. The question is, "What will we do with the time we have before that day comes. As Paul writes his letter to the Ephesian people, he also writes to those who will read his words in future generations. His final charge to them was *to be strong in the Lord, and in the power of His might.* With such a charge, comes a responsibility and accountability for which those who obey will easily recognize.

Strength comes from the Lord, and there is no greater power than His might. Those who know the final resting place for strength and might will rely upon the Source of those attributes over and over again. Those who do not will be limited to the strength and might that the Creator has given within a man and not the power of His God.

PRAYER

Dear Heavenly Father, I know there is no greater strength than Your strength, and there is no greater might than Your might. I fall upon my knees today to be strong in You and Your power. In Jesus' name I pray. Amen.

_____

_____

_____

December 27

FORT

*I have set thee [for] a tower [and] a fortress among my people,
that thou mayest know and try their way.*

Jeremiah 6:27

Forts are set up all over the United States. Whether it is Fort Benning in Georgia or Fort Bragg in California, from coast to coast, these fortified structures are meant for protection, training and security of the people who live within their territory. The widespread usage of forts exemplifies the need for protective forces for a people to live in peace.

The ultimate fortress is in God. There is no greater hiding place than in Him because His protection is eternal. Even if we should die, the fortress He provides goes well beyond this life and reaches into the life beyond. Jeremiah was told by God that the people of Israel would be a fortress or a tester of metals among His people. The idea is to find out of what they were really made of.

It is in the fort that protection is provided. It is in the fort where the true test is made, and it is in the fort of God where we discover the truth about ourselves and the protection that we need.

PRAYER

Dear Heavenly Father, I desire to run to and stay within Your fort. Protect and purify me as I enter into the holiest fort of all, Your presence. In Jesus' name I pray. Amen.

December 28
FORTUNE

*The earth [is] the LORD'S, and the fulness thereof; the world,
and they that dwell therein.*

Psalm 24:1

One of the benefits to conquering in the battles of history was those who were able to haul off with the loot at the end of a battle. Gold, silver, diamonds and rubies were commonly reported to have been taken. Today is somewhat different—fortunes that were off-limits to many at one time are often readily accessible to the conquerors.

The trouble with fortunes is that they are temporary and actually belong to the Lord. The entire earth is His and He has ownership of it all. There are no lands, jewels, currencies, or precious metals in which he does not hold title deed. In other words, it's all His.

The sooner we realize that the real ownership of all the toys belongs to God, the sooner we know that we are merely a steward and not a real owner. After we receive this knowledge, we will be prone to be careful how we manage the fortunes He provides.

PRAYER

Dear Heavenly Father, I know that everything I have and will have belongs to You. Help me to keep that in mind as I journey through this life and manage the things You have put into my care. In Jesus' name I pray. Amen.

_____

_____

_____

_____

_____

_____

_____

_____

FORMAL

When thou art bidden of any [man] to a wedding, sit not down in the highest room; lest a more honourable man than thou be bidden of him;

Luke 14:8

Military personnel know the importance of dress clothing. Their wardrobe isn't complete without the dress uniform. Formal affairs and high-ranking meetings require such attire be worn and worn sharply without stains or wrinkles. Those who disregard this formality will be met with rebuttal.

The Lord Jesus knew of formal affairs. He attended them and knew the bantering for position that was normal among people. Usually people who wanted to be seen or recognized tried to place themselves near the head of the table, if not sitting at it. Jesus says this shouldn't be the way it is. Jesus' approach to being honored was to take the lower position. The risk of individuals being placed above us is higher when we assume that we should be highly honored.

Honor and formality should come from God first. Obedience to His ways and His direction is one of the most formal positions that a person will ever know.

PRAYER

Dear Heavenly Father, I know the natural tendency to be recognized formally among men. I ask You to help me to keep my desire for acknowledgment directly related to You. In Jesus' name I pray. Amen.

FOREWARN

One woe is past; [and], behold, there come two woes more hereafter.

Revelation 9:12

Warning! Danger! Do not Enter! Signs and signals of various kinds are posted to give advance notice of possible trouble ahead. Those who interact with dangerous materials and machinery know exactly what this is about. Warnings upon military equipment and devices are imperative. The operators of such devices must comply with standards or be harmed.

The Bible gives forewarnings, and many of them are in the book of Revelation. The Scripture reading for today relates to the tribulation period where troubles will be upon the Earth like never before. In stages of "woe," an angel proclaims the dangers ahead and these dangers cost millions of lives.

We would do well to take heed to warnings ahead of time, well before the engagement of the danger arrives. We who follow Jesus know that perilous times are coming and those who are wise take heed to the forewarning.

PRAYER

Dear Heavenly Father, I see the warnings ahead in Your Word. Please help me to heed them as I know You love me enough to keep me in times of danger. In Jesus' name I pray. Amen.

———————————————————————

———————————————————————

———————————————————————

———————————————————————

December 31

CHECK

See then that ye walk circumspectly, not as fools, but as wise,

Ephesians 5:15

One of the most frightening places a soldier ever walks is within a landmine field. Carefulness and skill must be at the highest level or sudden injury or death might occur. Wise soldiers take their time and check very carefully every place that a landmine might be set. Though the task is tedious, the results are well-worth the effort.

Christians must also check areas within their lives. There are places that are like landmine fields, where extreme care must be employed or else their Christian walk will be compromised. There is no room for error in many instances and the ability to regain that which has been lost may never be available again.

As the little children song goes, "Be careful little eyes what you see, Oh be careful little ears what you hear, Oh, be careful little feet where you go, for the Father up above is looking down with love, so be careful ..."

PRAYER

Dear Heavenly Father, please help me to check my steps as I walk through this world. I realize the enemy of my soul has traps set for me out there, and I want to walk carefully in step with You. In Jesus' name I pray. Amen.

POSTSCRIPT

The key to understanding Biblical principles is through obedience. After reading through these inspirational devotions, we will benefit by re-reading them during the following year. This devotional is meant to become a part of our daily lives and will serve each reader for as many years as they will read it. May everyone who reads, re-reads, and reads again the writings in this devotional be blessed by the Lord God Almighty and His Son, Jesus, each time they open its pages.

CPSIA information can be obtained at www.ICGtesting.com
Printed in the USA
BVOW07s0715150115

383290BV00002B/48/P